W9-BDA-322

This is the South

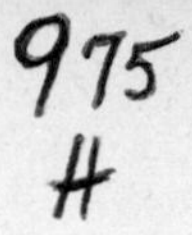

This is the South

Edited by ROBERT WEST HOWARD

ILLUSTRATED

RAND McNALLY & COMPANY

Chicago New York San Francisco

FIRST PRINTING, AUGUST, 1959

Library of Congress Catalog No. 59-11972

PRINTED IN THE UNITED STATES OF AMERICA
BY RAND MCNALLY & COMPANY

TO THOSE FAMILIES
WHO ARE SHAPING THE BEST OF YESTERDAY
INTO A BETTER TOMORROW

Acknowledgments

THIS BOOK was conditioned—indeed, prefabricated—by thousands of people. Each, as an individual, in a casual encounter, revealed another facet of the South's mores and environment to be explored by the authors. Grateful thanks, then, to these nameless co-operators, typified during my own Southland adventures by the Gullah berry-vendors on Pawley's Island; the Georgia hill farmer who, sharing a bench with us at a performance of *Unto These Hills,* vowed the play "The best thing's ever happened for history teaching in this whole country"; the gas-pump operator at Cleveland, Tennessee, who delivered a splendid thirty-minute lecture on Coppermine's history; the flower women of Charleston; an ensilage crew on the levee near Stoneville, Mississippi; the retired Marine sergeant at Venice, Florida, who first identified a Carcharadon tooth for me, and that proud, beaming giant who parks his pickup truck beside U.S. 78 near Aiken on July weekends to sell the largest, sweetest watermelons we've ever seen.

Special thanks, for numerous important reasons, are due Mrs. Carrie Greene of Lemon Bay Road, Englewood, Florida; Dr. Glenn W. Burton, Coastal Plains Experiment Station, Georgia; Dr. Elizabeth Gambrell, Decatur, Georgia; Drs. Frank Cyr, E. deS. Brunner, and Harry Carman of Columbia University; Kitty and Clayton Hoagland of Rutherford, New Jersey; Warren A. Ranney of Ithaca, New York; Wesley Hardenbergh of Lake Zurich, Illinois; and Dr. Vernon E. Loescher, pastor of the Union Church, Hinsdale, Illinois.

Simultaneous dealings with thirty-one authors, plus an editor, is a stellar achievement in human relations. The principal challenge for tact, clarity, and leadership fell on the trim shoulders of Cynthia Smith, Rand McNally's "trade" editor in New York City. Miss Smith's success as co-ordinator of the project, coupled with her devotion to detail, has brought spontaneous requests from the authors to "Give a big Thank You to Our Gal."

Two transplanted Texas sisters went far beyond any call of duty as typists and secretaries in preparation of the manuscript drafts. Very special thanks, then, go to Mrs. Gwen Olmsted and Mrs. Lorraine Brown of Skokie, Illinois.

Finally, as any professional knows, the work environment is actually more important than "the idea." An atmosphere of Faith, an infinite capacity for patience, a host of small and large sacrifices, the mysterious magics of intuition are all vital "fuels" on the long road from Idea to Manuscript. My wife, Elizabeth Zimmermann Howard, provided all of these during the stress of this book's genesis. If you like the organization of *This Is the South* . . . if it chants in harmony the ancient glory-song that is The South, the real credits for editing belong to her.

ROBERT WEST HOWARD

Chicago
May 1, 1959

Contents

PART V: *THE HERITAGE*

PART VI: *FOR KISSIN' COUSINS*

APPENDIX

List of Illustrations

Introduction

ROBERT WEST HOWARD

Look Away

A CENTURY to a mountain is another veil of loam, a few tons of shale, some frost cracks in surface rock. A century to a nation is four generations of eyes, ears, and noses, hands, minds, and hearts, each individual reacting so violently to environment that perspective and truth are often hidden beneath the loams of yesterday's emotions. Yet a few seconds in the right place at the right time can reveal in full perspective the constancy of cultures as well as mountains.

It happened for us that March morning. For fifteen seconds, by stop watch, the sun resting on the Georgia peaks anchored a vast rosy cross of light in the mists of the lake beneath our window, its south-flung arm outswept over the Field of the Great Canoe at the crest of Brasstown Bald. Then the two planets rolled on; sunlight spread down the valley.

To Brasstown Bald the last century had been a second of thin loam and cracked rock. To us, the last hundred years were a mystery of misconception and emotion as veiled from truth as the rock beneath the loam. We had come to this highland retreat to discuss it. No spot could have been more meaningful, no sunrise more portentous.

From the window of a new home we were staring across a great new lake in a pioneer North Carolina valley. Our view stretched over to the highest range of mountains in Georgia where the 4800-foot bulge of Brasstown Bald dominated the misty ridges. That grassy slope at its crest, Cherokee legend tells us, is treeless because it marks the spot where their ancestors landed in a giant canoe "after the Great Flood."

The present, recorded past, and legend had found a meeting ground in our sunrise. The second, the century, the variants of perspective became one in that instant of the roseate cross. But there was no miracle. There was no science. It was no more than the business of being at the right place at the right time . . . and knowing what you were looking at.

That was precisely why the nine of us had come together for the weekend: a college president, a banker, two editors, an economist, a veteran conservationist, a young theologian, and—because he cannot honestly be classed as anything short of a gray-thatched, owl-eyed ball-of-fire—Jim Sells. Our quest was simple enough, so deceptively simple that everyone seemed to have overlooked it in all the adrenal surges since 1859. We wanted to learn what *is* The South—and how did it get that way? We suspected we'd have to go all the way back to 1521, or beyond, to find out.

The weekend, and the plan behind it, had been a decade in the making, and grew as unconsciously and naturally as the Field of the Great Canoe. The taproots reached back, certainly, to the moment I first saw redbud in bloom one smoky spring morning of 1939 as my train crossed Tennessee. The dream must have germinated the night in 1946 when Jim Sells, as director of rural work for the Methodist Church in the Southeast, zephyred into my hotel room in Jackson, Mississippi, to give a Yankee magazine hack a spelldown on the meaningfulness of Governor Hugh White's "Balance Agriculture with Industry" Plan for rural improvement in Mississippi. The humor and fervencies that came out of Jim during the next three hours opened an exchange of correspondence. This led to a 1950 lecture on the values of book reading before the hundred rural preachers at Emory University's Church & Community Workshop. Midnight sessions over platters of catfish, fried chicken, and watermelon with distinguished rural clergymen of rival Protestant denominations fueled my curiosity about the South's perspective.

John Smith . . . tobacco sheds . . . the Founding Fathers . . . Whitney's cotton enGin . . . slavery . . . the Civil War . . . Thaddeus Stephens' crippled snarl . . . Tobacco Road . . . Miami real estate . . . a hangover in the Vieux Carré. Were these the Alpha and Omega of the area called the South? The clergymen didn't talk that way, nor did the forensic Jim. Who were the Crackers, and why? Why did the State of Rhode Island and Providence Plantation eventually drop the word "plantation" in favor of "farm"—which actually means "land leased by a peasant"? Why did an area economically tied to physical slavery, as contrasted to the "farm's" implications of economic slavery, take over the proud, free word of Plantation? What was a Planter, anyway? Did he perennially traipse around, as the books implied, with an open Bible in one hand, a glass of neat bourbon in the other, and a blacksnake whip tucked under one arm?

The questions about the South naturally multiplied like cotton bolls. Beggin' the pardon of the Civil War Roundtables, there was a lot more to this than Lee-on-horseback surveying a TVA dam site! How *did* the Western cowboy's Quarter Horse trace back to race tracks in seventeenth-century Virginia? Whatever happened that made the South march into Civil War battles singing a national anthem written by Daniel Decatur Emmett of Mount Vernon, Ohio, while the North surged out against them chanting a Unitarian preacher's inane and un-Unitarian verses to William Steffe's Southern camp-meeting tune, *Say, Brothers, Will You Meet Us?* Why *do* the mountain counties of the Carolinas and even Alabama vote Republican?

It wasn't too much of a surprise, then, to have Jim Sells charge into Chicago in November, 1957, after *This Is the West* was published. This time he didn't bother to stare me down or circle his quarry like an old foxhound enjoying the starlight. "Mr. Bob," he barked, "when are we going to do *This Is the South?*" (In ministerial context, "we" often means "you.")

This actually was why, on a March morning in 1958, I found myself standing at the window of Walter Moore's home Wonderview, watching the sunrise across glimmering new Lake Chatugi. Besides the Moores and Jim Sells, the rest of our group came because of friendships developed during trips south: Dr. Robert F. Poole, president of Clemson College; J. W. Fanning, chief of agricultural economics at the University of Georgia; Ivy Duggan, now vice president of the Trust Company of Georgia; Alex Nunn, the executive editor of *Progressive Farmer;* Ross Freeman, director of field work for Candler School of Theology; Joe Douthit, one of the Southland's great soil conservation pioneers; and Cully Cobb, 4 H Club pioneer and president of the Ruralist Press of Atlanta. Mrs. Douthit, Mrs. Cobb, and Mrs. Sells were part of the group, too.

Typically, it was Jim Sells who had suggested the meeting place where we would determine whether the book was feasible. Atop the bluff behind the Moores' lovely home, another of Jim's dreams was being built, the Harold H. Hinton Rural Life Center where his country preachers and rural leaders could gather for year-round retreats and seminars.

Walter Moore home-cures hams and bacon with brown sugar, peppercorns, and hickory; Mrs. Moore, long a home demonstration agent, makes buttermilk biscuits that given a tiny push could float from kitchen to dining room. Friday afternoon Dr. Poole strode in the front door a half-hour before dinner with an armful of peach and strawberry preserves from the Clemson College kitchens.

"If we're gonna talk South," he rumbled, "let's eat up to it."

At six o'clock, Jim beckoned me toward the dining-room door. He opened it, sniffed, sighed. A huge Lazy Susan table of antique pine dominated the room. Fairly sagging it to the groaning-board stage was the most dazzling Southern meal I have ever seen—steaming napkined mounds of buttermilk biscuits; pitchers of redeye gravy; gold monoliths of butter; bowls of pickled crab apples and carrot sticks; a sectional tray gleaming with eight or ten varieties of jams and relish; crowning it all, a monstrous pewter platter, sputtering beneath two dozen mahogany-red ham steaks crowned with parsley.

"Thought you might like to see this before the stampede," Jim muttered. "I have a sneaking suspicion the Moores want this book written, too. Brother, if this doesn't fetch it, we might as well have an early breakfast and go back to Atlanta."

There wasn't any question of success by midnight.

At dinner, the ladies, with the deftness of their tradition, veered the conversation to books before the ham platter could become a gleaming parsley desert. With the strawberry shortcake, they expressed their convictions about the need for "a book about the South that will just r'ar back and tell the whole story." Thereupon, with the majesty of Supreme Court justices, they picked up their coffee cups and adjourned to the television set in the living room.

A tape recorder went into the ham platter's position at the center of the Lazy Susan. The first coat was shed at 7:45. By 9:30, all nine of us had our sleeves rolled up and shirt collars open. When we headed for bed at midnight, *This Is the South* was a-borning.

The group had the endurance of Stuart's cavalry. Breakfast was at 7:30. The tape recorder was back on the Lazy Susan by 8:45. We debated an outline and argued folklore and fact until 12:30, then took the afternoon off to break into muttering teams of two and three for an inspection of Jim's Rural Life Center and a run down the valley to the Campbell Folk School.

The final pattern for *This Is the South* began to shape in the Saturday night session. The greatest basic driving force of the South, we all agreed, had been . . . and is . . . the Family. Our emphasis, then, would be on the families and the economic and geographic forces that influenced them from Jamestown on. The geographic boundaries of the South would, obviously, not parallel its ethnic and socio-economic boundaries. The influences of the South, for instance, on the cultural patterns fixed in the nineteenth-century West is a subject of fascinating research potential. We arbitrarily fixed the geographic boundaries of the South as follows: south of the Potomac and Ohio rivers; west to the Mississippi, plus Arkansas, Louisiana, and east Texas.

Scores—perhaps hundreds—of books about the South would be written between 1960 and 1965. Most of them would spotlight the Civil War and the grim decades of Reconstruction, as thousands have already. "Lot more important," Dr. Poole was the first to say, "is to report on the events that caused these high lights to be high lights. What really shaped up to Sumter and Bull Run? What kind of people marched off to be killed or, worse still, came home to put the pieces back together afterwards?"

Naturally we turned to the Family's most familiar Southern pattern, "homesteading." The book would be divided into six sections, titled progressively: 1) The Clearings, 2) The Molders, 3) The Building, 4) The Folks, 5) The Heritage, 6) For Kissin' Cousins. The Molders, as Cully Cobb and Ivy Duggan pioneered the notion, must be the individualists who, as representative of the basic economic and ethnic groups, actually shaped the future of the South to an area of individualistic regions. The Indian, the Negro, the Planter, the Preacher, the Woman, the Cracker, the Factor—these were the human foundations of the South. Only the section on The Building would depart from this strict pattern of the Individual and the Family to span the economic and social evolution of the saga years between the winning of the Old West and the winning of the New South.

All important, the pattern developed for *This Is the West* would be used. Each of the book's chapters would be researched and written by a specialist in that particular category.

Cully Cobb capped it finally at one o'clock Sunday morning. "Bob's a-going back up North," he mused. "We have just got to keep our hands off and let him do what comes natural. We're looking for the truth about our South . . . every facet of it . . . from white man and from Negro. We don't think this should be a book to take sides, because its got to be democratic. It should lay the facts on the table and challenge every citizen to absorb its contents and adjust his convictions accordingly. If Bob needs me, he can call on me."

I don't know why, five hours later, the first flare of sunrise drew me to the window. Yet there I was, perky as a tanager, staring out at that unbelievable huge cross of light. There was a rustle across the room. Ross Freeman was out of his bed too, standing before a corner window, arms folded behind his back. He stared with me until the cross vanished, and the gold mat was rolling with unbelievable speed north to the Smokies, south down the gaps and piney gullies to the dazzle of Crescent Coast. Ross turned then, his face as grave as the horizon-etched mountains.

"Perspective," he whispered. "Follow the gleam."

From Wonderview's weekend and the beneficent promise of that sunrise this book grew, just naturally. With the best of our co-ordinated abilities, thirty-two authors from North and South have come together for a new Look Away—a considered look away at the amazing role the South has played in building the U.S.A.; the tortures it has endured, the errors it has, with sincere human instinct, made or been forced into; the long road to a future now shining as brightly as that sunrise cross above Brasstown Bald. Look Away . . . from seventeenth-century Clearings to the New South's tomorrow . . . with forty-five million Americans in democratic resurgence from, literally as well as geographically, Jamestown to Nieman-Marcus. Dixie's future, and hope, is in Kissin' Cousins who understand what they're lookin' at.

Part 1

The Clearings

Preceding page:
Spanish explorers in Florida

It is the goodliest and most pleasing territory of the World; for the continent is of an huge and unknown greatnesse.

RALPH LANES, 1585

JAMES MCBRIDE DABBS

The Clearings

THE PEOPLE made the clearings. Where they made them, and what they made on them, rested with the land. The land was here already. Kings could grant it, but they couldn't change its harbors, its rivers, its mountains, or its climate.

The Appalachian barrier drives deep into the South. Meeting it, the westward tide of settlement would pause. Along the valleys a tide from the more populous north would now halt on the Virginia-Carolina piedmont, now flow around southerly escarpments into Georgia, Alabama, and Mississippi.

Chesapeake Bay and all its estuaries—James, York, Rappahannock, Potomac and the rest—would entice men far into the present Virginia and Maryland. Cape Hatteras and the sand bars along the North Carolina coast would warn them away. At Albemarle Sound, the Roanoke River would receive them only to lead them shortly into southern Virginia. The Yadkin, the Catawba, the Broad would pour much of North Carolina's commerce down to the Pee Dee and the Santee rivers, across South Carolina and into Charles Town. Even without this trade, the Charles Town harbor itself, at the junction of the Ashley and the Cooper, protected by offshore islands, must by its very location become one of the chief ports on the Atlantic seaboard.

One other geographical fact would help channel the South to its course: the Fall Line. Westerly rim of the coastal plain, its cascades and bluffs would become headwaters for navigation on the rivers. Thus, like

Richmond at the falls of the James, and Petersburg at the falls of the Appomattox, it would develop the "change-over" settlements where boat and horse interchanged their burdens. Southeasterly, across the sites of Weldon, Orangeburg, Augusta, Macon, the Fall Line arched into horizon-wide bands of sandy plain, shadowed by pine forests, here and there pocketed by rich riverside fields that Indians had tilled for five thousand years. Between it and the sea quavered a lush tidewater jungle, intermittently broad savannah, canebrake, and swamp, all domed by the cathedral soar of chestnut, oak, or cypress. Northwest of the Fall Line rolled the Piedmont, with rich but shallow soil, well drained and covered mainly by hardwoods.

These were the great contours of the land—the basic structure—that indicated where the clearings should be. Here. Not here. What of the texture? The forests opened, how frequently we do not know, into the used or abandoned fields of Indians, and here and there into "prairies," especially in the Piedmont, "abounding in tame grass and wild peas so thick that they prevented crossing." Writing of the low country, Bishop Asbury said: "Crossed Little Pee-Dee at the Potato-Bed ferry. Beautiful deep sands, live-oaks, lofty pines, pimeta swamps, with intermingled gums and cypress, variegated by evergreens of bay and laurel, and twining jessamine flinging its odors far and wide"; and again: "Passed this day over expansive savannahs, charmingly decorated with late autumnal flowers." Many writers have commented on the great pine forests, so open that "even small objects could be seen at a great distance," in the spring covered with grass and dotted with wild flowers—the "dark retreats and stately forests" of the historian Drayton.

William Bartram, in his *Travels*, noted this grandeur. Of lower South Carolina he wrote in the 1770's: "I soon entered a high forest, continuing the space of fifteen miles. . . . This ancient sublime forest, frequently intersected with extensive avenues, vistas and green lawns, opening to extensive savannas and far distant Rice plantations . . . captivates the senses by scenes of magnificence and grandeur." On the same trip, in Alabama, Bartram "entered a vast open forest which continued above seventy miles . . . the stately trees scatteringly planted by nature, arising straight and erect from the green carpet, embellished with varying grasses and flowering plants." As for the fauna, Thomas Ashe wrote a hundred years before Bartram: "There is such infinite herds that the whole country seems but one continued Park."

Such was the seductive land that lured European settlers, swallowed some of them up, and changed them all. What were the European forces that urged them hither?

They were concentrated in three empires: Spain, France, and England.

Spain tried to settle the Carolina coast as early as 1526; France tried it in 1562; England came last, in 1585. Spain left stories about "the land of Chicora"; France left the name "Port Royal" and a tale of Jean Ribaut; England's first effort left the haunting legend of Lost Colony, with Virginia Dare, well named, the first English child born on these shores, vanished with the rest of Roanoke's hundred, and the word *Croatoan* carved on a tree. Its founder, Raleigh, was detained in England to take part in the defeat—and with the help of the winds of God, the destruction—of the great Armada of Spain. The little colony in Virginia was lost—to Indians? Spaniards? the sea itself?—while Drake's fireships and Irish Sea gales veered the course of history.

But Spain had already planted forts and missions from Saint Augustine to Santa Elena, the present St. Helena at Beaufort, South Carolina. She held this coast line for one hundred fifty years, threatening the Charles Town settlement of 1670. The French, having failed in the southeast, searched far north along the Atlantic coast and settled Quebec in 1608. Then, for three-quarters of a century, they explored west and south, until La Salle rode the Mississippi to the Gulf in 1682, d'Iberville settled Biloxi in 1699. Now, with the help of the Spaniards in Florida, they had the British pinned down on twelve hundred miles of the Atlantic seaboard. It was 1763 before this encirclement was broken. Around 1700, during the early days at Charles Town, it was nip and tuck for the English. Before that time, however, Virginia had been permanently settled.

Why was Virginia settled before Carolina? Partly, one would think, because of the presence of the Spaniard in Florida, and along the Guale (later Georgia) coast. England, gloried on by the Armada's defeat and her sea captains, was rising to challenge Spain; but it would have been foolhardy to challenge her too boldly or too soon. When we seek the motivation for the settlement of Virginia, we find national interests combining with hunger for personal gain. Still, we must not read back into that great age—Elizabeth had died only four years before—too much private motivation. Under the mercantile theory, all trade was a national affair. Englishmen, seeking private gain, also sought national security and honor. Here is a list of the products they wanted: wine, hemp, flax, cotton, silk, dye products, rice, sugar, spices, medicinal herbs, pineapples, oranges, olives, currants, pitch, tar, turpentine, masts and other lumber, pearl and soap ashes, salt, gold, silver, copper, iron, and precious stones. The precious metals need no explanation. England's forest products came from Sweden; she wished to shake off that dependence. The other needs were subtropical or Eastern, and Portugal controlled the Eastern trade. Seeking the East, Columbus had sailed west. Throughout the nineteenth century, Englishmen still sought the Northwest Passage to Asia.

THE CLEARINGS

The Virginia Company of London, organized in 1606, was composed of "certain Knights, gentlemen, merchants." They were called "adventurers," and they were—both for commercial and political, for individual and national, ends. Raleigh failed to establish the Lost Colony partly because it had been too individualistic a venture. The Virginia Company succeeded because it foreshadowed in its organization the modern corporation: businessmen united for adventure. How much religion was involved it is hard to say. The Company was chartered partly to carry the Protestant Gospel to the heathen Indians. In a stirring appeal in the spring of 1610, after the *Sea Adventure* had been lost amid the "still vex'd Bermoothes," the directors called for further support: "The eyes of all Europe are looking upon our endeavors to spread the Gospell among the heathen people of Virginia, to plant an English nation there, and to settle and trade in those parts which may be peculiar to our nation, to the end we may thereby be secured from being eaten out of all profits or trade by our more industrious neighbors." These people were close to the Middle Ages. Catholic Spain was still a real threat to Protestant England.

So, with a fanfare in England, Jamestown was finally planted on the James, on a peninsula chosen for defense and exploration rather than for subsistence, a colony driven in the starving time of 1609–10 perhaps even to cannibalism, one-third of its twelve hundred members massacred by the Indians in 1622, the Company a failure by 1624 and control reverting to the Crown.

Even the initial plan of settlement, the company plantation, had failed. In 1618 the Company surrendered its monopoly in, and planned use of, the land. It substituted with "the headright system," granting an average of fifty acres to each colonist. Out of this, American democracy developed. From its misuse grew the great estates and a Southern aristocracy.

Before this land policy was adopted, John Rolfe, who is remembered chiefly for his marriage to the Princess Pocahontas, the resultant peace with King Powhatan, and the fathering of many of the blue bloods of later Virginia, experimented ominously with tobacco. By 1614, he had cured leaves good enough for export to England. It was Rolfe's tobacco, more than anything else, that destroyed the Virginia Company's ideal of the English town, which was to become an actuality in New England. In its place developed the type of settlement described in the heading of this chapter, The Clearing. Here began the centuries of our historic figure, the American Settler: the lonely individual, moving from clearing to clearing through an almost endless forest, over the Blue Ridge, down the valleys, into the West.

Tobacco, combined with the individualistic land policy, was the chief factor in the spread of the farms, first northward along tidewater, then westward up the river valleys of Virginia. It was tobacco that, with the lack of sufficient indentured labor, suggested African slavery, and all the splendor and the evils incident thereto. The "headright" land policy, selfishly used, created the great tobacco estates and the spread of slavery. And finally it was tobacco, the soil depleter, that caused the wasteful use of land. With labor dear and land cheap, more profit came by clearing new fields and abandoning the old. By 1650 "the Old Field and the Old Field Pine served to give men a peculiar sense of age in a society that was really new." By 1676 this expansive process was, despite all treaties, pressing so hard upon the Indians, and had carried the frontier so far out from Governor Berkeley and the tidewater rulers of Virginia, that Nathaniel Bacon rose and, exactly one hundred years before the Declaration of Independence, staged a preview of the American Revolution.

The best-laid plans of the new Company went awry, too, when faced by these actualities of soil, climate, and tobacco. King James I even wrote a book against tobacco. With restrictions that would make 1959's farm program look like child's play, the Williamsburg Assembly tried to control it. The only effect was to make rich tobacco land more valuable and to speed up the soil depletion that would expand the crop clean out of Virginia across the mountains to Kentucky.

A word about the religious life of the colony, and incidentally of the colonial South. It differed from that of New England. The difference was due in part to the settlers themselves. "New England," says Wertenbaker, "was largely East Anglia transplanted to America: Virginia east of the Blue Ridge was a cross section of all England shaken apart and reunited in a different pattern." Virginia took its tone before the Puritan conflict became sharp in England. By happy chance, it missed the Plymouth settlers of 1620. Sir Edwin Sandys, member of the London Company and liberal reformer, had obtained permission from the King for the Pilgrim Fathers to be brought from Holland and settled as a "hundred" in Virginia. But storms carried them to Massachusetts.

Those who came to America in the Great Migration of the 1630's were fleeing the persecution of Archbishop Laud. Most naturally they turned to the northern colonies. Several hundred Puritans did settle in Virginia. During the 1640's they appealed to their brethren in Massachusetts to send missionaries south. Three were sent but, for political rather than religious reasons, were refused entry. The entire Virginia group of Puritans then left for Maryland, where, in short order, they took over Lord Baltimore's liberal government. (He got it back.)

Nonetheless, religious requirements were probably as strict in Virginia as anywhere else. Craven suggests that the town life of New England made

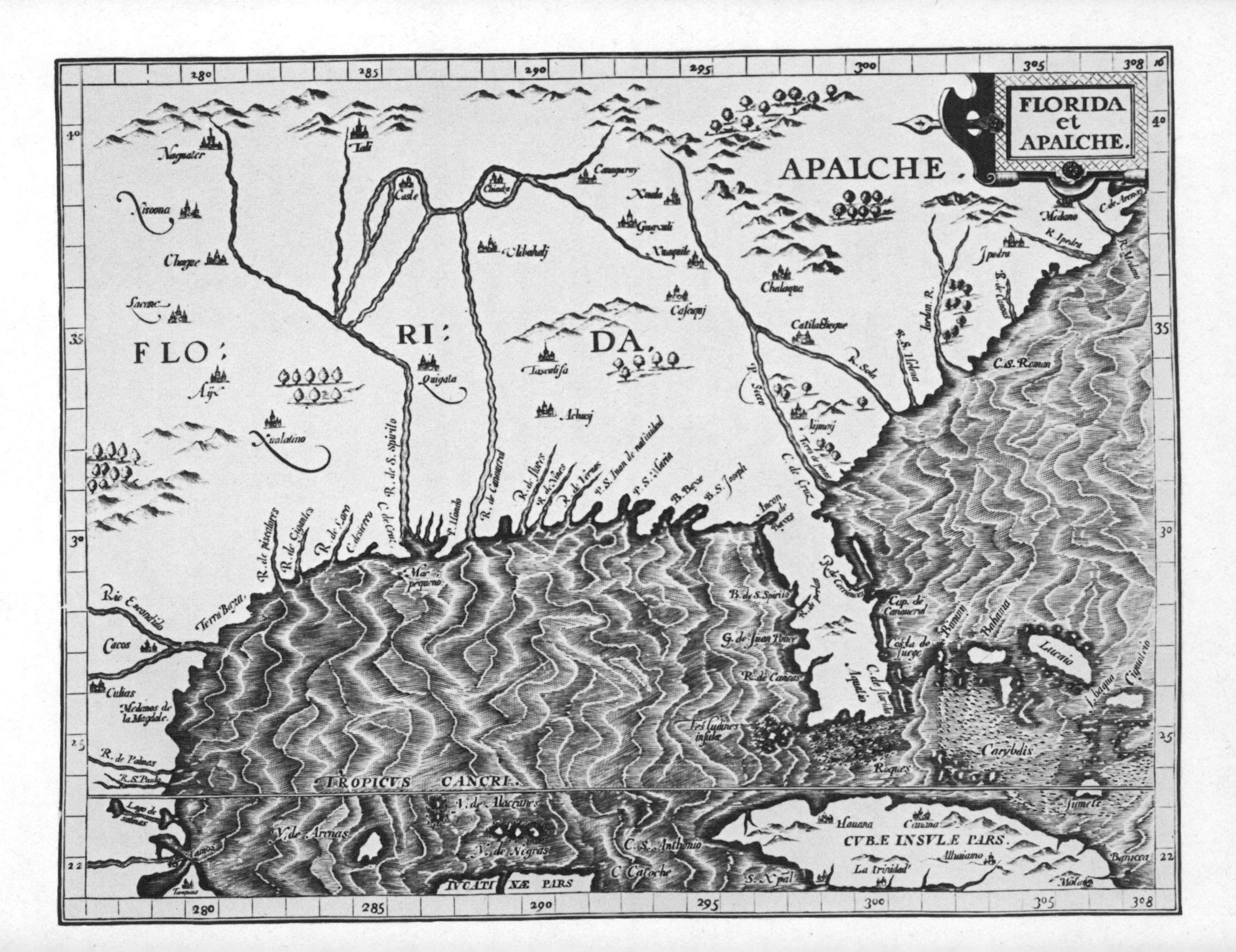

FLORIDA et APALCHE.
APALCHE.
FLO: RI: DA.
TROPICVS CANCRI.
CVBÆ INSVLÆ PARS.
IVCATI NÆ PARS
Hauana
La trinidad
Caribdis
Lucaio
Bahama
C. de florida
C.S. Anthonio
C. Catoche
C. de Cruz
Rio Escondido
Cacos
Culias
Nagnaier
Tali
Casle
Quigata
Chalaqua
Catilaftegue
Tascalisa
Achusi

their enforcement relatively effective there, while life in the plantation clearings made it ineffective in Virginia. It does seem that the Virginian never took "conscience," either his own or another's, as seriously as did the New Englander. As for religious observances, they were a part of civic life. In brief: civic temper and country life married in the South; a religious temper and town life bundled in New England. That, perhaps, has made all the difference. When, in the South, the civic temper faded in the later colonial expansion into the back country, religious life faded with it, for a while.

Within fifty years of Jamestown, Virginia traders and settlers were pressing southward into territory later to become North Carolina, obeying perhaps the spirit of the Virginia Company's advice to Sir Thomas Gates in 1609 when he was setting out for Jamestown—that he should be guided by the general principle of seeking the south, "which is under God the first cause both of health and riches." The first North Carolina settlements were made just below the Virginia border, in Albemarle. The slow development of the province, both as a geographical unit and as a state of mind, was due mainly to lack of harbors and a poor intrastate river system. In the early days St. Augustine was Spanish, Charles Town was English, but what was Albemarle? Nobody knew. For Albemarle—and North Carolina—was that as yet unnamed mixture which was to become American. Leaving it, then, to its retarded but perhaps more truly American future, let us pass on, as the English did in 1670, to the settlement of Charles Town.

It is erroneous to think that Charles II, over a glass of wine in 1663, casually handed Carolina to the eight Lords Proprietors. "Politically, these men were closely identified with the framing and administration of imperial policy." Economically, they were outstanding business promoters, Lord Ashley's "Carolina business" being but one of their many colonial schemes. Profit from commerce was probably their chief aim in Carolina, but land itself offered them a second value. To judge from the Fundamental Constitutions, they intended to set up a belated feudalism. They failed in most of the details, but did set a trend toward large landed estates. This slowed the settlement of the colony, and marked the entire history of the area.

Though Carolina was clearly an outpost against Spain, Charles Town being only two hundred and fifty miles north of the Spanish fortress at St. Augustine, one gets the impression that in its genesis the settlement lacked somewhat the Elizabethan largeness of the Virginia settlements of two-thirds of a century before. Profit had become more important. Yet the tropical, the exotic, vision still lingered. Supplies for the experimental farm included cottonseed, indigo seed, ginger roots, sugar cane, vines, and olive sets. Men were still misled by degrees of latitude, and apt to equate the

Carolina climate with that of North Africa and the Mediterranean. Indeed, even in 1805, Thomas Spalding, of the Golden Isle Sapelo, speaking as the first president of the Union Agricultural Society, could declare: "Gentlemen, we are in the climate of Chaldea and of Egypt, of Greece, of Tyre, and of Carthage. We are in a land where rice, wheat, and cane, sugar, indigo, cotton, and silk, where the olive and the vine not only grow but will find their favorite home if man will only lend his aid."

It wasn't, of course, just a misunderstanding of latitudes. It was partly the West Indies background of the majority of the early Carolinians. Anyway, they missed their guess. Rice, which was to become their first great crop, wasn't even considered by the Lords Proprietors. Indigo was, but it would be eighty years before it came into its own. Of cotton, which a century and a quarter later would make and then unmake the state, Governor West remarked in 1671: "I feare this will not prove a cotton country."

Even before rice came in about 1700, the land itself was teaching the settlers what it would produce. In the vast canebrakes that covered miles of lowland, men began to herd cattle and to export barreled beef and pork, including the marked hog ears to prove the meat not stolen. By 1682 some planters had herds of from seven to eight hundred cows. In the endless forests of the pine barrens, they produced tar, pitch, turpentine, and lumber. From these same forests and canebrakes came the thousands of deerskins—within thirty years, fifty-four thousand a year—brought in by Indian hunters and destined to enrich, and for a brief moment to endanger, the life of the colony.

The Indian trade can be seen at its best—and worst—in early South Carolina. Even New York's "bush runners" did not rival as explorers the Charles Town men, who, within a dozen years, were trading along the Coosa, seven hundred miles to the west, and, by 1705, had reached and crossed the Mississippi. But they overreached themselves. Fomenting tribal wars among the Indians and buying up the captives for slavery, they finally aroused too much resentment. Their Carolina allies, the Yamasees, revolted in 1715, and with them the more westerly Creeks and Choctaws. They drove their attacks to within twelve miles of Charles Town itself. If the Cherokees had risen too—and they came within an ace of doing so—they would have poured thousands of warriors out of the hills and swept the Carolinians into the sea.

Crusty Cotton Mather remarked, fairly aptly: Carolina "is newly destroy'd by the dreadful Judgments of God, for which an uncommon measure of Iniquities had ripened it." It isn't recorded what he thought of New Englanders buying Indian slaves, delivered in Charles Town vessels—in New England vessels, too—nor of the South Carolina justification for the trade: "that it both serves to lessen their numbers before the French can arm them, and it is a more Effectual way of Civilizing and Instructing [them] than all the Efforts used by the French Missionaries."

Virginia, too, had fallen into slavery: Negro slaves, for lack of indentured servants, and Indian slaves, as incidental to Indian warfare. South Carolina assumed slavery: Negro slaves as necessary to the plantation, Indian slaves as a valuable native product. Thus the broad Elizabethan vision dimmed and narrowed.

Finally, in 1733, Georgia was settled both as a buffer state against the Spaniards, now strengthened by new Indian allies because of the Yamasee War, and also as a refuge for worthy debtors. The debtors and the others—especially South Carolinians who wanted to move to Georgia—objected to the initial absence of rum and slaves. But even after the founding of Georgia—and she was England's last colonial adventure in America—South Carolina preferred to be known as "the Southern Frontier." It is probable that the frontier experiences of South Carolinians between 1670 and 1760—settled, as Joseph Dalton said in 1671, "in the very chops of the Spaniard"—facing great Indian nations who were being egged on by France and Spain, and with no help from England and little from the other colonies, combined to develop the pride that South Carolinians still feel. Charles Woodmason said of them in 1771: "It being a Maxim with these proud People, *Not to copy after others*—But to have something of their own."

Final primary ingredient, for both the pride of South Carolina and the course of the burgeoning South, was the tremendous eighteenth century movement of Scotch-Irish, English, and Germans down the valleys of the Appalachian "divide" as far as Georgia. The Palatine German tide into the Valley of Virginia, out of upstate New York and Pennsylvania, was so strong that it slowed the tobacco planters' land-mining push west across the Fall Line. Further south, the Scotch-Irish stalking west into Carolina's piedmont could not yet bend Calvinist convictions to the commercial-plantation economy. The times and their pressures would wreak change. Within a century, Scotch-Irish John Calhoun would begin his fluent prelude to the South's great crisis.

Thus, before 1750, from the Potomac to Oglethorpe's Fort Frederica on St. Simon's Isle, from Cape Hatteras to Great Smoky shadows, the South's future took shape and firmed. Scotch-Irish, German, English all still accepted a future as subjects of London's King. The mores and convictions of the South as a region, as a begetter of specific North American types, would grow nonetheless from the Clearings, and those Foundation groups established by the Clearing's individualistic pattern by word, deed, and economic decision determined the building of the South.

Part 2
The Molders

Preceding page:
Settlers in South Carolina

With fish, oysters, bread and deere, they kindly traded with me and my men, beeing no lesse in doubt of my intent, then I of theirs.

CAPTAIN JOHN SMITH, 1608

WILLIAM S. POWELL

The Native

"YESTERDAY OUR two barks lay quietly at anchor all during the fourth of July. The day was hot but the land breeze hinted of a sweet-smelling garden just beyond the trees. We kept a careful watch for other human beings, but it was not until today that we saw any of the strange creatures who occupy this paradise. They must have been gathering courage for several days to approach us for when they came they filled many dugouts. They are a handsome and goodly people, much the color of dull copper. The brother of the king came in one of the boats and from him we learn that the king is called Wingina and the country is Wingandacoa.

"When we went ashore to visit them, they showed no signs of fear. Their clothes are only loose mantles of deer skin or perhaps an apron, and their weapons are simply bows and arrows and flat-edged clubs.

"A little investigation has disclosed that their towns are very small with ten or twelve houses, or at the most twenty. A house is made of many small poles gathered at the top in arch form (much as our arbors in the gardens of England) and covered with bark or rush mats. Some houses are but twelve or sixteen yards long, but we have seen others up to twenty-four.

"These trustful people, with whom we are being very gentle, have traded many deer skins for our bright tin dishes. One of them offered a great box of pearls for some of our armor and a sword. They have heaped our decks with venison, rabbits, and fish, fresh fruit, melons, nuts, and vegetables. Our copper kettles and bits of bright cloth they esteem highly, and knives and swords are much sought after since they have no sharp-edged implements."

This was the early summer season of 1584. Captain Arthur Barlowe was reporting to Sir Walter Raleigh, who had sent this expedition to the shores of "Virginia," now North Carolina. The Indian of the South was also getting a close look at white men, his conquerors-to-be. The curtain was about to rise on two hundred fifty years of warfare, enslavement, plague, and final banishment. All of this is seventh-grade history. But only today are excavations revealing the story of the South's red man before that 1584 calm.

Archaeologists have shown that the Indian inhabited the Pacific slope and the Southwest for at least fifteen thousand years. He was a comparative late-comer in the Southeast, probably arriving about 3000 B.C. While some information has come to us from early writers and from traditions, many questions are being answered by modern exploration. Frequently under the direction of the Smithsonian Institution or in connection with the National Park Service or a state park agency, sites of important Indian villages, council houses, and ceremonial mounds have been excavated. They reveal such a variety of information as the shape, size, and construction details of various buildings; goods acquired by the Indians in trade with distant tribes; burial customs; items of personal adornment; and household implements. In many cases reconstructed Indian villages have been restored, and excellent museums display the relics found on or near the site. Ocmulgee National Monument at Macon, Georgia, with modern facilities of this nature, has become a center for prehistoric research and survey of the Southeast's Indian peoples.

Broadly speaking—a semantic trap studiously avoided by the Amerind archaeologist—nineteen Indian cultural areas existed in the Old South when European "invasions" began. North to south on the coastal plain lived the Pamunkey, Mattapony, Chickahominy, Powhatan, Tutelo, Croatan, Catawba, Yuchi, Seminole, and Timuquanan. West of them, in the Appalachians, ranged the Shawnee, Tuscarora, Cherokee, Upper Creeks, and Lower Creeks. On the west slopes, Mississippi Basin, and Gulf Coast the Quapaw, Choctaw, Natchez, and Biloxi dominated.

These Indians were great travelers. Their earliest trails, made by wild game, generally led to water, a salt lick, or sources of food. Through constant use and extension, a mass of crossing trails existed throughout the South by the early colonial period. Indians are known to have traveled up to two thousand miles, and to have been absent from home for two months or more, on visits to distant friendly tribes. Iroquois from the New York area went into South Carolina to attack the Catawbas, and into Florida in a campaign against the Creeks. A network of trading paths led from settlement to settlement. They crossed rivers at the best fording places and followed natural gradients, so provided ready-made routes and foundations for the paths and roads of the white man. Many of the cities of the South developed at the crossroads of Indian trails; Nashville and Chattanooga each stands at the junction of at least five Indian trails. Charlotte, Charleston, Savannah, Jacksonville, Montgomery, and Jackson all were terminals of Indian trading paths.

The white settler soon adopted Indian crops and the natives' methods

"The manner of their attire and painting themselves when they goe to their generall huntings or at theire solemne feasts." Drawing by John White, a a member of Raleigh's first colony

of growing them. The red man had determined by trial and error which of the plants growing around him were poisonous, which pleased the palate, and which could best be adapted to provide him food that would last through the winter. He also determined the proper seasons for planting and harvesting, how to fertilize a hill of corn, how to store grain for the winter and also save seed for another year's crop.

Nearly every facet of the land had an Indian legend to explain it. Thunder and lightning, birds and snakes and lizards, the sun and moon—all were fair subjects for the grandmother tales. Many American folk legends ordinarily attributed to the Negro were actually Indian in origin. The Indian slaves of early settlers worked side by side with Negroes in the fields; the tales they told were adopted by the imaginative Africans. The famous "tar baby" story was a Cherokee legend. Such other Southern folk beliefs as Groundhog Day, the Lucky Rabbit's Foot, and the ill-boding Falling Star fall into the same category.

The Indian's techniques for hunting and fishing were copied by his new neighbors, too. Stalking game, or driving it into the open by firing woods or canebrakes, were common practices. The tribes had developed different kinds of weirs for coastal and inland fishing; they used bone hooks and fiber lines, nets and snares, shot fish with arrows or speared them. Sometimes fish were attracted by fire, or stunned by poison in small pools, then taken out with drags or by hand. Remains of rock fish weirs built by Indians survive in and near the southern Appalachians.

From the Indian's skill in woodcraft, the colonist learned many valuable lessons which stood him in good stead not only as an individual but later when he and his neighbors struck the blow for independence from England. Early observers discovered that the native could find his way through thick woods or across nearly barren plains without a compass—he knew that a certain kind of moss grew on the north side of trees. On such excursions the warrior-hunter subsisted on the berries and nuts of the country through which he passed. When crossing an unfamiliar river or lake at night or during a fog, Indians found their way by tossing sticks out at intervals and observing their drift. By 1709, when John Lawson wrote of his association with the Indians of North Carolina, their methods of marking trails were understood. Their skills at camouflage, and their ability to take advantage of the terrain in concealing themselves, soon became second nature to the frontiersman, too. Before long, he was beating the Indian at his own game.

But the give-and-take between the red men and the whites was not on a cultural-exchange basis. The first few men to step ashore in Virginia in 1607 at the establishment of the first permanent English settlement in America were attacked by warriors, and two of the intruders suffered arrow wounds. Subsequent events favored first one and then the other of the opposing forces. At times, the friendly native unselfishly shared his meager food with starving colonists; at others, he shot whites in the back as they poached on his ancestral hunting and fishing grounds. The newly arrived settler frequently took Indians into his household as servants, to be trained in the ways of the white man and taught Christianity. But he seldom hesitated to take advantage of the poor savage in trade, to steal his corn, and usurp his land. A bloody assault by once friendly Indians on the Virginia colonists on March 22, 1622, reduced the colony from 1140 to only 894. The war waged against the natives during the next decade designed to serve as "a sharp revenge upon the bloody miscreants, even to the measure that they intended against us, the rooting them out from being longer a people upon the face of the Earth." By 1642 the Pamunkey tribe had given up and was in confinement on America's first Indian "reservation."

This pattern, in the main, was repeated all across the South, although "Indian troubles" did not end until America's first gold rush to the Dahlonega "strike" in Cherokee territory in 1830 hastened the cession of remaining Cherokee lands in Georgia to the state and foredoomed the exile of ten thousand Cherokees over "The Trail of Tears" to Oklahoma. The Five Civilized Tribes of Oklahoma, in 1850 totaling fifty thousand Indians and their "several thousand" Negro slaves, were all exiles from the South: Choctaw, Chickasaw, Creek, Seminole, and Cherokee. Yet they avidly supported the Confederacy during the Civil War; because of this, the Federal government "put aside" all their treaties. Meanwhile, before the Revolution, most of the Tuscarora fled north to become the "Sixth Nation" of the Iroquois Confederacy in New York State. Remnants of the Seminole fought on from the fastness of the Florida Everglades; to date, the Seminole have never made a formal peace treaty with the United States.

Place names on the land today serve to remind us that these proud and devoted people lived in, and loved, the South. Perhaps it was the name of the native king, Wingina, which reminded England's Queen Elizabeth of a Latin term sometimes applied to her, so that she decreed that the new land be called Virginia. Many streams and mountains still bear ancient Indian names. Tallahassee is derived from the Creek *talwa*, "town," and *hasi*, "old." Tulsa is a variation of the same words. And, some contend, so is Tennessee. Alabama is from the Choctaw *alba*, "plants" or "weeds," and *amo*, "to cut" or "to gather"—that is, "those who clear the land." Oklahoma as a name for the Indian territory was coined by a Choctaw chief in 1866 from *okla*, "people," and *homa*, "red." Chattanooga, in its Creek original, meant "Rock that comes to a point." Centuries before the War, the Creeks prophetically named Chickamauga, their phrasing for "Dwelling place of the war chief."

Many words of Indian origin in everyday use today in the South were first recorded by Captain John Smith and others in Virginia between 1608 and 1612. Among them are: canoe, chinquapin, moccasin, opossum, pohickery (which soon became "hickory"), pone (corn pone), raccoon, tomahawk, and tuckahoe. Hammocks were mentioned by early writers, as were "hurricanes." Hominy was first referred to in Virginia in 1629. Bayou is Choctaw. Names of some of the unfamiliar birds, animals, and fish retained their Indian names in the conversation of the early English colonists. Chipmunk and manhaden, for instance, are Algonquian names.

Even a hair-raising Confederate technique appears to be of Indian descent. Early fox hunters in the South adapted an Indian war cry to the purposes of the chase. Just 276 years after Captain Barlowe traded tin dishes for deerskin with King Wingina, that war cry evolved into the Rebel Yell.

Those who labor in the earth are the chosen people of God.

THOMAS JEFFERSON, 1787

WEYMOUTH T. JORDAN

The Planter

THE DESIRE for land-ownership hungered down the centuries from Roman villas and slaves, medieval manors and serfs. Most of the South's colonists crossed the appalling Atlantic for economic reasons. They and their sponsors longed for precious metals—Baron de Graffenreid wasted almost thirty years looking for gold in Carolina—but Land was the force which pulled them to America. If tenure of land brought economic, social, and political security and privilege in Europe, they reasoned, it ought to do the same thing in America. They came to Virginia to get land. They went westward for the same cause. And they found, until Andrew Jackson's time, that land ownership did indeed bring American privileges similar to the Norman's "ville" and the Englishman's barony.

Only a few Southerners became great land magnates. But point a finger at any hard-working, shrewd farmer in the South from Jamestown to Fort Sumter and beyond; there stood a potential planter. There were hundreds of them by 1775. They had to have a money crop, and they found it first in tobacco, then in rice and the blue-black dye source, indigo. Later, they would find greater profits in cotton and sugar.

A planter also had to have a labor force. White, Indian, and Negro indentured servants were tried for a time, but all failed to serve the purpose of large-scale farm production. What the planter needed was a permanent and dependable labor force. Slavery became a confirmed institution in the 1660's, as a result of Virginia's legal sanction and the introduction of both slaves and slave codes from the West Indies to Carolina. Since Virginia was the cultural hub of the Upper South and South Carolina the hub of the Lower South, slavery spread to their hinterlands. In 1775 slaves made up at least two-thirds of the population of the five Southern colonies. By 1860 the South had 8,000,000 whites, 4,000,000 slaves, and 250,000 free Negroes.

There were also some mulattoes. Their status was determined by the mothers. The saying prevailed that "Motherhood is a matter of fact; fatherhood is a matter of opinion." The Old South was not a brothel, but miscegenation went on, particularly on the more lonely plantations.

About one-fourth of the white adults in the South owned slaves in 1860; about 100,000 of the owners were planters. The average planter then held something like 1,000 or more acres of land, 20 to 40 slaves, and was engaged in producing a staple commodity for sale purposes. A total of 30,444 whites owned 20 to 40 slaves; 13,546 owned 40 to 100; 1,980 owned 100 to 200; 224 owned 200 to 300; 74 owned 300 to 500; 13 owned 500 to 1,000; and one owned more than 1,000. (In 1852, Samuel Hairston, of Pittsylvania, Virginia, held between 1,600 and 1,700 slaves, managed another 1,000 belonging to his mother-in-law, and was said to be worth between $3,000,000 and $5,000,000.) Every Southern state seems to have had at least one millionaire before the War, their wealth based largely on land and slaves.

Very few planters were aristocrats in the fullest sense of the word. Lord Halifax was the only titled aristocrat in colonial Virginia. Most planters were of plebeian origin, and became quasi-aristocratic during slavery time, this being especially true in the Lower South. This is not to say that they lacked gentlemanly traits, for men of that character abound in fact and in legend in the region. It is only to say that very few of them were aristocrats. Most planters were simply farmers with a highly exercised speculative bent who succeeded in their business operations and elevated themselves to planter status.

Look at the Georgian who went to Alabama and made his million in cotton and Negroes. While touring Europe in his private railway car, troops of a petty German prince tried to eject him from his car so that it could be used by the prince. The old planter, completely aroused, stormed at the soldiers, "Money are power, and I are got it." He refused to budge. Returning home, he resumed his activities as a member of the board of trustees of the University of Alabama and studied the progress of the two other colleges, the church, and the railroad he had founded and endowed.

The experiences of this man's family were typical of the large planter class of its time and place. Leaving Georgia in 1819, he and his brother moved to central Alabama, where everyone just then, according to a local slave trader, was "talking about cotton and 'niggers,'" adding, "Every man we met, either wanted to buy a 'nigger' or take a drink."

Starting with a credit purchase of about a thousand acres of land and a few slaves, the brother amassed nearly eight thousand acres, one hundred eighty-six slaves, and numerous other properties before his death in 1852. His son carried on the operations, and, by 1859, operated six plantations. He sold 1725 bales of cotton to his Mobile factor for $96,846 between 1852 and his own death in 1860. On each plantation he specialized, in addition, in the production of certain crops—peas, fodder, grain, hogs, beef cattle, and so on. He was not self-sufficient. Nearly all of his business transactions were done on credit. One day in town, as operator of the six plantations and worth hundreds of thousands of dollars, he signed notes (i.e., "drafts") totaling $14,320, then borrowed five dollars from a merchant in order to pay a pressing debt of $3.88 and get a haircut! Nevertheless, he left his family financially secure in 1860. After the War they turned to the share-crop system, with Negro and white labor, and remained comfortably solvent.

In operating its plantations, this family followed the usual practices of its class. Primarily they were agriculturists engaged in a capitalistic undertaking for profit. They were on their own. In pre-War days, planters received little aid—other than cheap land—from their government. The first agricultural appropriation granted by Congress—the sum of one thousand dollars to collect statistics—was not made until the year 1839. This family's problems were about the same as a manufacturer's: capital investments, production methods, labor management, credit, and the distribution and sale of products. Hard work and keen management were essential to success. As stated in the *Southern Quarterly Review* of Charleston, South Carolina, in January, 1848, "The truth is, a cotton plantation soon becomes a dead expense unless it is managed with great care and energy. Those who own slaves are forced to a system of sleepless activity, or the expense of their labor will soon consume all the profits and sink the capital."

The heirs of these transplanted Georgia brothers were typical large planters in practically every way. They bought land and slaves on credit and produced crops for sale. They worked their Negroes by both the gang and task systems under overseer management, then sold their crops through factors on a two and one-half per cent commission. They lived comfortably, educated their children, and contributed liberally to charities. As the benevolent gentry and leaders of thought in their communities, they were usually willing to help unfortunates and to advise whites of their own and of a lesser class. Most men approached them hat in hand; they laid their hands on the shoulders of most men. Some served in the Alabama legislature. Others held high positions in the courts of their state, some appointive,

some elective. They sponsored education and religion. By the turn of the twentieth century they reached a place in the society of their state matched by few people.

These families were, of course, far above the average. Most planters put three hundred fifty to five hundred acres to the plow each season. Census returns show that nonslaveholders owned as much land as slaveholders. County tax records prove that small farmers were not pushed off "all of the best lands" by planters. Many history books indicate that planters cultivated only "money crops": cotton, sugar, or rice. The truth is that corn was the largest crop in the Old South. The reason that this fact does not show up in most records is a simple one: Southerners produced corn for their own use. There was more livestock on a per capita basis in the pre-War South than in the North. So the corn was consumed at home by the millions of mules and horses, by the chickens, and—Amen, brother—by planter and slave alike in the a-maizing array of grits, hoecake, shortenin' bread *ad gustorum.* Corn wasn't sold. Planters couldn't be bothered keeping records on it.

Planters, more than any other Southerners, advocated and practiced diversified farming. They were the chief founders and supporters of the agricultural press, societies, and fairs. Some even said that "a good farm paper is more important than a good wife." Many encouraged the use of Peruvian guano, the potent sea-bird manure, introduced into the South through Baltimore. Carolina planters found it increased their cotton yields by two hundred pounds to the acre. One tall tale was circulated about a small boy who fell asleep on some bags of guano stored in a barn and woke up to find he was "a giant eight feet tall"!

The columned mansion with veranda and other trappings is as tall a story as the guano-giant, insofar as the vast majority of planters were concerned. In most of the South, planters were not long or far removed from the frontier. Too often interested only in mining the soil for quick profits, they did not want mansions as much as shelter, and sometimes were satisfied with cabins. Instead of cognacs, mint juleps, and "cock-tales," the planter generally preferred raw, hard liquor and home brew. A few purchased expensive liquors and wines through factors; the majority "made their own." Beer was made by placing a pound of treacle, two bay leaves, and one-fourth of an ounce of powdered ginger in eight quarts of water, boiling the whole for fifteen minutes, then working it with yeast. A recipe for "good bitters" calls for one ounce each of pulverized columbo root, gentian root, orange peel, red sanders, black snake root, and Peruvian bark, blended in three pints of "Jamaica spirits," set in the sun for ten days, and then strained.

Planters often took "the pledge," but didn't put their hearts in it any more than their descendants who voted against Al Smith in 1928. The region was—and is—noted for its hard drinking, which may explain why John Gorrie, of Apalachicola, Florida, in 1851 patented an ice-making machine. One of the most lamentable events in Southern history, to many a planter, occurred in New Orleans in 1830 when hard cider and beer had to be used to douse a building ablaze on Custom House Street.

Planters liked to gamble, like other Americans, on horses and almost anything else. (One Mississippi planter bet $50,000 on the size of the Southern cotton crop in 1834.) They loved parties, housewarmings, weddings, and even funerals. Of all games, they seem to have been most interested in "kissing games." One editor advised them, "If you want to enjoy a kiss in all its raciness—get your little charmer into a corner of a sofa, before a cozy fire of a freezing night—steal your arms around her waist—take her hand gently in your own—and then draw her tenderly towards you. Kiss her a long sweet kiss, as if you were a bee sucking honey from a flower." Another warned, "Don't make a noise over it, as if you were firing percussion caps, or trying the water-cocks of a steam engine, nor pounce down upon it like a hungry hawk upon an innocent dove." One planter, at least, complained of the "sneak stage kisses" prevalent among the actors on the Mobile stage. Kisses, he vowed, ought to be "real old-fashioned smacks as loud as bursting goat bladders."

The chief reading interests of planters were newspapers, farm magazines, and the Bible. Most of them were Baptist, Methodist, or Presbyterian. They loved the Georgia Presbyterian minister who openly prayed that two Baptists would move out of his community and be replaced by members of his own denomination, and were equally delighted by the story about a preacher who was arrested for making and circulating counterfeit bank bills so "that he might be able to do more good, and send more missionaries to the heathen." In 1841 they applauded a jury in Oberlin, Ohio, for only fining some local students "who lynched a fellow student for writing anonymous letters soliciting a private interview with a female scholar." They understood when an eighty-one-year old plantation grandmother "put burglar bars on her windows to keep from bein' raped."

In politics, planters really "searched their souls." Many had remained loyal to the British Crown during the Revolution, probably because they received Crown "bounties" (now we call them "parity payments") for production of tobacco, indigo, tar, pitch, and turpentine. In the early Republic, most planters followed Thomas Jefferson because he supported Agrarianism and Expansion. They split on Andrew Jackson and John C. Calhoun, and turned to the Whig and Know-Nothing parties. By the eve of the Civil War, they were back with Calhoun precepts; these seemed best for Southern interests and states' rights. Thus in 1860, in the fifteen slaveholding states, Lincoln polled votes only in Missouri (17,028), Delaware (3815), Maryland (2294) and Virginia (1929), for a total of 25,066 out of 1,276,979 cast in the South. There is no doubt that planters had a great deal to do with influencing the way Southerners voted before the Civil War.

One of the most important responsibilities of the planter was management and care of his slaves. Rules and regulations were necessary in handling a slave force. Most of these seem to have been humane. Slaves were punished when they broke a master's regulations. Cruel and sadistic treatment of a capital investment was not unheard of, but it was not common. However, slaves had very little freedom of movement. They were chattel property bound by law to their owner. It was this earlier lack of freedom of movement which caused so many Negroes to take to the roads after 1865, "to see the elephant."

Housing, food, and clothing for slaves were among the chief concerns of planters, all usually being no more elaborate than necessary. Some religious instruction was furnished, often by Negro ministers whose chief accomplishment was an ability to talk fluently. (Praying for a departed brother, one of these ministers remarked, "Lord, I pray he am whar I know he ain't.")

Unusually close attention was given to the slaves' health. Fevers, agues, smallpox, dental problems, and epidemics, such as the cholera which swept the South in the 1840's and 1850's, could ruin an effective working force. Negro nurses on plantations often became expert practitioners.

Very few planters were completely self-sufficient in their operations. There was always the temptation of concentrating on a staple, money crop, and hoping that it would carry the load. Thus, as plantations developed across Mississippi, Louisiana, and into Texas, greater dependence was placed on the money crop. Between 1820 and 1845, James Westfall Thompson estimated, Southern planters spent nearly $1,000,000,000 in the North for horses, mules, cattle, sheep, hogs, hay, and farm implements.

Location and quality of soil, plus the individual traits of planters, had much to do with profits, of course. Planters on adjoining places could and did come out differently, one failing while the other succeeded. Hence the successful planter was at the top of the ladder in the Old South. Cheap land, slaves, planters, and staple crops largely made the Old South what it was.

There is no such person as a typical planter any more.

The rough rider of the plains, the hero of the rope and revolver, is first cousin to the back woodsman of the southern Alleghanies, the man of the ax and rifle; he is only a unique offshoot of the frontier stock of the Southwest.

THEODORE ROOSEVELT—"Ranch Life and the Hunting Trail"

ROBERT WEST HOWARD

The Cracker

TWO MYSTERY RIDERS dominated the western sky line of the pioneer South. One was the Chickasaw warrior of northern Mississippi, who bred the Chickasaw pony. The other was the Cracker, the cattleman who pushed the South's frontiers west from 1650 to 1800. Through them, J. E. B. Stuart's cavalry became American immortals, the cowboy and his Quarter Horse grew to demigod stature in the Far West, and horsemanship, a rich source of both humor and affection, became an essential of Southern life.

While Englishman and Spaniard glowered at one another through the gunports of Fort Frederica and St. Augustine, the Cracker–wild cattle–Indian pony alliance they unknowingly had fostered was developing in the groves and pea-vine pastures of the Piedmont. Only King Cotton's plundering march across the Mississippi would force these antecedent pioneers on to glory-roles in the high plains and up the long trails from Texas.

In 1521, Juan Ponce de Leon attempted, on the jungle shore of Charlotte Harbor (ninety miles south of modern Tampa), the first permanent European settlement in what is now the U.S.A. Indians forced abandonment of the stockade within a month, after Ponce de Leon had received a fatal wound.

History's smirch on the name of King Ferdinand's former page boy glares from neon signs along Florida highways which depict him as a bumbling searcher after a Fountain of Youth. But his true role is Gargantuan; the records indicate that he imported the first domestic livestock—horses, swine, cattle, and probably sheep—into a nation destined to become the world's greatest producer of cattle, of horseflesh, and the associated profession-sagas. Ponce de Leon's true Fountain of (and for) Youth was: the Sioux and Apache warrior, the cowboy, the Tennessee Walking Horse, the plantation horse, the Quarter Horse, the C.S.A. cavalrymen, and one of the greatest sources of America's humor, the mule.

Other Spaniards attempted Gulf Coast conquest during the next twenty-five years. Cabeza de Vaca (his name translates to "Head of a Cow"!) abandoned his horses, too, wandered inland for years, and returned to Spain to write the book that set off the three-century legend of the golden Cities of Cibola. Narváez tried it . . . and left more livestock. Finally, Hernando de Soto invested much of his Peruvian plunder in the 1539 expedition that slashed across two thousand miles of tidewater, highland, and river valleys to end with De Soto's burial in the waters of the Mississippi and the dispersion of his pigs and horses among the Indians of Mississippi, Arkansas, and Louisiana.

Historians now concede that the millions of wild horses thundering the Great Plains and the Pacific slope by 1800 were descendants of the herds abandoned by Ponce de Leon, de Vaca, Narváez, De Soto, Coronado and other Spanish explorers. The razorback hog, a cornerstone of Southern humor from Davy Crockett's *Journals* through Mark Twain to twentieth-century vaudeville, traces back, too, to the three hundred sows and boars de Soto's swineherds bred up during his two-year march.

Proof positive of the historians' concession is the Chickasaw pony that became the darling of the South's frontiersmen. Small, seldom over thirteen and one-half hands high, but spirited and beautiful, the pony was named for the first mounted Indians with whom colonial scouts and hunters came in contact. "The Chickasaws," Eggleston reported in his *Husbandry in Colonial Times*, "were fully aware of the value of the breed and carefully guarded it from intermixture. They even tried to prevent the sale of their horses to the whites, and most of the horses in South Carolina and Georgia were stolen and smuggled out of the Indian country."

The existence of a veritably "patented" breed of horse, jealously guarded by an Indian tribe in the hills of north Mississippi before 1700, indicates one of the most exciting, and least researched, chapters in American history. Although Gulf Coast tides persistently wash petrified teeth of pre-historic horses ashore near Charlotte Harbor and on the Venice and Englewood beaches, the animal vanished from the North American continent before the Indian migrated out of Asia.

Only the Spanish importation of horses and the amazing increase of these "strays" in the Southeast and on the high plains of the West after 1540 enabled the Apache, Sioux, Cheyenne, and other great cavalry tribes to achieve their nineteenth-century stature. The famed cayuse was named for the Oregon tribe who did precisely what the Chickasaws, Creeks and early Seminoles did: capture wild horses, crossbreed them, and produce a carefully controlled strain of wiry, fast pony. The Chickasaw pony was thus the first American example of domestic livestock inbreeding.

But, although the Chickasaw pony implied these potentials of an American future, the actual role of translator and developer-into-fact was performed by a great pioneer whose name became a slur, almost an epithet, in the American language.

By the 1750's, during fall and spring, long drives of cattle, horses, and pigs, sometimes totaling five thousand head, took the trails toward the seaports. The men and boys who "trailed 'em" carried stocky leather and

The landing of De Soto at Tampa Bay, Florida, 1539

wood whips with rawhide or linen strings braided to the tip. With practice, and a strong wrist, a cowboy-drover could flick a fly from a cow's nose at fifteen feet, or make the strings crack like a rifle shot against the flank of an errant sow halfway up a creek bank. (Not until 1958 did scientists discover *why* the whips cracked. They finally measured the speed of the tip as it flicked, discovered that it "bangs" because it has broken the sound barrier.)

The trails ran out of the Sea Isles to Charleston, and from the Five Points trail-crossing that was one day to be called Atlanta, over the hills to Augusta, Columbia, Camden, and Elizabethtown—then on north through Wake Court House, Warrenton, Petersburg, and Richmond to the Baltimore, Philadelphia, and New York paths. Even Boston knew the flavor of South Carolina and Georgia beef before the Revolution. The Cheraw bacon cured in Charleston was famous throughout the South and many of the West Indies.

Into town the droves clattered. The livestock squealed and bawled through clouds of dust; the drovers howled like banshees and cracked the long whips at everything in sight. Perhaps a pretty girl began it as a tease; perhaps a paunchy, scowling shopkeeper jammed his Sunday wig in place and stormed off to complain to the City Council. Whoever did it, the drovers soon had the city nickname of Cracker. Dr. Johann Schopf, a keen observor and agricultural authority, toured the South the year after the Revolution ended. In Wilmington, Raleigh, Charleston, whenever he asked about livestock drovers and herdsmen from the highlands, people said, "Oh, you mean the Crackers," then explained about the long whips. Schopf went back to Europe and wrote about the Crackers in his book, *Travels in the Confederation, 1783-4*. It was a pretty proud nickname, by then.

Before 1600, cattle had joined the Spanish horses and pigs that went "native" in the southern highlands and Gulf Coast savannahs. Florida Spaniards called them "the cimmarones" or "wild ones" . . . a name that would not strike the American fancy until the movies reintroduced it in fixed association with Oklahoma (and Edna Ferber). Thousands of wild black cattle, descendants of Andalusian stock imported for Florida settlements, were roaming the Georgia and Carolina piedmont when the first adventurers from the English colonies reached there in the 1680's.

Fortunately, Nature "rigged" this, too. The first Virginians were not good stockmen. England went all-out for a sheep economy during the twelfth century. The Irish, the Scotch, and the Germans were the prime cattlemen of England's world. Ireland had been cattle-country since the sixth or seventh century A.D.; the word "cowboy" first appears in ancient Gaelic poetry. The Scotsman, blessed with highland pastures and a natural bent for "the beasties," sailed willy-nilly back and forth across the Irish Sea from the dawn-days. And so did the Welshman.

Meanwhile, from the Dutch Lowlands to the Alpine passes, Germans and Dane-Marchers developed superb strains of milch cattle. Guernsey, Holstein, Jersey, Fresian, and Brown Swiss all had ancestry there, just as the Hereford, Angus, and Durham Shorthorn would emerge from the border counties of Scotland and Wales in the eighteenth and nineteenth centuries. Logically, on July 7, 1620, the directors of the Virginia Company resolved that "200 cattle, 400 goats, 80 asses and 20 mares" be imported *from Ireland*. The following year, three hundred Walloons landed in Virginia, bringing the colony's first imports of Flemish cattle.

Compelled possibly by the profits of the tobacco crop, the Indian wars, and urges to create an American aristocracy, the Virginian continued to neglect animal husbandry. Horses were essential; horse races provided excitement and an opportunity to gamble. He did import good strains of "horseflesh" and bred them up to race on turf-tracks a quarter of a mile long. Here, as Wayne Gard has shown in his excellent book *Fabulous Quarter Horse: Steel Dust*, the sires and dams of the Western cowboy's Quarter Horse actually surged toward birth as a distinct breed.

But the pioneering of the South's livestock industries was left to the highlander; and Nature had carved a path for him. Germans and Scotch-Irish . . . some in flight from New York tax-collectors, others "fed up" with New England's narrowness and Pennsylvania's frontier policies . . . began marching down the Great Valley of Virginia, far west of the colony's tidewater towns and plantations. Some drove in herds of livestock. Others discovered the Spanish cattle, wild-horse herds, and snag-tusked hogs wandering in the Piedmont woods, then scouted the valleys and ridges to discover Cherokees, Creeks, and Chickasaws industriously herding livestock and growing corn and wheat for winter feed-supplies.

Ancestral instinct quickened. Irish prisoners from Cromwell's pillage of the Emerald Isle, now fleeing Virginia indenture, joined refugee adherents of Nathaniel Bacon's 1676 revolt against Williamsburg's gentlemen. Mennonites and French Huguenots trekked in, too. By 1700 they had set up the animal-husbandry pattern that was to cross the continent.

Sugar plantations on Jamaica, the Barbados, and the Leewards needed huge annual supplies of meat, lard, and horses. The Germans, Scotch-Irish, and Mennonites teamed to build V-shaped wooden pens. Whooping and firing guns, they flushed herds of wild horses and cattle and pigs out of the glades and drove them into the pens. They were in business.

Branding irons were as common to them as hip boots. If you didn't want to scar an animal's hide with the hot iron, it was a simple matter to cut your mark on the ears or tail-butt; that's what the Puritans were doing in back-country Massachusetts and New Hampshire.

By 1722, Gray reported in his classic *Agriculture in the Southern States to 1860*, herdsmen had crossed to the south side of the Savannah River, thus forcing the development of Georgia. A decade later, the General Assembly of South Carolina voted to contribute 133 head of breeding cattle to "the Georgia experiment."

Quickly, a string of crude "wild and woolly" settlements grew along the Piedmont and over into the Blue Ridge and Smokies themselves. They became the master-pattern for Dodge City, Abilene, and other cow-towns of the Far West. Going under the name of "cowpens," the communities consisted of a cluster of log cabins, a series of wooden corrals for horses and cattle, large fields of corn, and natural stands of pea-vine or bluegrass pasture. "It was usually," said John H. Logan in his *History of the Upper Country of South Carolina*, "officered with a superintendent and a corps of subagents, all active men, experienced woodsmen and unfailing shots at long or short sights with the rifle." (Even then, avowed Gray, these herdsmen were known as "cowboys.") Pastures were burned off every year or two in the belief that this improved the grass and killed the ticks.

By 1704, South Carolina shipped beef, pork, soap, candles, butter, and cheese . . . all livestock products . . . to the Leeward Islands. Two years later, the colony ruled that butchers "and all others engaged in killing cattle" must present animals to a Toll Master before slaughter. Slaves were forbidden to brand the stock, save in the presence of a white person. When pork was sold in barrels, the animal's head had to be packed with the ears on so that inspectors could examine the brand-mark and make certain the meat was not stolen goods.

The Crackers of the 1790's having done potent shooting with Morgan at Saratoga, with George Rogers Clark at Vincennes, and pretty much by themselves at Kings Mountain and Cowpens, kept right on going in history. Before 1805, they opened stockrails down through Staunton and Abington into the new village of Nashville. They pushed a path on south by southwest across the Tennessee River, through the Chickasaw-pony country into Natchez. Here, too, they found thousands of wild black cattle feeding in the savannahs of pea-vine and sweet grass.

Back along this Natchez Trace they'd pounded, hundreds of new settlers got into the livestock business: Scotch-Irish "freeholders" who had stalked west beyond the grasp of the rice and indigo planters; the nine thousand or more Scotch Highlanders who stormed into the Carolinas after Bonnie Prince Charlie's 1746 rout at Culloden. County clerks in Knoxville and Nashville took down the books two or three times a day to enter a new brand-mark—"The Mark and Brand of Nicholas Gibbs are, Mark half Crop off the Right Ear and Split and Under bit out of the under part of the left Ear. Brand, N. G."

East across the mountains, the three most eminent Virginians cheered the Crackers' efforts and became their "idea men." Long before the Revolution, George Washington reached the conclusion that tobacco and Indian corn were dangerous, soil-depleting crops. By 1773, he had cut tobacco production on Mount Vernon's six thousand acres back to five thousand pounds a year in order to concentrate on a program of land restoration through cover-crops, rotation, and livestock production. He tried to domesticate bison and painstakingly experimented with pig and sheep breeding. He planned, until called to the Presidency, to devote the rest of his life to the development of sheep particularly suited for east-coast farms. So, in 1784, he hired James Bloxham out of England to develop plans for the improvements of livestock and "the implements of husbandry necessary thereto." There were 270 head of cattle on the Mount Vernon range that year; each carried the big "G.W." brand on its right shoulder.

Over in the Charlottesville area, neighbors Thomas Jefferson and James Madison were similarly engaged. Jefferson urged the importation of Merino sheep; he and Madison maintained experimental herds. Both preached for, and practiced, a "scientific animal-husbandry."

Cotton and the mule changed the picture. Mules began to be imported from Cuba after the Revolution. The King of Spain presented Washington with two jacks in 1795. Their progeny, known as Royal Gift, spread across the tidewater. Connecticut traders, long the shrewdest horse dealers on the seaboard, imported shiploads of Spanish mules and sold them through Norfolk and Charleston. The mule's stoic toughness helped the spread of inland cotton caused by Whitney's invention of the gin. By 1815, contemporaries reported, cotton planters with processions of slaves, household goods, and mules were crossing the Mississippi meadows "like ancient caravans."

The more daring stockmen pushed west, some into the Red River valley, some out to the Ohio country. Kentucky, the Iroquois' "Land of Rolling Meadow," burgeoned as the Crackers applied their skills to its bluegrass and "bottom" land. Horse and cattle herds from Kentucky and neighboring Ohio created the trails that later became routes for the Baltimore & Ohio, Pennsylvania, and New York Central railroads. Henry Clay imported some of the first Herefords ever seen in America to his Lexington plantation, and did his oratorical durndest to popularize the poker-faced critters.

In those same years, other Southerners reared in the proud Cracker tradition headed toward Texas . . . Stephen Austin from Virginia, via Missouri; the Bowie brothers from Georgia; Davey Crockett and Sam Houston from Tennessee. There they, and the Crackers who followed them, found the selfsame conditions of wild, longhorn cattle ("The Texas lions") milling through tumbleweed and mesquite. The Crackers' skills, blended with those of the Southwest vaqueros and Comancheros (rigged out in Mexican hats and such fancy Spanish words as *ranch*, *lariat*, *rodeo*, *hombre*), prepared for the postwar depression of 1866–67 that ennobled the saga of The Cowboy on the High Plains.

His words and gear might be Southwestern Indo-Spanish; Texas might claim all his glory. But from the tunes he spun into his haunting songs to the Southern stature permanently given him by Owen Wister's *The Virginian*, the cowboy could look back over his shoulder to the Carolina highlands and call the Cracker "Daddy."

As for Daddy's home-clinging heirs, they fell on hard days. Land prices forced them out of the bottom lands into the red clay hills. They toiled grimly on forty acres with a mule, slowly falling through poverty, lack of schooling, and inbreeding to the category of "poor white." Yet the title "Cracker" hung on like a chigger . . . now a term of scorn and sadness . . . a name of unknown ancestry.

Perhaps eventually, with livestock's resurgence across the South, the day will come when cattlemen again, from Kissimmee to Tupelo, will straighten their shoulders and say "I'm a Cracker, dammit . . . the tallest and oldest and best cowman of them all." Perhaps by that time, too, Florida will realize what Juan Ponce de Leon's Fountain of Youth really was.

"Thus now, as always, the evils which men fear they shall be called upon to encounter as a result of doing what is just and humane, are discovered, when they are really encountered, not to be evils at all, but blessings pure and simple."

Report of the Committee for
Securing Colored People in Philadelphia
the Right to Ride in Street Cars (1866)

LAURENCE C. JONES

The Negro

THE NEGRO'S COMING to this country was dictated by the demand for labor and labor only. In his coming as a chattel, and not as a human being, he probably influenced American life and history more profoundly than any other single factor.

Within the last few decades a vast and increasing change has so transformed the lives and fulfilled the hopes of sixteen million Americans that it has obscured what has been taking place gradually for centuries. In less than a single generation American Negroes have marched further, and moved faster, toward their long-dreamed participation in American affairs as full citizens than any other group in history.

We have earned this right not only through the contributions of such well-known people as Booker T. Washington, George Washington Carver, Marian Anderson, Ella Fitzgerald, Louis Armstrong, Jackie Robinson, Eartha Kitt, Sammy Davis, Jr., and Ralph Bunche—to mention only a few—but have also earned it through the economic and cultural contributions of "the only element of the American population which came by special invitation, with their passage paid"—our ancestors, the slaves.

In the beginning, to create our America of today, there was a vital and insistent need for labor—strong backs and brawny muscles to clear forests, build roads, work mines, dig ditches, build houses, plant, cultivate and gather crops, cook the meals, care for the sick, and to take the brunt of countless other activities. A large part of this labor in the country as a whole, and almost all of it in the South, was performed for two and a half centuries by Negro slaves without pay.

It was the Negroes' labor that made tobacco the first staple crop of the New World. The Negro alone could live and work in the miasmic coastal swamps where rice was grown. The first successful sugar plantations and refineries, located mostly in Louisiana along the Mississippi River, were manned by Negro workers. The folk ballads that grew up around John Henry came from Negro levee workers and stevedores. When Eli Whitney's cotton gin revolutionized the textile industry, it was Negro labor that planted, cultivated, and picked the snow-white fiber for the hungry mills of Europe and New England.

To understand the Negro's economic as well as cultural contributions, his life must be considered in relation to that of the whites whom he served. Domestic and rural work made intimate contacts unavoidable, hence brought about the rapid assimilation of the white man's civilization, language, religion, and folkways. This of course was speeded by wide interbreeding, which leaves not more than a third of the colored population today as pure Negro.

To think that the Negro came empty-handed or empty-headed to this new land is naïve. He had many varieties of tribal languages, none of them written. This led to more oral memory than dependence on the written word. He had innumerable superstitions and myths, as well as definite concepts of morality and religion. Furthermore, to come to an economy of scarcity when you had lived in the rich extravagance of the tropics; to be forced to be punctual and prompt when time had been a hazy intermission; to be forced to read, write, and calculate when you had never seen a pencil or a book; to be controlled by rules and regulations when only haphazard natural pain and pleasure had been your master—all of these influenced the Negro in his contributions.

As the Negro took off the garments of primitiveness and donned those of civilization, he did so in the South on three different levels. There were the privileged house servants—sometimes half-brothers or half-sisters to the white children of the family—who were well cared for and, if they kept their place, had many privileges and advantages. They did the cleaning and the cooking, the nursing, and were the Mammys who looked after the children. Some of them were the hunting, fishing, and riding companions of the boys, though never quite on an eye-to-eye level.

Below the house servants were the artisans, who also occupied a privileged spot. Many of them were quite skilled; among them—some of them freedmen—were noted inventors, although no accurate record is available since a Negro could not obtain a patent in his own name. A Maryland Negro, Henry Blair, in 1834 invented a successful corn planter; a Louisiana Negro, Norbert Rillieux, worked out a complicated vacuum pan that revolutionized the refining of sugar; and another Negro, Jan E. Matzeliger, in 1842 constructed a machine that took bootmaking from handicraft to factory work, thereby reducing the cost of manufacture by over 50 per cent. Since slavery days many thousands of patents have been taken out by Negroes.

Most of the carpentry and blacksmithing work on the plantation was done by Negro artisans, as was the shoemaking. The shoes worn by President Monroe at his inauguration were made by a Negro bootmaker. Many were millers and stone masons. When Harriet Martineau visited America she marveled at the exquisite patterns of the tiling in Thomas Jefferson's Monticello, the work of a Negro. The delicately patterned hand-wrought iron porticoes, trellises, and galleries in New Orleans were the handicraft of Negro artisans, as were most of the great mansions that symbolize the Old South.

A Virginia newspaper mentioned a slave who was an "extraordinary sawyer, a good carpenter and currier, made shoes and is a good sailor." A twenty-six-year-old Maryland Negro, by trade a blacksmith, was also a shoemaker and capable of reading, driving a carriage, and shaving and dressing hair. Another slave was a weaver and an expert musician. Others were listed as barbers, brewers, bricklayers, cabinet makers, carpenters, caulkers, coopers, cordwainers, distillers, glovers, goldsmiths, locksmiths, painters, pipe makers, shipwrights, tanners, and upholsterers.

Some of the women possessed skills far superior to those of the average domestic, excelling in cooking, washing, and other forms of household work. Many were spinners and seamstresses, soap and starch makers, and dyers.

Although the Negro had few opportunities in the South before the Civil War in the fields of science, medicine, and education, the mention of only a few names indicates the breadth and wealth of his contribution since attaining freedom. George Washington Carver, in an ill-equipped laboratory at Tuskegee Institute, developed more than three hundred new uses for peanuts, sweet potatoes, and other Southern products which, when the coming of the boll weevil ravaged the economy of that region, brought to it many millions of dollars in replacement. Dr. Daniel Hale Williams not only opened the way for the training of Negro nurses and doctors, but was a pioneer in heart surgery. Booker T. Washington made Tuskegee Institute, one of the first of its kind, world-famous for the training of Negroes in sciences and crafts. His famous statement, in connection with his goal of giving economic opportunity to the Negro, that "The white man can't keep the Negro in a ditch without crawling in with him," still has a tremendous lesson for all of the world.

As evidence that a greater contribution from colored people could have been made in the South toward industrial education, my maternal grandfather and his brothers, after escaping from the South by the underground railway, founded and chartered "The Woodstock Manual Labor Institute"

A primary school for freedmen at Vicksburg, Mississippi, about 1866

at Addison, Michigan, in 1849 to give to all people who wanted it "a Christian education of hand and head." This was before Hampton and Tuskegee—the first time in the educational history of our country that education was conceived to be the training of the hand and heart as well as book education.

As valuable as these contributions were, however, the entire order of the South rested on the "bent and lash-scarred back" of the menial workers, those who constituted a peasant class. It is here that we must look for the greatest contributions of the Negro to the South and to America. These pioneers toiled, suffered, and only by a miracle of emotional endurance survived; it is out of their suffering that our greatest legacy came. To survive they had to share their burdens and sorrows with each other, and at the same time present an individual front to their masters that masked their deepest longings.

Held together in a common bondage, a true folk culture developed that was an admixture of what the Negro had brought with him from Africa, what he got from the white culture of which he was such an intimate part, and the uses he made of the mixture. Paradoxically, his position as a slave affected this vitally. The dominant whites, living in the artificial vacuum of a transported feudalism, could have accepted the folk contributions of the poor whites. This they scorned to do, while being almost unconsciously affected by the Negro's contributions, which they could afford to tolerate from their dominant position. Thus out of the Negro's humor, emotional makeup, mystic superstitions, nonchalance, and sentimentality came a folk art that made him the official jester of the South.

Because this comic side offered no threat to the dominant class, it richly colored the local and regional culture and became a wide source of amusement. From its dancing, singing and jigging came the "blackface" minstrelsy and, later, the vaudeville and musical comedy that dominated the stage of the United States for three-quarters of a century. Later this flowered to jazz and ragtime, to popular dance idiom, to the matchless balladry of the "blues," secular work chants, folk-tale ballads, and "sinful" songs that constitute by far the greatest body of folk music enriching the American heritage.

And there was an even more important and significant contribution that went unnoticed until after the Civil War. This was the superb "spiritual," first recognized by an army officer, Colonel Thomas Wentworth Higginson of one of the Negro regiments during the War, who encouraged William Allen to collect such songs. Not until the Fisk Jubilee Singers began singing them in 1879, however, was the spiritual's uniqueness realized, and its extraordinary folk genius revealed. The South that gleefully heard the secular songs had paid little attention. All Negro singing to them had been a way of "carrying on." Time has proven what the spirituals really were—a religious vitalization of Christianity and the Bible that, along with their use of humor, reflected the most serious and intimate aspects of the slave Negro in his life-sustaining hope of heavenly salvation and of earthly freedom. It saved his spirit from breaking, and was also a triumph of folk art.

The secular song and dance, and the spirituals, in addition to their intrinsic contribution, are regarded as even more precious in their potential value as material for fresh artistic reworking. Already contemporary musicians and folklorists, Negro and white, are turning back more and more to Negro folk music.

Another means for escape other than musical, and quite as useful for survival through the emotional exhausts of laughter, ridicule, and even mockery, were the folk tales; those attributed to Uncle Remus by Joel Chandler Harris are among the best examples.

These cultural contributions of the Negro have been for the most part dominant, fundamental, and enduring, rather than merely superficial or transitory. As such, they add up to a substantial portion of the native American art forms and play an unusually large part in molding and sustaining the entertainment life of the nation. Strange indeed that the section of the population most subject to oppression and suffering should furnish such a large proportion of the population's joy and relaxation!

But not so strange was another more momentous contribution. "Go down, Moses, tell ole Pharaoh to set my people free," goes the spiritual that brings Christianity and the Bible alive, and "Moses," in the spirit of a people dedicated to democracy, listened. Strange and wonderful things happened. The progression of the Negro from chattel to freedom, to legal citizenship, to increasing equality of rights and opportunities, to a recognized status as a neighbor and compatriot, represents perhaps the most dramatic testament to the vitality and the dynamic character of democracy.

The presence of the Negro in American life, as a slave the very antithesis of democracy, has been democracy's catalyst that may keep it forever alive. Actually, the more slavery spread and deepened, the more the Negro became the concern and obsession of the enslavers—the goad to their consciences. In the words of Gunnar Myrdal, the Negro became the "great American Dilemma" that must be solved, or freedom will perish. The struggle is that simple. It has never been a racial one, but whether a nation committed to democracy can live half free and half slave. The progress toward freedom of the Negro, with his increasing usefulness and added strength, is a living proof of Lincoln's immortal words.

Once again today, with democracy's stake in the future of the world in balance, the Supreme Court decision of May 17, 1954, brings this challenge to the forefront. And in its contribution to democracy, the Negro must again bear the brunt of the struggle. But he and his white co-workers are better able to bear it because of the gleeful trumpet of Louis Armstrong and the golden voice of Marian Anderson singing "We are climbing Jacob's ladder."

In all convenient places are kept stores or ware-houses of all sorts of goods, managed by storekeepers or factors, either for themselves or others in the country or Great Britain. This trade is carried on in the fairest and genteelest way of merchandize by a great number of gentlemen of worth and fortune.

HUGH JAMES, 1724

IVY W. DUGGAN

The Factor

THE FACTOR and factoring in the South are as old as John Rolfe's discovery of a curing method for Virginia tobacco, as new as the $230,000,000 "broiler" industry of Georgia and the spotless "pig-parlors" of Alabama. Not quite a merchant, a banker, or a broker, the factor performed some of the functions of all three. As sire of the mercantile system developed around tobacco, rice, indigo, naval stores, and cotton, he was the Founding Father of Southern industry and the power behind King Cotton's throne.

To call the factor "another commission man" is gross misstatement, even though he sold and bought goods for others on commission. His power reached every alcove of Southern life, including the nuances of marriage-broker. He could buy and sell in his own name, and was entrusted with the possession and control of goods. In most of the South, as well as in Great Britain, the factor was legally empowered to pledge the goods entrusted to him. Traditionally, too, he could extend credit to his clients, then, as a side line, operate a retail business. Vis-à-vis, the merchant sometimes "factored" just as a country grocer did when he accepted eggs or butter in trade.

During the Colonial period, the position and influence of the English factor and his agents, as far as the South was concerned, were second in importance only to those of the governing officials. In fact, the commercial policies of England toward the Southern colonies were largely shaped by the wishes and demands of the factors and trading companies engaged in handling plantation products.

Factors were essential in carrying on the trade of a new and developing country where there was a shortage of capital and of people, no manufacturing, and a very limited market for the local crops. They supplied these needs and wants, and since their services were essential and scarce and involved considerable risk, the business advantage was heavily on the side of capital.

"It was said to be one of the stipulations between the principals of these houses and the young men they sent to Virginia as clerks," wrote Lewis C. Gray, "that they were not to marry in Virginia. They came with the prospect of being admitted as partners in some branch of the central establishment, and it might weaken the sordid attachment to their patrons if they formed an attachment of a purer tenderer nature to the fair daughters of their customer."

The factor performed a variety and number of functions and services. He received and sold tobacco and other agricultural products on consignment or under contract. When the products were disposed of in England, he deducted the necessary expenses and commissions and placed the balance to the credit of the planter. But the planter seldom saw this money. The factor instead bought quantities of goods from English merchants, either on consignment or on his own account, to be shipped to his American client. (Some of these clients seemed to be heavy consumers of beer, wine, rum, and whisky. The ledgers of the merchants and factors of the day carried many entries for pipes of wine, casks of Madeira, and other alcoholic beverages.) This was the planters' principal source of credit.

Sometimes a factor acted as guardian of a client's children, sent back to England for their education, or perhaps was called upon for service of an even more intimate nature. There is the instance of a young planter who ordered, with his annual supplies, ". . . a young woman of the qualifications and form following; As for portion I demand none, let her be of an honest family between twenty and twenty-five years of age; of a middle stature and well proportioned; her face agreeable, her temper mild, her character blameless, her health good, and her constitution strong enough to bear the change of climate. . . . If she arrives and conditioned as above said, with the present letter endorsed by you . . . that there may be no imposition, I hereby oblige and engage myself to satisfy the said letter by marrying the bearer at fifteen days sight." No explanation was offered for the fifteen days' waiting period.

The amount of credit that a planter could get, or the quantity of goods he might purchase on credit, was the gauge of his financial and social standing. Obviously, this criterion was to become a fixed characteristic of Americans.

Thus fulfilling the function of international banker, factors accepted bills of exchange, collected bills drawn on persons in England, extended considerable amounts of credit, and often allowed clients to overdraw their accounts. The latter practice, of course, often led to bitter feelings. Yet it persists today in the "supply" and "furnish" merchants, in "installment plan" buying, and in other manifestations of "Spend tomorrow's income today."

By its very nature, the system placed the planter at the merchant's mercy. Communications were slow and uncertain. The planter was forced

Account Sales of 15 Bales Cotton received for Sam Dale and sold on account and risk of Mr Samuel Wright to Messrs Peabody & Purvis

S.W. 15. 534 600 648 606 538 698 508 616 600 630
586 662 574 642 664 = 9.046 lb @ 5 3/8 ¢ $ 486.22

Charges

Freight $15 Wharfage 75	15.75	
Weighing 1.20 Drayage .94	2.14	
Storage 2.25 Mending 50	2.75	
Charges at Montgomery	16.88	
Commission 2½%	12.15	49.67
Nt Cr Saml Wright Esqr		$436.55

E.E.
Mobile December 20 1844

Tarleton Scott & Cummings
pr J. C. Mauri

Record of a shipment of cotton from the Auburn, Alabama, area through Montgomery to the factor in Mobile in 1884 to sell on the merchant's terms (a condition which many claim still exists today) in almost a "blind market." There were abuses in the form of "juggled" accounts and excess charges. Some factors seemed to follow the practice of "when all else fails, tell the truth." In 1768, George Washington wrote: "I have lost [at least] four years out of five by my consignments, having better prices offered in the country than my tobacco had sold for in England."

Thomas Jefferson, too, was convinced that "The advantages made by the British Merchants on the tobacco assigned to them were so enormous that they spared no means of increasing those consignments. The powerful engine for this purpose was giving good prices and credit to the Planter until they got him more immersed in debt than he could pay without selling his lands or slaves. They then reduced the price given for his tobacco so that, let his shipments be ever so great and his demand for necessities ever so economical, they never permitted him to clear off his debt. These debts became hereditary from father to son for many generations so that the planters were a species of property annexed to certain mercantile houses in London."

The annual interest paid under such circumstances often averaged at least 20 per cent. This is reminiscent of some present-day "small loan" companies. Certain practices seem to prevail for centuries.

Little wonder, then, that Southern factors and merchants violently opposed the Revolution, with few exceptions. New England merchants suffered under the Navigation Laws of Great Britain. But Southern merchants and factors were prosperous. To be a Tory was sound economics.

The Revolution cut these ancient connections. The London factors were replaced by enterprising men, some of whom had been export agents and correspondents for the British houses. What London had been to colonial Tidewater, Richmond became to the Piedmont, Charleston and Savannah to the Eastern Cotton Belt, New Orleans to her great hinterland, and Memphis to the Mississippi's Upper Delta. Minor markets arose at lesser seaports, at the heads of steamboat navigation—Fayetteville, Columbia, Augusta, Macon, Columbus, Montgomery—and along the great rivers.

It was in cotton that the factorage system reached its greatest development and became most powerful. The cotton factor's functions were about the same as those of his English progenitor. Some factors operated their own mercantile businesses; others did not. In either case, they filled orders, extended credit and delivered goods to their clients. The nineteenth-century factor outstripped his English prototype in the magnitude of his operations, was less cautious of real security for credit extended, and assumed, through his close association with the planter, a position of considerable influence in society and politics. Cotton factors extended millions of dollars of

Shipping cotton from Charleston to foreign and domestic ports

credit to planters, often with little or no formal security. This offered an opportunity to many men with little or no capital to obtain backing for large-scale cotton production, and played a dominant role in pushing cotton production in the South toward its zenith. Many of the largest and most successful cotton planters of the South started with factor "angels."

The factor's only "open" profit came from interest on loans and from commissions for selling the crops and making purchases for his clients. But there were innumerable charges to the planter for drayage, weighing, sampling, storage, insurance, etc., on which the factor received rebates. (Just as it is customary in automobile financing today for the automobile dealer to receive rebates of a portion of the insurance and financing charges.) Also, on occasions, a factor bought cotton for his own account, competing with his client's interests.

About this time there grew up in the South the saying, "De ducks got it." It grew out of the experience of planters and tenants who found at settlement time at the end of the year that the deductions of advances for food, clothing, fertilizer, and other goods and supplies equaled the gross income for the crop; when these deductions were made the tenant had little or no funds for the new year. The phrase "De ducks got it" became a part of the vernacular of the South.

Since the factor's markets constantly expanded, and he was in the "driver's seat," two features of the plantation contracts, the penalty clause and the requirement that every bale of the planter's cotton be consigned to the factor, were of great advantage to him. Under the penalty clause, a planter agreed to pay the factor a certain amount (ranging as high as four dollars) for each bale by which his crop fell short of the number originally agreed upon.

One of the primary effects of the factorage system was to concentrate capital in the cities serving as factorage points. The factors were usually located in prominent sections of Southern cities, and came to be identified with certain streets. The section of Reynolds Street in Augusta where the factors had their headquarters was known as "Cotton Row." It is still illegal to smoke on Reynolds Street. In Savannah, a section of Bay Street overlooking the waterfront is still called "Factors Walk." At Charleston, East Bay Street and Vendue Range were factor land. In Memphis everyone knew that the factors were to be found on Front Street. In New Orleans they centered on Gravier, Perdido, and Poidras Streets. Worth Street in New York City became the headquarters for factors in the textile industry.

Just as the Revolution brought about changes in factoring, the War between the States set developments in motion which were to mark the end of the seaboard factorage system. The railroads and the land-mortgage companies were two of the important successors. Cotton could be shipped directly by rail from the point of production to points of consumption and overseas shipment, which developed dominant interior markets. The land-mortgage company enabled planters to obtain credit on the basis of land alone. His current crop then could be transferred, on the security of a crop lien, to smaller interior merchants and factors. The country banker and merchant also became important in extending credit for cotton production.

A death blow to many cotton factors, especially in the Mississippi Delta area, came with the cotton price debacle of 1920. Cotton prices soared through 1919, and land prices followed; factors gave easy credit. Then the bottom dropped out of the market. Only the hardiest survived. One Memphis factoring firm is reported to have lost $500,000 on a single account. The federal farm programs, including price supports and loans, added the final blow to the cotton factor. Almost the only cotton factors in existence today are the few in Memphis.

While the tobacco, rice, and cotton factors have almost passed out of the picture, there are others who are still important to the national economy, particularly in textiles and processing enterprises. By supplying credit services and working capital, factors perform many necessary and worth-while services for industry. Although about half of the present factoring volume is done by several large companies in New York City, there are factors in other industrial centers as well. Three commercial banks, The First National Bank of Boston, The Bank of America in California, and the Trust Company of Georgia in Atlanta, have factoring departments, each of which does in excess of forty million dollars business annually.

It may be that the ghost of the factorage system is being seen again in Southern agriculture. Within the past few years there has emerged throughout the South a new source of farm change and uncertainty, described by the term "vertical integration." It refers to the joining together of two or more successive stages of production and marketing. In the South's new and huge broiler industry, the contractor (usually a feed dealer who is often financed in whole or in part by a feed manufacturer) supplies the grower with chicks, feed, medicine, fuel, and litter, and provides the managerial supervision through field men. The contractor retains title to the broilers. The grower supplies the housing, the labor, and the equipment. By this method, the farmer can obtain capital and technical guidance, expand his scale of operation, and be relieved to a great extent of the money risk. Also, he relinquishes his opportunity to make managerial and marketing decisions and reap a larger portion of the profits. No one will question the important role this system has played in expanding broiler production in Georgia from an annual output of $230,000 in 1935 to $150,000,000 in 1957. Many "pig-parlor operations" are vertically integrated. Beef cattle production is often on an integrated basis. Contract farming of vegetables and many other crops now has elements of integrated farming.

Vertical integration and the factoring system have much in common, as well as some differences. What effect will vertical integration have on "the family farm"? Will it lead to corporation farming, just as the factorage system produced the plantation system in the South? Is vertical integration good or bad?

Ask the preacher, ask the merchant, ask the farmer, ask the consumer, ask the agriculturist, ask the banker, and, last, ask the politician. They will all be debating the question for another twenty-five years. Meanwhile, fully in tune with the folkways, mores, and economics of his homeland, the Factor may rise again. This time, though, he'll shy clear of marriage brokerage.

A Seminary of learning is greatly necessary for the Instruction of our Youth, and ought to be one of the first objects of attention after the promotion of Religion.

GEORGIA LEGISLATURE STATUTE, 1783

ALFRED D. STEFFERUD

The Teacher

THEY WERE missionaries, clergymen, scholars.

They were opportunists, slaves, indentured servants, ne'er-do-wells, drunkards, tradesmen.

They were the first schoolmasters and (let us not quibble) the teachers.

Some teachers stood tall against the yardstick of boys they trained to greatness. Some were bad or incompetent by any yardstick. They were underpaid or unpaid, homesick, bumbling, and harrassed by the miasmas and worries of a wilderness land. The wonder is they were as good as they were.

The burghers wanted them, and the burghers wanted *education;* why had they come to these raw colonies but to get a better living for themselves and their children? In theory, that is. But taxes have a way of twisting theory. And people have a way of confusing education with training-to-make-money.

But the colonial leaders, did they want the teachers? No. They could send sons to Eton and Oxford to learn gentlemen's ways. They could pat their paunches and burp the dictum of Governor Sir William Berkeley of Virginia in 1671: "I thank God, there are no free schools nor printing, and I hope we shall not have these hundred years, for learning has brought disobedience, and heresy, and sects into the world, and printing has divulged them, and libels against the best government. God keep us from both!"

Or the privileged could utter the crass profanity of King William's attorney, General Seymour, when the Rev. James Blair asked him for two thousand pounds and a charter to start a college for the good of the souls of people in Virginia. "Damn your souls!" he yelled. "Make tobacco!"

But such was the light and drive and guts of the James Blairs that the foundations were laid for learning. (What later Berkeleys and attorneys general put on those foundations is something else.) Among the Blairs were men like young, energetic Thomas Morritt; Thomas Bray, a big organization man; the spellbinder George Whitefield; and Thomas Jefferson, who never taught but was still a teacher. And many more who wrote no journals and lived out their plodding lives without getting into print or trouble, yet left some mark on the boys and girls who made the South.

When Thomas Morritt took over the Charleston Free School in 1723, he introduced a program that would scare the daylights out of any high school or college boy today.

"The Latin tongue is the Intent of my Mission and for that Method I shall observe no other than what is usually practis'd in other Gramer Schools in Engld," he announced. "I shall chiefly use Lilly for the rudimental part & then I shall proceed to Sententia puerites, Corderii Colloquies, Latin Test., Erasmus. . . .

"Those boys wch I shall have constantly in the House wth me & such as are boarders I do intend to make them read 3 times a week at least if not every night Classick History. those books I will cause to be read at nights between 8 & 9 & I shall not omit at that time to instruct them in Cronology & Geography & teach them the use of the Globes."

Thomas Morritt was one of 353 missionary-teachers sent out by the SPG—Society for the Propagation of the Gospel in Foreign Parts—which was chartered in England in 1701 to provide "the ministrations of religion for our countrymen in the Colonies, and of bringing the surrounding heathen to the Knowledge of the truth."

They had a pretty hard time of it.

James Blair, the Bishop of London's Commissary for Virginia, and the Rev. Thomas Bray, the Commissary for Maryland, started feuding almost at once. The SPG'ers in South Carolina had to cope with dysentery, yellow fever, malaria, a high death rate, and Quakers and other dissenters. Governor Tryon of North Carolina pleaded with SPG to stop sending "the sweepings of the Universities but some clergy of character."

Thomas Morritt had his troubles, too. Maybe it was just his jealousy or fear of competitors—the Congregationalists, who had their own school, and those tutors the wealthier citizens engaged to "educate their Youth-a-la-mode." Anyway, Thomas Morritt was moved to demand that SPG suppress "intruders" as schoolmasters: "They're a great hindrance. It is Customary here for a Newcomer to set up for a Schoolmr and in a little time either grow weary or meet with some other employ. In the meantime these Intruders amuse the people and baulk the Publick School. . . ."

Missionary-Teacher John Urmstone wrote in blood and anguish to SPG from North Carolina in 1721. He had had no letters from home, he announced. Indians and Quakers were ruining this poor country. Dangers and expenses were great; he had to buy a couple of Negroes and a canoe to help him get around. He had too few books.

From Newbern, North Carolina, in 1765 SPG got this report: "The schoolhouse is now in building, but the work goes slowly. Men, money, and material are wanting, but money chiefly. Mr. Tomlinson continues a useful Member of Society and attends his school with very great diligence. He is the first person that ever taught school in Newbern for any considerable time without complaining of bad pay and very loudly; such complaints have been nailed up at the Church Door. Mr. Tomlinson is obliged to lodge in a public house which he says is very disagreeable."

Close to SPG were the redoubtable Dr. Thomas Bray's Associates. Armed with a bequest from King William's private secretary and a decree in chancery in 1731, they aimed to establish libraries and teach Negro children in the British plantations.

Before long they discovered their big problem: many people do not send their young Negroes to school "upon right Motives, because They do not suffer them to continue at School long enough to be properly instructed, but keep them at Home as soon as they can be of the least Service in the Family. The Planters urge it a sin & politick to enlarge the understanding of their Slaves, which will render them more impatient of Slavery."

It was not a problem only of Dr. Bray's Associates, though. Education in much of the South—and elsewhere, for that matter—had to contend with the forces of feudalism and greed that wanted to keep slaves, hired help, sharecroppers, tenants, other people's children in their place.

Georgia began under glorious auspices of philanthropy and benevolent paternalism. People in England eagerly contributed money and books for the Colonists. There are long lists of the donations: "Receiv'd from an Unknown Hand for the Use of the Colony of Georgia, 40 Bibles Minion, 50 Duty of Man, 100 Horn Books, 100 Primers, 100 The Young Man Instructed, 200 Friendly Admonition to the Drinkers of Brandy, 10 German Grammars."

The Rev. George Whitefield founded the Bethesda Orphan House on five hundred acres near Savannah—the outstanding institution of learning in the colony before the Revolution—on the pattern of a famous school at Halle, Germany. A man of tremendous energy and zeal, he toured the colonies and England to raise money for it. Franklin wrote about Whitefield in his *Autobiography:*

"I happened soon after to attend one of his sermons in the course of which I perceived he intended to finish with a collection, and I silently resolved he should get nothing from me. I had in my pocket a handful of copper money, three or four silver dollars, and five pistoles of gold.

"As he proceeded I began to soften and concluded to give the coppers. Another stroke of his oratory made me asham'd of that and determin'd me to give the silver; and he finish'd so admirably that I emty'd my pocket wholly into the collector's dish, gold and all."

An old-time schoolmaster

It is agreed between A. B. Stroud, and W. W. Wright, School Trustees of Township Eighteen Range Twenty five in Macon County and State of Alabama, and M. E. Williams, a School Teacher of the same County and State, that the said M. E. Williams will take charge of the Public School no two of said Township, locataed on the Wright Road near Charles Wrights, for the term of Ten months, beginning on the 23rd day of February 1863 that she will exert the utmost of her ability in conducting said School, and improving the education and morals of the pupils, keep an accurate register of their attendance, and, at the close of her term submit, on oath an abstract of such register to the Trustees, and that she will conform in all respects, to the laws regulating the Public Schools. And for such services, properly rendered, the said Trustees will pay to the said M. E. Williams the pro rata share of the educational fund of said Township for the year 1863, to which said School may be found to be entitled, which, amount, when ascertained and paid, shall be appropriated to discharge, as far as it may go, the tuition of the Pupils of said School, according to the number of days each may attend. In witness whereof the said parties have hereunto set their names the 23rd day of February 1863

In presence of
J. L. Wright
James Wright

A. B. Stroud Trustees
W. W. Wright
M. E. Williams Teacher

Contract between the school trustees and a schoolteacher in Macon County, Alabama, in 1863

Of the location of the orphanage, Whitefield wrote in his journal, "I choose to have it so far off the Town, because the children will then be more free from bad Examples, and can more conveniently go upon their Lands to Work. For it is my Design to have each of the Children taught to labour, so as to be qualified to get their own Living."

His twenty-three orphans, "the most pitiful Objects that I ever saw," began immediately to learn how to spin and card, farm, tend cattle, learn the catechism, and "live in order."

Whitefield petitioned the Council of the Colony for a charter and land for an endowment so he could make Bethesda into a "seminary of literature and academical learning." He pointed out that he had spent more than twelve thousand pounds sterling for buildings, the purchase of Negroes, and the care and training of many orphans, and that "several Gentlemen, who had been obliged to send their Sons to the Northern Provinces, had much rather have them educated nearer Home."

The General Assembly approved the petition, but the British Government insisted on impossible conditions.

Bethesda Orphan House was a forerunner of the many manual labor schools, which mixed geography, smatterings of ciphering, and odds and ends of reading and writing with work in barns, workshops, gardens, fields, orchards, breweries. Such schools flourished before the Civil War. Manual labor, people thought, was the best kind of exercise for students, for it was natural to man, yielded moral benefits, was practical, encouraged the manlier features of characters, and lacked the faults of ordinary education, which made their minds effeminate, imperiled morals, fostered laziness, and was undemocratic.

The early teachers in Georgia, Virginia, and the Carolinas had to have certificates from the Anglican Church and the permission of the Bishop of London or his representative. Since schools are so personal, local, and parental, it is strange that people let their schools be for so long the pawns of kings and bishops three thousand miles away.

I submit therefore, as something to be cherished and applauded, some individualists who tried to do something on their own.

The Winyaw Indigo Society, a club of planters, met once a month in Georgetown, South Carolina, "to talk over the latest news from London, which was never less than a month old, to hold high discourse over the growth and prosperity of the Indigo plant."

An early historian goes on: "And so it came to pass that the exchequer became plethoric of gold, and hearts of our founders overflowed with the milk of human kindness. . . . And hence it became the question of the hour, to what good purpose shall we devote our surplus funds.

"As the tale runs, the discussion was brief, pertinent and solid. At the close of it, the Presiding Officer called on the members to fill their glasses; he wished to close the debate by a definite proposition. If it met their approbation, each member would signify it by emptying his glass.

"He said: 'Knowledge is indeed as necessary as light and ought to be as common as water and as free as air. . . . I move, therefore, that the surplus funds in the Treasury be devoted to the establishment of an Independent Charity School for the Poor.' The meeting rose to its feet. The glasses were each turned down without soiling the linen."

The school flourished from 1756 to 1861. At least twenty-five children attended it each year. The Civil War devalued the Society's funds; troops occupied the school building; the library was scattered. Funds were raised later for a new endowment; the school continued until 1886, when it became a public school. The Society still keeps its organization and library.

Of another stripe was James J. Selby, tailor. "On the 3rd Monday of February, 1822 being the forty-sixth year of American Independence," the Court of Pleas and Quarterly Sessions at Raleigh, North Carolina, ordered that "A. Johnson, an orphan boy and son of Jacob Johnson, deceased, 14 years of age, be bound to Jas. J. Selby till he arrive at lawful age to learn the trade of a Tailor."

We can guess what happened between that time and June 24, 1824, when James J. Selby advertised in the Raleigh *Gazette:*

"Ten Dollars Reward: Ran away from the Subscriber, on the night of the 15th instant, two apprentice boys, legally bound, named William and Andrew Johnson. . . . They are much of a height, about 5 feet 4 or 5 inches. The latter is very fleshy, freckled face, light hair, and fair complexion. I will pay the above Reward to any person who will deliver said apprentices to me in Raleigh, or I will give the above Reward for Andrew Johnson alone."

We could skip the episode but for two details. Andrew Johnson became the seventeenth president of the United States. James Selby represented the apprentice system, which was a common method of mass, compulsory, general education until well into the nineteenth century. The need for skilled artisans was great, and apprenticeship was a way to get them.

For those who did not go abroad and did not fit into the category of orphan, slave, apprentice, or free schooler, there were tutors and the "old field," or community, schools, which people in a neighborhood set up.

Hundreds of advertisements of schools and schoolmasters appeared in newspapers.

John Walker, lately arrived in Williamsburg from London, undertook to instruct "young Gentlemen in Reading, Writing, Arithmetick, the most material Branches of Classical Learning, and ancient and modern Geography and History; but, as the noblest End of Erudition and Human Attainments, he will exert his principal Endeavours to improve their Morals. Mrs. Walker, likewise, teaches young Ladies all Kinds of Needle Work; makes Capuchins, Shades, Hats, and Bonnets."

John Davis, a man of letters newly arrived in New York, called on a bookseller and told him of his plan to become a tutor. He got a barrage of questions: Can you passively submit to being called schoolmaster by the children and *Cool Massa* by the Negroes? Can you comply with humility to giving only one rap on the door that the family may distinguish it is the private tutor and then wait half an hour with good humor on the steps till the footman or housemaid condescends to open the door? Can you carry the children's Bibles and prayerbooks to church twice every Sunday? Can you rise with the sun, and teach until breakfast; swallow your breakfast, and teach till dinner; devour your dinner, and teach till tea-time; and from tea-time to bed-time sink into insignificance in the parlor?

No? Well, then, said the bookseller, you will not do for a private tutor. The labor of Sisyphus in hell is not equal to that of a private tutor in America!

The Rev. James Maury has a special place among the "old field" teachers. Brought to Virginia by his Huguenot parents, he attended the College of William and Mary, taught in its grammar school, went to England for Holy Orders, and finally became rector of the extensive Fredericksville Parish in Albemarle County. He had three churches and a chapel and, he said, a postboy's life. To educate his own sons and to eke out his clergyman's pittance, he set up a small school in a log cabin.

Tom Jefferson began attending James Maury's little school in 1758, when he was fourteen. Soon after he arrived, Tom was a baptismal sponsor for the ninth Maury child.

James Maury had a strong influence on Tom. Maury was the standard bearer of the clergy and public officials against Acts that involved their salaries and must have made Tom aware of his feelings about separating church and state and schools. Jefferson came to share Maury's strong enthusiasm for the classics.

He absorbed also Maury's interest in education, precision in English, and love for reading. Maury enjoined him: "I would recommend it to you to reflect, and remark on, and digest what you read; to enter into the spirit and design of your author; to observe every step he takes to accomplish his end; and to dwell on any remarkable beauties of diction, justness or sublimity of sentiment, or masterly strokes of true wit which may occur in the course of your reading."

Jefferson remained close to education all his life, and his influence on education is as great as any man's. He cherished the idea of a national university. He kept a critical love (as many of us do) for his alma mater, the College of William and Mary in Virginia, the second oldest college in the country. He labored manfully for the University of Virginia. One of the great documents of American history is his "Bill for the More General Diffusion of Knowledge," which he introduced in 1779 in the Virginia General Assembly. It has been called the first definite proposal of sound principles for public school support and control in this country and the first plan for a complete state school from the elementary schools through the university ever made in the Western world.

The preamble is pure gold: ". . . . It becomes expedient for promoting the public happiness that those persons, whom nature hath endowed with genius and virtue, should be rendered by liberal education worthy to receive, and able to guard the sacred deposit of the rights and liberties of their fellow citizens, and that they should be called to that charge without regard to wealth, birth or other accidental condition or circumstance. . . ."

Virginia did not accept the plan; it would have given district and county officials too much authority. It was two centuries ahead of its time.

The document has always been a challenge to the teacher, though, and a charter. It has sustained him in war and reconstruction, when education all but died; in the days when people were forgetting the provisions in their state constitutions for public education; in the years of struggle over the idea of *equal but separate*.

We have sometimes despaired that the teacher in the South will ever get his intellectual and financial due—despaired, that is, until we get a reminder from J. Lupton Simpson, who taught my children in Lincoln, Virginia, and who to thousands of children and parents is everything the teacher can be and should be.

The mantle of Whitefield, Maury, Jefferson, and many more unnamed are upon him when he says:

"Let there be virtue among you, if not genius. Learn, by the education we offer you here, to guard the rights of others. This education is for all, regardless of wealth or circumstance."

There are problems, he goes on, and every boy and girl in the auditorium is breathlessly still as he tells them what the problems are and how they can be met.

"We have tradition, and vision, and our ways of doing things," he concludes, "and hope."

To show the unhappy state of the Church in Virginia I shall give a brief description of the manner of our Peoples scatter'd Habitations there; next show the sad unhappy consequents of such their scatter'd Living.

REPORT TO THE BISHOP OF LONDON, 1662

JAMES W. SELLS

The Preacher

THE PREACHER has always been a child of his own day and age. Each had to be true to his training and doctrines. And, if there was not a denomination that taught the Bible and its doctrines as his understanding of the Bible caused him to believe, he would go out and organize a church of his own.

Each preacher felt a divine call and urgency to save souls, to proclaim the Gospel, to establish the Kingdom on some far frontier. He was called Preacher because he preached the truth as he understood and believed it, full knowing that some would welcome him with friendship and pure love, some would regard him with veiled respect, and some would hurl the word "Preacher" from their lips as a simile for derision or disgust. Frontier trail to superhighway, these forces have shaped all our lives.

My first circuit included three churches in Sullivan's Hollow and two churches in "The Free State of Jones." This is the section of Mississippi depicted in the novels of James Street, who was once a Baptist preacher. Jones County won its "Free State" title by the steadfast refusal of its residents to secede, and join the Confederacy, in 1861. Sullivan's Hollow, settled by eight brawling, boisterous brothers from South Carolina in 1810, was a synonym for recklessness throughout the state.

The churches were small town, smaller village, and open country from four to eight miles from a branch-line railroad. I could borrow Brother Clark's mule and ride four miles out to Fairmount to preach on Sunday morning. At the other end of the circuit, I could hitch a ride on Saturday morning, or "mos' an' generally" walk the eight miles out to Old Hebron.

Fairmount was the place where I learned to preach. Every fourth Sunday we had "all day preachin' and dinner on the ground." At the afternoon service, the ladies of the congregation spread blankets and quilts on the floor between the pulpit and the first benches, and placed their babies on them. When the babies cried, you kept on preaching. If you were good, you held the attention of the adults over the crying of their children. In the eyes of the people, when the Lord called you to preach He gave you words of wisdom to speak and eyes of understanding to see. Otherwise, they reasoned, why should He have called you?

After service hurry from the church, walk up the lane to the cemetery, and watch the men finish the grave for a sixteen-year-old girl who should not have died if even the primary laws of sanitation and health had been known. In a few minutes the family drives up in the farm wagon, bringing her body in a homemade pine casket. On the casket is a bunch of yard flowers withered by the hot, dry heat of a Mississippi August sun. What do you say to the crowd gathered for a "burying" in a situation like this, facing that withered bunch of flowers, the mound of red clay, the dry-eyed father and the broken-hearted mother, the questioning looks of the friends and relatives?

You walk slowly, sadly back to town. There waiting for you is a wedding party, with all the joyous expectations of a healthy gathering of young people who want you to say the proper words so they can kiss the bride and begin the frolic. What should Preacher say then—or a few nights later when an irate father comes to your house at midnight, wakes you and demands that you un-marry his daughter, because he doesn't approve of the groom?

You serve. You go on. A man dares you to go home with him to his remote community and preach a revival meeting in an abandoned school house. No services have been held in that gun-toting community for so long that there are teen-age girls who have never seen a preacher. Later you go through the dark to the preaching place, carrying the one lamp that will furnish the light for the meeting. The host carries the baby; your hostess walks barefoot, toting the shoes she will put on just before she enters the building. You don't stand between the light and the open door when you preach that night.

You look out into the faces of your congregation each Sunday. You know the private life of every one of them. You know the men who have sinned, the women who have known sorrow. You know some of the men are as evil as the community says they are. And you know, too, that many want

A circuit preacher on his travels

to make amends and live a new life. You preach to them all as sinners; because saints are sinners saved by grace. The Gospel you preach is for them. Look what it has done for you. It can do the same for others.

These are some of the things to keep in mind about Preacher. He was a man who feared, and doubted, and made mistakes, and was human, yet gave his heart, his mind, his health and life to "reform the continent and spread scriptural holiness over the land." The preacher in the South went with a sense of mission, an inner urgency of being sent, of obeying a call from God, or forever-after remaining outside the pale of God's love and care. Hell was real, and punishment sure.

So he rode Indian paths and mountain trails to spread a fervent message of "personal redemption" and "God's Glory on earth." The thousand or more preachers who rode "the circuits" after 1780, and the host of educated school teacher-preachers and farmer-preachers who served in the piedmont, mountain, and delta lands, had greater influence on the permanent pattern of the South, and very possibly on the Far West, than any other educational force migrating from seaboard cities and cultural centers. Through them, the South retained the cohesive strength the Family had developed in the lonely, individualistic centuries of the Clearings. And for another century, in many areas, the preacher would be the community's only man of "learning"—the dispenser of books and "reading," the writer of letters to the outside world, the day-school teacher, and, in hours of stress, the man who combined book-knowledge of medicine with power-of-prayer until "Doc" could be brought out from town.

The reasons for the Wilderness Preacher, and the glory-powers he extended from palmetto through bluegrass to Southwestern prairie, sprang naturally out of the times. He was in regional harmony with the feverish expansion that swept the United States after the Revolution. The wagon-trains, daubed with the phrase "Ohio or Bust," clattered west out of Maine, Massachusetts, and Pennsylvania. Columbia College professors dubbed Rome, Ithaca, Pompey, Ilian and other classic Greek and Roman names on new towns in the Iroquois country of Upstate New York.

The North would call this period, because of the classical references in its oratory and the details of its architecture, "the Greek Revival." (A generation later, the same style of architecture and similar names of towns would be evident all across the South.) The South—because of the wilderness preachers, the democratic sociability of their camp meetings, the gospel music and spirituals that flowed out of them, and the reverence-for-church that followed—would title the same years "the Great Revival."

The South had been the land of the frontiersmen since 1607. Here the plot and counterplot of French, Spanish, and English performed their bloodshed. Here the individualist was bred by the environments of plantation clearings and cowpen-villages.

The Great Experiment, which poets would call "the American Dream," revolved around the spiritually dynamic drive of a new people, in a new land, and with a new idea. Could churches be established and become self-supporting, without dependence on—or domination by—the State? Could the State provide school education without the Church? Could the child of the mountaineer and the small patch-farmer have an education, as well as the child of the aristocrat? Could the Church, if it so desired, establish, maintain, and support schools, without direction or guidance from the State?

The Protestant Reformation had long severed ties between the South's Scotch-Irish, German, and English settlers and those Roman Catholic missionaries toiling bravely in Florida, Louisiana, St. Louis and distant "Tejas." The Church of England, powerful in the coastal cities but tepid in missionary work on the frontiers, officially vanished during the Revolution. Thereafter, its Episcopal successor developed principally in the cities. Outstanding churches such as St. Michael's in Charleston are magnificent evidences of such continuity of service.

The Baptists, Presbyterians, and Methodists, with the followers of Alexander Campbell and other smaller groups formed from the believers in "full, free salvation for anyone," fell heir to the missionary challenge of the lonely, lawless frontier. The Baptists, persecuted in New England, first migrated from Maine to Charleston in the 1680's. The Presbyterians, children of the glorious thunder of John Knox, traced American beginnings to the Irish missionary, Richard Makemie, and were a force in South Carolina and Virginia before 1700.

Spanish governors west of the Mississippi River banned the Protestant ministry. But the preacher was in the Natchez country on Old Man's eastern bank soon after the French and Indian Wars. The Rev. Samuel Swayze, Congregationalist, trekked in from New Jersey in 1767 to settle his mandamus-grant from the British crown and become pastor of the small colony there. The Rev. Richard Curtis, Jr., served the first Baptist church in Mississippi in 1781.

Methodism, youngest of all Christian faiths in the new U.S.A., was to prove the most vigorous frontiersman. In 1736–37, John Wesley served as chaplain to the daring families at Fort Frederica, Oglethorpe's tabby-and-sand defense post against the Spanish, on St. Simon's Island. His brother Charles was Oglethorpe's secretary during the first months of Frederica's construction. In spare moments, he jotted down verses, hummed snatches of tunes—harbingers of the 6500 gospel hymns that were to chant from his soul into the humming, whistling, choraling hearts of every Protestant sect on earth. Back in England, in the 1740's John Wesley put into action his convictions about "faith, sanctification and the privilege of full, free salvation to anyone, with pardon for the past, power for the present and promise for the future." So out of thoughts germinated, or at least rooted, in Georgia and Carolina experiences, Methodism was born.

Francis Asbury came to America as a Methodist missionary in 1771. His sympathies quickly swung to the Continental cause. On Christmas Eve, 1784, he became leader of the group of lay-preachers who met in Baltimore and organized the Methodist Episcopal Church. Asbury personally supervised the stationing of preachers and church strategy by traveling more than five thousand miles a year on horseback. The South became the principal scene of his efforts. A gossamer thread through towering mountains and misty glens, the Catalooche Trail had been a warpath of the Cherokee for a thousand years—from Charleston on the Coast to the Holston Hills and the connecting warpaths up through the Shenandoah Valley. Asbury and his preachers used it before the turn of the nineteenth century. Thereafter it became known as the Asbury Trail.

Many of the newer communities in Georgia, Alabama, Tennessee, and Mississippi were established "all-at-once," as pioneers moved in by families, with friends and kin-folks. They brought their civilization with them: their ministers, schools, and churches. Some of the preachers were graduates of universities and theological seminaries, shrewd scholars of human nature and worldly wisdom. Many others were farmers, lumbermen, hunters who had heard the call to "proclaim The Gospel and establish The Kingdom."

The first Methodist preacher to brave the old Southwest was Tobias Gibson of South Carolina. Appointed by Asbury in January, 1799, young Gibson left Charleston by horseback to ride the Cherokee Trail, over the stormy Appalachians and Cumberlands of east Tennessee, to a landing on the Cumberland River, near Nashville. There he sold his horse, put his saddle and saddlebags into a canoe, and paddled down the Cumberland, into the Tennessee, the Ohio, and finally the muddy Mississippi to Natchez. Thus did Preacher enter the country which was to be the channel for civilization's flow into Louisiana, east Texas, and the Far West.

Traveling as Tobias Gibson traveled, the precious stock of books and tracts in their saddlebags, their bodies often racked with malaria and fevers, the Methodist circuit riders pushed on over the wilderness trails. Of the first 672 listed in Methodist Church records, a third died before they had served five years or had reached their thirty-fifth birthdays. But their camp meetings chanted a glory-road from the Piedmont to the Missouri, Kansas, and east Texas prairie before 1820.

The first Methodist Sunday School was founded in 1786. The Methodist Book Concern was established in 1789. Church colleges followed naturally. So although the primitive ecstasies of wilderness camp meetings seemed a drastic method for curbing frontier evils, the blessings of education came with them. The theme of redemption emphasized democratic equality. The organization of local churches in every community was an object lesson and training ground in local self-government. They successfully answered the questions as to the building of a civilization on the separation of church and state.

Preaching to, then with, the Negro produced glorious rewards that would not become fully apparent until the spirituals began to charm the world in the 1880's. Black Harry, the Negro preacher who was Francis Asbury's traveling companion for years, became such a skilled and fervent minister that congregations demanded to hear him as well as their revered Bishop. One of the largest churches in Fayetteville, North Carolina, traces its origin back to a Negro preacher who, in his preaching to the other Negroes, became so popular that the white people built a tabernacle so he

Family worship on a South Carolina plantation, about 1863

could preach to both races. Later, one of South Carolina's greatest religious leaders, Dr. William Capers, distinguished himself and all of Methodism by championing the cause of educational and evangelistic missions to the slaves.

The Southern preacher's convictions of individual worth, exemplified by his examples of selfless service, developed him as a social force in giant proportion to his economic assets. Into the present, his fire and zeal influences all the hills, hollows, towns, and cities of the New South. Faith in God not only fills city and country churches to the last balcony rows on Sunday, but abides in family devotions, Bible-readings, and earnest effort to live up to the Golden Rule every day of the week.

The leadership expressed in William Capers' plantation schools for Negroes has been carried on in preacher campaigns, sometimes grimly misinterpreted, to achieve permanent harmony and friendship between the Negro and the white. In every Southern community, large and small, Negro ministers work with white ministers to carry the message of "redeeming love" to all men, everywhere.

Each summer, in recent years, hundreds of rural ministers from every Protestant denomination meet at the Church & Community Workshop on Emory University's campus in Atlanta. Similar schools for Negro ministers are held on the Campus of Gammon Theological Seminary, sponsored by the same group of concerned laymen. There they study theology, sociology, philosophy, psychology, hold seminars on community-relations and the year's best books and, like the circuit-riders, learn to become shepherds leading their flocks to a better life in *today's world.*

Looming now beside the Asbury Trail, at Lake Junaluska, stand the hotels and meeting places of one of Methodism's largest conference centers. To the east, in a thirty-mile drive, are Montreat, Ridgecrest, and other summer-assembly centers of the Presbyterians, Baptists, Lutherans, and Episcopalians. Thus, in appropriate symbolism, the vistas that beckoned the pioneer preacher to the challenge of "establishing His Kingdom" still inspire, still beckon the theologian or layman concerned with his church's desperately needed leadership toward tomorrow.

Sam Varnell, pastor of the Piney Flats parish in eastern Tennessee and a veteran at both Junaluska assemblies and Emory's Church Community Workshops, summed the challenge admirably for Harold H. Martin in the article "He Works in God's Back Pastures," published in the *Saturday Evening Post* in December, 1958.

"I believe that God is interested in our bodies as well as our souls," Sam said then. "The church, as the representative of God, needs to be concerned with anything that affects the lives of men. The county agent, the home-demonstration agent and the soil-conservation technician are doing God's work, too. They are expressing the Christian faith in action."

That was the Southern Preacher speaking, one hundred fifty years after the Great Revival, as Francis Asbury, Black Harry, Richard Makemie, Samuel Swayze, Richard Curtis, George W. Truett, and the crusaders of Wilderness Road spoke in their own way for their own time. Preacher's saddlebag was . . . and is . . . a potent symbol of the South.

Relying then on the patronage of your good will, I advance with obedience to the work, ready to retire from it whenever you become sensible how much better choices it is in your power to make.

THOMAS JEFFERSON—"First Inaugural Speech," 1800

MARGARET L. COIT

The Statesman

HE HUNCHED OVER a pine table, a lean man with blazing blue eyes and a touch of red burning in his bristling hair, lips clamped on a corn-cob pipe. He crashed his fist into a nest of papers.

"The people, Sir!" he said. "The people are with *me*."

They were. The people came first in the Presidency of General Andrew Jackson. And he was first with a lot else, besides.

Jackson is not the kind of Southerner we usually think of as the traditional statesman of the old regime. Yet, always, there have been three breeds of Southern leaders: the aristocrats, the plain people, and the demagogues—and still others, with elements of all three. All were subjected to the same fertilizing influence that made the South pre-eminent in national affairs. This influence was: Slavery.

The Old South was a school for statesmanship. For two generations—from the mellow wisdom of Jefferson to the narrow genius of Calhoun—the gentlemen of the South rode high in the saddle of the U.S.A. The "Virginia dynasty" was virtually synonymous with the founding of our country. And after the Founding Fathers had stridden from the national stage, except for John Quincy Adams and Daniel Webster, nearly every outstanding American political figure was a Southerner.

Some, indeed, called themselves Westerners. The brilliant Clay, "Harry of the West"; the original quiz-kid, "Old Bullion" Benton of Missouri;

Jackson and Polk of Tennessee, and flamboyant Sam Houston were Westerners in their own day, but Southerners for history. For they grew up in the old cotton states, and trained for leadership by managing plantations and slaves, who, like children, had to be handled with flexibility.

For two hundred years the slave system flowered, and generations grew up, ruling as if by divine right. Leadership passed from scion to scion of the great families: in Virginia, the Byrds and the Randolphs; in South Carolina, the Rutledges and Pinckneys. They stepped out to sit in at the signing of the Declaration and to help write the Constitution. Significantly, a frontier Virginian, Patrick Henry, sounded the trumpet of revolution. The aristocrats' day was over within a generation.

For the Revolutions had come, in France and in America, ending effectually the pretensions of the divine rights of kings. By the enraged loyalists, Washington, the military leader, and Jefferson, the spokesman, were both regarded as traitors to their class; certainly each helped lay the ax to the root of the very concept that brought them authority.

George Washington we honor today, but not only because his rag-tag army wore out the redcoats in the chase, and won freedom. Nor is he particularly remembered for the specific acts of his presidential administration, including his plea for isolation from foreign affairs—a doctrine which, like Christianity, has never been really tried. In the end, we remember the military hero for his talents in the art of peace—the beneficent, wise, human spirit who bound up the wounds of war and knitted together the states, standing them up before the world as a nation, free and independent and at peace while Napoleon scourged Europe.

Not the greatest American President, but perhaps the greatest American ever to hold the Presidency, was Mr. Thomas Jefferson of Virginia. Jefferson was like a Renaissance man. He was a philosopher. He was a musician. He was an architect and an interior decorator, an incorrigible gadgeteer and the best experimental farmer of his time. His presidential administration was marked by the gigantic acquisition of Louisiana, which put the West to the fore in national affairs; and marred by the abortive embargo, which wrecked the political and economic power of New England.

In the year after his Presidency, the great men of the time made pilgrimages up the mountainside to Monticello to drink of Mr. Jefferson's mellow wisdom, and to feel the majesty of the man himself, reflected in the world he had built around him. There, at Monticello, was the best of the past and the present, the old world and the new. You could stand with Mr. Jefferson on the portico and scan the green, terraced acres; you could share his delight in his home, the Roman design, the first parquet floors and the first French doors in America, the dumb-waiter and the swivel chair and the big clock in the hall, with the seven cannon balls to mark the days—all but Sunday. Sunday was down cellar.

Yet, always, you knew that the loose-jointed, sandyhaired, freckled man beside you was the philosopher who had breathed one Revolution into being and had watched the rise of another Revolution in France, and this was his strength and his weakness. In the end, he was perhaps colored too much by the forces of his own time. He was no Puritan. He could not believe that man was born evil, or with a saddle on his back, to be ridden by the favored few. He saw men as the prisoners of the political institutions that bound them—the slum cities that cramped them. He could not believe that men would voluntarily sacrifice agrarianism for the "benefits" of industrial civilization. He could not see that the tyranny of the many could be no less destructive to democracy than the tyranny of the few; or that democracy itself requires safeguards against its own citizens. These were problems that he would leave for later generations to solve.

Jefferson's friend and neighbor, James Madison, is, unfortunately, most remembered today for the passivity with which he let the War Hawks of 1812 hurl us into war with England; and for the sprightly charms and rouged cheeks of his wife, Dolly. But Madison's real claim to fame lies with his brilliant theorizing in the *Federalist Papers* which he wrote with Alexander Hamilton, and which helped sell the "egg-heads" of the time on the values of the American Revolution. He was also co-author, with Jefferson, of the Kentucky and Virginia Resolutions, invoked a generation later by John C. Calhoun in the doctrine of a state's nullification, or interposition, against a federal law.

Last of the Revolutionary generation to hold the Presidency, the last chief to wear a queue and smallclothes, was the self-effacing Virginian, James Monroe. Monroe was an army officer, Governor of Virginia, Senator, Minister to France, Secretary of State, and Secretary of War. But, as President, perhaps Monroe's greatest achievement was the caliber of the men he chose to serve him. John Quincy Adams was Secretary of State, authoring the Monroe Doctrine, which remained American policy for a hundred years; John C. Calhoun put the War Department on a footing that stood the tests of the Mexican and Civil Wars. Andrew Jackson was leading American troops on forays in the Southwest which not only thwarted the Indian menace there, but added huge territories to the American realm.

Jackson, duelist, frontiersman, romantic lover, had no illusions about his abilities. "Do they think I am such a damned fool as to consider myself fit for the Presidency?" he demanded. But like other military heroes, before and since, he was drafted into the job. He had been a hero as far back as most Americans could remember, the man who had loomed out of the powder smoke over the heaped cotton bales at New Orleans, to win a war after it was all over. He had been a hero in the old Creek War, living on acorns and holding off mutiny with oaths and an unloaded rifle. He had been a fourteen-year-old soldier of the Revolution, watching the slaughter of the Battle of Camden through the logs of a prison stockade. He was three times chosen President and twice inaugurated; his administrations were one running battle. Yet, historically, he was as significant as any President in American history.

He was the people's President. It was under Jackson, not Lincoln, that our modern, centralized popular democracy was born. Jackson first gave the laboring man a voice and a vote in the ranks of the Democratic party. Jackson, in his war with the United States Bank, dramatically illustrated that the power of Big Business could only be countered by a big government in Washington. Jackson called the bluff on the belief of the Southern Nullifiers that the power of a state was superior to that of the general government. Jackson himself was the living proof of Jefferson's doctrine of the natural aristocracy. Yet he perverted that doctrine. He failed to see the genius in himself. He felt that if he, a common man, could handle the Presidency, so could any other common man. This was a belief highly acceptable to the proponents of all-out majority rule. It marked the start of the lowering and leveling process which eventually tainted all national leadership, education, and mass entertainment. Not since Jackson's time has the goal of "Jeffersonian democracy" been to ferret out the natural leadership. Instead, the aim has been to prove literally that all men are equal, and to press all down into a single mold of conformity.

Several Southern-born Presidents, Benjamin Harrison, John Tyler, and Zachary Taylor, had undistinguished administrations. But James Knox Polk, a Scotch-Irish North Carolinian, by way of Tennessee, was of the same tough hickory stock that produced Jackson. He lacked Jackson's color and dash, but he had the same drive and determination and force of character. Men had dreamed of the United States spanning the continent; Polk put the dream into action. Under his lead, the Northwest boundaries were drawn and the vast Oregon Territory added to the Union. Under his lead, too, the Southwest came in—New Mexico and California and parts of Texas—though only at the cost of war with Mexico. Furthermore, this war made the "irrepressible conflict" all the more inevitable; hurled into the cockpit was a vast area that the North would never see Slave and the South would never see Free. But James Knox Polk was an empire-builder. If he led us into war, the conflict at least netted huge material benefits. Under Polk, the present dimensions of the United States were charted.

Henry Clay addressing the United States Senate, 1850.
From a painting by P. F. Rothermel

Meanwhile, different dramas were played out on the stage of the national Congress. "I don't like Henry Clay," John C. Calhoun said. "He's a bad man, an imposter, a creator of wicked schemes. I won't speak to him, but, by God, I love him!"

The remark was typical. The great Senators of the time got on each other's nerves. For all the Southern leaders were caught in the same web of slavery, and all, with the exception of Clay, were to die, disheartened and haunted men, repudiated for holding fast to what they had believed all along. Thomas Hart Benton, for instance, could not see why the system that had bred him was immoral; on the other hand, neither he nor Sam Houston could reject the patriotism that had sustained them through life. Benton and Houston died, convinced that the whole slavery question was whipped up to embarrass and defeat them; Clay and Calhoun lived, convinced that as each was Southern, each should think exactly the way the other felt on the slavery question.

The Congressional stage was too small to hold them all. These were heroic days and men were cast in giant mold, and without the benefits of radio or television, the image of each was stamped upon the national consciousness. They move in parade before us: ghostly John Randolph of Roanoke, with his wraithlike body and spidery limbs, the light of madness burning in his eyes and shrilling in his voice, yet with a wisdom in his ravings that foreshadows the philosophizing of John C. Calhoun; Sam Houston, an Indian blanket slung over his shoulders and a whittling knife in his hand, six-feet-six and vast as the empire of Texas, which he had ruled as President and as General; laughing Henry Clay and dark Calhoun and big, bull-like Benton of Missouri. It is as a personality, rather than as any real maker of history, that the memory of Benton survives: his fierce loyalty and fight and love of country, and his prodigious memory. There was almost nothing that you could find in a library that you could not get right out of Benton's head.

Like Benton, Henry Clay of Kentucky lacked intellectual profundity, but he was the most skillful political manipulator in American history. His patriotism was simple, his loyalties undivided; the United States was his country, of which he could say, truthfully, that he three times saved the Union: in 1820, with the Missouri Compromise; in 1833, with the tariff settlement; and again in the 1850's, with the Omnibus bills, which held off the Civil War long enough for the North to gather the strength to win. Clay was the master of the immediate. He did not penetrate the basic causes of the wounds that were rending the body politic apart; he did not share the tormented vision of his colleague, Calhoun. He was convinced that you could bring any groups together and make anything work, if only you worked hard enough at it. For his own time, he was successful.

John C. Calhoun, a lean Scotch-Irishman from frontier South Carolina, was of a different breed. "The thinking machine," they called him. It has been said that he penetrated deeper into the causes of things than any man of his time. He grappled with two problems, primarily: how to reconcile the interests of the slave South and the Federal Union, and how to reconcile minority rights inside the Union with a central government strong enough to act in a crisis.

Calhoun was the most profound political thinker of his time, possibly the greatest logician produced in this country. He lacked Jefferson's width and cultural background; yet by viewing the French Revolution as an incident in a history book, he was better able to put it into perspective. A Puritan and Calvinist, he did not believe that any revolution could basically change the evil nature of man. He picked up the questions that Jefferson had dropped and found answers for them. From the original theory of nullification, he developed his doctrine of the concurrent minority, or the group interest veto, which has become part of the unwritten law of the land: that no legislation may be passed or any political candidate chosen in violation of the will of a major interest group. Calhoun worked out his idea in behalf of the Southern slaveholders; it is invoked today to protect the rights of the Southern Negro.

With the passing of the Great Generation, lesser men took their places. As President of the Confederacy, the frustrated army general Jefferson Davis ruled with courage, but with the rigidity of his heritage. And his counterpart across the Potomac—Abraham Lincoln—was he a Southerner? The blood of Kentucky and Virginia flowed through his veins; their drawling speech was on his tongue. But Lincoln was not Southern, any more than he was Northern or Western. As President of a divided country, he was still above any stage or region, completely and authentically American.

The last President from the old slave-South was the first from the silent, unspeaking South, the "mud-sills" called out to fight the war the leaders had made. Silenced and sacrificed on the altar of postwar hatreds was Andrew Johnson, the tailor's apprentice from Tennessee. Only the memory of his fight and courage lingers. . . .

The Civil War virtually ended Southern statesmanship. Confederate officeholders were rounded up and imprisoned, some living on like Davis, to become tragic and silent symbols of the defeat. Several of the most brilliant, like Judah Benjamin and Robert Barnwell Rhett, escaped into exile. Much of the potential leadership, of course, rotted in death; the military commanders, even Lee, were stripped of their right to vote or to hold any office.

A few raised their heads, even above the debris. In South Carolina, General Wade Hampton rode his Red-shirts to victory in the bitter fracas of 1876, taking possession of the State House by sheer armed force. From Mississippi, Lucius Quintus Cincinnatus Lamar rose to Cabinet rank and, by gentle words over the death bier of Charles Sumner, helped heal the gaping wounds between North and South. In Georgia, Henry Grady and a generation of Southern leaders decided that defeat meant that Southern agrarianism was wrong, and called for the building of cotton mills. Industrialism was under way.

Meanwhile, the poor whites, who had always said that it was "a rich man's war and a poor man's fight," paid the penalty for the war they had not wanted and the slave system in which they had taken no part. Stripped of their meager lands, reduced to cropping and tenantry, the "mud-sills" found a scapegoat in the luckless ex-slave and the "natural superiority" of all white men. The demagogues moved in. Some, like Ben Tillman of South Carolina, who threatened to ram a pitchfork into the side of President Grover Cleveland and the bitter "agrarian rebel," Tom Watson of Georgia, were intelligent men from the upper strata of Southern society. One of the most ludicrous examples in modern times was Senator "Cotton Ed" Smith of South Carolina, who spent a lifetime concealing his graduate degree from Vanderbilt and who lived through the rise of Adolph Hitler and the beginning of the atomic age still discoursing on "the sanctity of white Southern womanhood."

The Great Depression closed down. Cotton mill workers got five dollars a week, when working; croppers existed on cash incomes of two hundred fifty dollars a year. A new generation of Southern demagogues was rising from the depths, the most talented and dangerous being Huey P. Long of Louisiana. You could laugh at Huey, red-faced and bulbous-nosed, arms flailing in the United States Senate, as he discussed "pot-likker" and "every man a king." But Long had a genius for weaving together the dissident and displaced elements of American society: the followers of the radio-priest, Father Coughlin, and of the gentle old-age pension advocate, Francis Townsend; the mobs who cheered suspender-snapping 'Gene Talmadge in Georgia, and the half-starved mine workers of John L. Lewis. Only the New Deal and the assassin's bullet saved America from a possible Fascist state, imposed by American means in American terms.

Yet the traditional genius of the Old South still flickered—in Georgia-born William G. McAdoo, Wilson's dynamic, hard-headed, fiery Secretary of the Treasury, and in Carter Glass of Virginia, author of the Federal Reserve system. It burned like a flame in Woodrow Wilson of New Jersey, a Virginia native and son of a Confederate chaplain. He was the staunchest constitutionalist since Jefferson; he conceived and put through the New Freedom, which foreshadowed the New Deal by a generation. He was of the same tough, knotty, Scotch-Irish stock that had produced Jackson and Polk and Calhoun; this gave him the strength to see through to fulfillment his dream of a League of Nations, and the rigidity which made its success impossible.

The flame burned on in a few others—Cordell Hull, Walter George, Bernard Baruch, James F. Byrnes, perhaps—in the test of time—Harry S. Truman. Southern statesmanship is still alive.

It is harder to preserve than to obtain liberty.

JOHN C. CALHOUN, 1848

WAYNE GARD

The Law

RUGGED JUDGES often were needed to enforce the law in the early South. The Texas Republic had such a one in Robert M. Williamson, the salty frontiersman who in 1837 went into the backwoods of Shelby County to set up its first district court.

Some of the residents of that haven for fugitives made it plain that they wanted no court. When the judge sat down behind a dry-goods box to open the session, one of this group stood up to announce that an assembly of citizens had resolved that no court should be held.

"What legal authority," asked Williamson, "can you give for such procedure?"

The ruffian drew a bowie knife from his belt and slammed it on the improvised bench. "This, Sir," he snarled, "is the law of Shelby County."

As quickly, the judge whipped out a long-barreled pistol and laid it beside the knife. "If that is the law of Shelby County," he thundered, "this is the constitution that overrules your law."

Duels, feuds, terrorism, and lynchings flourished in the early South largely because the law was slow in exerting its full force. The prevalence of such practices, in turn, slowed the progress of the law. That was especially true in the backwoods, where population was thin and social organization was fragile. Where courts had not yet been established, or officials were unable to keep order, many fell back on primitive ways of attaining what they considered to be justice.

The rural nature of most of the South tended to keep local constables and police officers from attaining much authority. Usually the most effective enforcement officer was the county sheriff. Often the sheriff not only held law enforcement in his hands but wielded much political power. A great deal depended on the type of man who held this post.

As courts were set up on the frontier, conditions changed only slowly. Lack of secure jails made it advisable to punish culprits as soon as possible after they were caught. In such circumstances, drunks and other offenders sometimes were confined in rail pens or placed under an inverted wagon box. Whipping was a common punishment.

Some of the harsh punishments of the frontier South were carry-overs from the seaboard colonies, which in turn had inherited them from Europe. Preventing the stealing of horses, cattle, and hogs was a serious problem, especially in the backwoods, where much of the stock ranged unattended on public lands. Georgia had a death penalty for livestock thieves but in 1773 found it ineffective "because of the tenderness of prosecutors and witnesses."

In Tennessee in the 1780's, James Fulsome and John Wilson were convicted at Jonesboro as horse thieves. The court sentenced them to be confined in the public pillory for an hour, to have both their ears first nailed to the pillory and then severed from their heads, and to receive thirty-nine lashes on their bare backs. Finally each man was to be branded with an "H" on his right cheek and a "T" on his left. The court directed that the sentence be carried out "this afternoon."

The trend in other colonies was in the opposite direction. South Carolina, which had provided for death without benefit of clergy for the second offense for stock thieves, changed its law in 1784 to inflict death for the first offense. Two years later North Carolina made the same change.

A carry-over from this era of severe punishments is the Alabama law which still permits the death penalty for robbery, with or without arms, regardless of the amount. To date, this penalty has never been imposed on a white person, but several Negroes have been put to death for robbery. It was imposed again in 1958 on a Negro farm hand who had robbed a white woman of $1.95, but for the first time the sentence was commuted.

In the frontier era, backwoods judges often carried pistols to protect themselves from desperadoes. Traveling from place to place, they held court in log homes or schools or, in mild weather, under the trees. Court Day usually brought into town a crowd of country people who spent their time in trading, swapping news, and betting on the ponies raced through the streets.

Since colonial days, police officers in the South have faced—some heroically, some fearfully—the "devil's twins" of Mob Law and Personal Honor. These outbursts ranged from jungle-type gougings through formal duels and family feuds to terrorist bands and lynch mobs.

Judges, lawyers, and clients going to court in pioneer days

In the backwoods of the early South, the gougers were typical of those who took the law into their own hands. On the frontier, they felt capable of personally righting their wrongs. These hand-to-hand encounters often took the form of biting off noses and ears and gouging out eyes. Major Erkuries Beatty saw barbarous clashes in pioneer Louisville. "When two men quarrel," he wrote in his diary, "they never have any idea of striking. They immediately seize each other and fall and twist each other's thumbs or fingers into the eye and push it from the socket until it falls on the cheeks, as one of those men experienced today. It chilled my blood with horror."

Another observer, Isaac Weld, told of frontiersmen who fought "like bears, biting, kicking, punching, and gouging." That form of combat became so common that Virginia, followed by other states, enacted laws against mayhem. The Virginia law provided jailing for twenty days to six months for anyone who had "unlawfully and willingly disabled the tongue, eye, slit or bit the nose, ear, or lip of another."

The Southern gentleman, meanwhile, preferred to settle his disputes with a dirk, a sword-in-cane, or a pistol. Hundreds of quarrels were thus resolved on the spur of the moment, often bringing death to one of the combatants.

The formal duel was indulged in, as a rule, only by the elite. Thomas H. Benton, later a Missouri Senator, killed Charles Lucas in a duel on Bloody Island in 1817. Henry Clay in 1826 fought a bloodless duel with John Randolph on the Virginia bank of the Potomac. Andrew Jackson fought two duels, killing his opponent in one, and barely missed several other encounters. Sam Houston, before going to Texas, wounded a man in a duel. At a dinner in 1834, while Stephen F. Austin was in prison in Mexico City, John A. Wharton proposed a toast: "To the Austins, may their bones burn in hell!" William T. Austin defended the family name in a clash in which he shattered the right arm of Wharton. Dueling became so common in Texas that the Constitution of 1845 banned duelists from holding public office. Until 1939, every Texas state official had to take an oath that he never had taken part in a duel.

Occasionally the duel became a popular social event. One outside Vicksburg in 1838, in which Colonel Alex K. McClung faced the planter John Menifee, drew crowds from interior towns. New pistols were obtained from New Orleans. Many bets were made on the outcome. The surrounding hills were covered with spectators as the firing took place and McClung killed Menifee.

Early laws against dueling did not have much effect. Even more difficult to check were the bloody feuds. They spotted the whole South, especially in the Reconstruction period, but were most common in the mountains. Starting over a stolen horse, a love affair, or even a batch of gingerbread, a family or factional quarrel might last for generations and take many lives. The most famous was between the Hatfields and the McCoys. It started soon after the Civil War as a quarrel between two families on the Kentucky-West Virginia border, near the junction of Tug Fork and Big Sandy River. More than a score had been killed before the law stepped in and led the surviving gunmen off to cool their tempers in prison cells.

Another informal law was the authority of the planter over his slaves. Killing of a slave was unusual, partly because it destroyed valuable property. Whipping was the most frequent punishment.

For more than a century and a quarter, the South had another peculiar form of punishment in the lynching mob. By this means several thousand Negroes were killed, usually by hanging or by burning, without trial, by mobs of white men. Many of the victims were taken from jails where they awaited trial. Some obviously were guilty of serious crime. In other cases no evidence of guilt was at hand.

The word "lynching" was derived from a Quaker patriot in the American Revolution, a man who would have been shocked at such misuse of his name. Colonel Charles Lynch, born in Virginia in 1736, was a member of the House of Burgesses in 1776. Despite his Quaker scruples, he became a colonel of militia and formed a regiment.

Tories were stealing horses from patriot farmers and selling them to British troops. With the court at Williamsburg more than 200 miles away, the farmers decided to take justice into their own hands. They appointed Colonel Lynch their emergency Judge, with three of his neighbors as associates. Horse thieves brought before Lynch were given a fair trial. Those proved guilty were sentenced to forty lashes on the back, then ordered to shout, "Liberty forever!" Other Tories who conspired to seize stores of the Revolutionists were tried before Lynch, convicted, and sentenced to prison. In 1782, the Virginia Legislature passed an act justifying and exonerating Lynch and his associates.

This Virginia measure, sometimes called the Lynch law, by no means countenanced the mob murders later done in its name. Lynching, rare before the Civil War, became a commonplace horror of Reconstruction. The worst year for lynchings was 1892, when 235 were cited.

Frank Shay, who made a penetrating study of lynchings, found that most of the instigators of this mob-frenzy were planters, landlords, or employing farmers. Those who carried out the dirty work, though, were more likely to be "young men between their teens and their middle twenties, with a sprinkling of morons of all ages. Its members were native whites, mostly the under-privileged, the unemployed, the dispossessed, and the unattached."

Lynchings became rare after World War II, with some years entirely free from them. But another manifestation of mob rule proved harder to root out. It stemmed from the Ku Klux Klan of Reconstruction days. The original Klan, formed by a group of young men in Pulaski, Tennessee, in May, 1866, was intended as an innocent social organization. It soon added "dens" in other towns. Then within a year or two it was transformed to furtive fraternity, with secret ritual and goals of social regulation. It opposed "carpetbag rule" and misconduct by the Negroes. The Klan quickly became guilty of so many outrages against individuals that the better citizens deserted it. In 1869 the Grand Wizard, General Nathan Bedford Forrest, dissolved the organization. But local branches continued to flourish and indulge in disguised lawlessness. By 1873 the then-outlawed Klan had become a synonym for clandestine murder and masked rebellion.

As the harsh Reconstruction ended, the Klan died out, only to revive in 1915 as an organization of hate for Negroes, Catholics, and Jews. This time it swept across the continent. In 1921, when it was investigated by Congress, the Klan had a sorry record of floggings, tar-and-feather parties, and intimidation. It dominated politics in communities and states, dictated employment in industrial plants. These outrages brought its downfall in the middle 1920's. Yet agitation against racial integration in the public schools revived it again in a few communities, both South and North.

Against such floutings of statutory law, sheriffs, judges, and other enforcement officials had a stupendous task. They were further handicapped by inadequate budgets for prisons and police forces—a product of Reconstruction poverty plus voter fears of the law that traced back to Jamestown whipping posts and British dungeons.

For decades, Southern prisons lagged far behind those in other sections of the country. Conditions were extremely unsanitary. Prisoners were flogged for such minor offenses as putting their hands in their pockets or failing to have their hair properly combed. One survival of barbarism was the practice of working prisoners in chain gangs. The men, with shackles riveted to their ankles, lived in tents or in cages with tin roofs. Beginning early in the 1920's, however, exposures of shocking conditions in Southern prisons aroused public opinion to demand improvements. Most states modernized prison housing. Some did away with whipping.

The low pay offered and the difficulties of the official duties did not encourage well-qualified men to seek law-enforcement posts in the South in early days. The result was that many places were poorly filled. It was common everywhere in America's frontier days for lawyers, justices of the peace, and judges to use a pompous manner to hide ignorance. In Mississippi one unlettered judge, who had just made a ridiculous decision, became irritated when an Irish lawyer rose with a law book. The judge reminded the attorney that the question was settled. The lawyer then remarked: "If Your Honor plase!! Far be it frum me to impugn in the slightest degray the wusdom and proprietay of Your Honor's decision! I marely designed to rade a few lines from the volume I hold in me hand, that Your Honor might persave how profoundly aignorant Sir William Blackstone was upon this subject."

Fortunately, those frontier judges who were ignorant of the law and who were cowed by bullies soon were outnumbered by others who knew the statutes and had the courage to enforce them. In 1802, when Andrew Jackson was a circuit judge at Jonesboro, Tennessee, the sheriff reported that he had been unable to arrest an indicted man, Russell Bean. This culprit, having clipped the ears of an unsponsored baby born to his wife and beaten her seducer, sat at home with a rifle by his side and a pair of pistols in his lap. Judge Jackson told the sheriff to bring in Bean, even if he had to summon every man in town to help him. So, as the court recessed for dinner, the sheriff eased up to "Old Hickory" and said, "Then I summon Your Honor first."

"By the Eternal, I'll bring him in!" Jackson roared. Leveled pistol in his hand, he stalked into Bean's home, with a challenge to surrender or be shot down. Bean, a veteran of the Battle of Kings Mountain, gave up his weapons and meekly preceded His Honor to the courthouse.

The number of spunky, forthright judges and skilled police officials swelled slowly toward a proud heritage of the host of Southern jurists and statesmen who rose, from plantation home, cropper's cabin, and mountain lean-to, to national honor.

Today the Law is mirrored in the drawling courtesies of highway patrols and the determination of most police officials and courts to live up to the 1810 dictum of Thomas Jefferson: "Cherish, therefore, the spirit of the people, and keep alive their attention. Do not be too severe upon their errors, but reclaim them by enlightening them. If once they become inattentive to the public affairs, you and I, and Congress and Assemblies, Judges and Governors, shall all become wolves."

We also send as many maids and young women as will make upp the number of fiftie . . . and disposinge of them in marriage (wch is or cheife intent) we leave to your care and wisdome.

VIRGINIA COMPANY OF LONDON, 1621

CELESTINE SIBLEY

The Woman

THEY DIDN'T GO to do it, maybe, but the book-writing, play-making geniuses of the world have unwittingly perpetrated on a gullible public literature's biggest fraud. All the way from Harriet Beecher Stowe to Tennessee Williams (with an assist, it must be admitted, from the locals who like the publicity) they have created a languishing, lily-handed, sugar-mouthed monster known as: *The Southern Lady*.

She is as pretty as a Cherokee rose. She moves with the airy grace of a sprig of honeysuckle stirred by the flight of a mockingbird in the April twilight. She smells faintly of magnolias and her speech is a cross between a ballad played on a mountain-made dulcimer and a pan of chocolate fudge. She is also devious, deceitful, conniving, and darned near useless—and, crossed, she may crack you with her riding crop or bash in your skull with an ancestral syllabub churn!

This is not to say the lady doesn't exist.

There's a touch of that saintly, golden-haired tyke, Little Eva, in the women of Talking Rock, Ga., just as there is in the women of Brooklyn, N.Y. There's a faint suggestion of Amanda Wingfield's granite whimsy and, thank heaven, a dash of Scarlett O'Hara's ruthless drive in women everywhere. There are professional and perennial "Southern belles" in Tivoli, Italy, and Two Egg, Fla. (They have read the books, too.) But what doesn't get around is the word that this character *isn't* and *never has been* the typical Southern woman.

To arrive anywhere near a true picture of the representative Southern woman you'll have to set the pretty flower similes on the shelf and get you an entirely new batch of ingredients. That honeysuckle-magnolia stuff is mere garnishment, anyhow.

You have to start with the pioneer spunk of the kind that made them follow their men to these shores on frail sailing ships in the early 1600's—like the twenty women who landed with their children at Jamestown, Virginia, on the ship *Blessing* in 1609 for "the better strengthening of the colony." You have to give them credit for what Ellen Glasgow called a vein of iron, the thing that enabled them to stand up to the agues and the fevers and the murderous and pillaging Indians who reduced the population from five hundred settlers to what a historian described as "not past sixty men, women and children, most miserable and poore creturs, and those were preserved for the most part by roots, herbes, acornes, walnuts, berries and now and then a little fish."

You have to throw in the high venturesomeness of the maids who packed their boxes and their baskets and set sail for Virginia and Georgia and New Orleans to make marriages with men they never saw before and found homes in a strange and sometimes terrifying land. You have to take into account their different national backgrounds—poor and middle-class English, haunted by fear of debt, the pious Salzburgers and Moravians, Scots, Irish, Swedish, and the Spanish and French along the coast of Florida, Alabama, Mississippi, and Louisiana.

What happened in Georgia in colonial days was fairly typical of what was happening everywhere. General James Oglethorpe, founder of the colony at Savannah, was anxious to establish a settlement to be called Frederica on what is now St. Simon's Island, to hold off the encroachments of the Spanish, who were in Florida. Settlers had been brought from England with glowing promises of a rich and productive country where they might earn "content and affluence." When they arrived in Savannah they found Oglethorpe unable to get the ships to carry them on to Frederica. He explained this to the settlers himself, admitting that the 130-mile journey in open boats with exposure to the cold wintry rains and frosts would be too much for the women and children.

The women made the decision. They were ready to go.

Their new homes were palmetto-thatched shelters, buffeted by the chill Atlantic winds and within easy shooting distance of the Spanish on the south and the Indians on the west. But they stuck it out. Prey to recurring disappointment, almost constant fear, and probably hunger, they neverthe-

Arrival of wives for the settlers at Jamestown

less set about establishing what Oglethorpe himself proudly noted were "orderly households."

Women were wanted in the South. What Oglethorpe said was freely admitted by all. Bringing women to these shores was "a cheap way of increasing the colony." Women were fruitful and multiplied. They made homes. And because they were a valuable commodity with responsibilities that were to grow tremendously with the passage of time, they have historically enjoyed more recognition than their sisters elsewhere. From earliest colonial days girl children were allowed to inherit lands and trained to supervise their cultivation. Although they prettily disclaimed the intelligence to participate in public affairs and solemnly affirmed that politics was for men, they got in their licks behind scenes for their favorite candidates and sometimes heatedly petitioned legislatures for needed reforms. Young women in North Carolina felt so strongly about the American Revolution that they organized associations and publicly announced they would not "receive the addresses of any gentleman who failed in his military duty."

Mary Musgrove, daughter of an Indian mother and English father, is seldom remembered when the subject of Southern ladies comes up, but she was one of the earliest. She could speak the Creek language as well as English; she had great influence over the Indians and was such a skillful diplomat that Oglethorpe secured her services as an interpreter and adviser on Indian affairs. She owned acres of valuable land, she ran a brisk trading business, and when food was scarce she supplied the starving colonists with provisions at her own expense. She set up a trading post on the Altamaha river to keep an eye on the Spanish for Oglethorpe. She made treaties with the Indians for him, and when hostilities began she rallied her warriors to Oglethorpe's side.

Nancy Hart isn't the kind of Southern lady who gets in the stories, but Georgians think so much of her they named a town and a county for her—the only one in the country to be named for a woman. No magnolia, Nancy was a rawboned, red-headed, cross-eyed backwoods woman who left her remote log cabin and brood of children occasionally to operate as a spy for the American Revolutionists. She is credited with having spit tobacco in the eye of an Indian peeping-Tom (the Indians called her "War Woman"), and she personally supervised the hanging of many a Tory. Nancy would have been filled with raucous merriment at the fancy picture of the legendary Southern lady. She was Southern from the top of her red head to the soles of her big feet, and her neighbors described her as "a honey of a patriot but a devil of a wife."

Pioneer days were followed by a period of prosperity and comparative ease for many Southern women. The white-columned mansion came along and so did coveys of slaves, ostensibly eager to take over the drudgery while the ladies of the household furrowed their pretty brows over nothing more important than the latest fashions from Paris. It was the time when the South of legend was born, and, like most legends, it has a high incidence of fantasy. There were comparatively few slave-owning, mansion-dwelling Southern families, and in those the responsibility for running the plantation often fell on the woman.

It's true it was a period when gentler arts flourished. Homes and gardens were memorably beautiful, hospitality was brought into full and glorious flower. Social graces, the talent for being charming and amusing, were stressed.

But oddly enough, they did nothing to soften or nullify the essential toughness, the sturdy vigor and valor of the Southern woman, as the Civil War was to prove. Matthew Page Andrews, writing in 1927 of the women of the South, said: "Southern women, suddenly and violently plunged into the midst of an economic cataclysm, rose equal to the occasion and showed that they were even more ingenious than the men; for they were called upon to establish new processes and to provide substitutes for a much greater variety of things."

They boiled sea water or washed the dirt from their smokehouse floors to get salt, nowhere else available in the South. They made cooking soda from the ashes of corn cobs. They parched rye, wheat, and corn and dried sweet potatoes for coffee and made tea from sassafras. They gathered myrtle berries to make candles or labored over their account books and their mending by the light of rag wicks burning in bowls of grease or by pine-knot torches elsewhere. They used thorns for pins and persimmon seeds for buttons and made themselves corn shuck and palmetto hats.

One woman, following "Sherman's sentinels"—the chimneys of burned houses—to Atlanta, salvaged half a bushel of corn out of the cracks of bureau drawers where horses were fed and used it for seed to replant. Old diaries and journals are filled with matter-of-fact accounts of such women's stubborn determination to survive. Erstwhile pampered "ladies" turned scavenger and searched the battlefields for spent bullets and Minié balls to trade to the Confederate commissary for a little meal and molasses.

But because of their peculiar conditioning, their training in smiling and being agreeable no matter what, they never allowed themselves to become grim in defeat or tragedy. An old book called *A Virginia Girl in the Civil War*, written by Myrta Lockett Avary and published by D. Appleton & Company in 1902, contains this testimony:

"There were hunger and nakedness and death and pestilence and fire and sword everywhere and we, fugitives from shot and shell, knew it well but somehow we laughed and sang and played on the piano—and never believed in actual defeat and subjugation."

A group of women who had known the wide acres, the spacious comfort of plantation life, were holed up in one room in a house in Richmond, starving gaily together and jubilant when they were able to report: "We did get hold of a lean chicken and tied it to the foot of the bed and tried to fatten it with boiled peas."

These same women saw the fall of Richmond and its occupation by their enemy. They vowed they would never "draw rations from the Yankees," and they held out for a long time. But eventually hunger and the wistful certainty that but for their stubborn pride they could be living "high on the hog," drinking tea and coffee and sweetening it with sugar again, prevailed.

Wearing the pooled finery of the group as a bolster for their pride, two aging and stately matrons set forth as emissaries to ask food at the Yankee depot. The daughter of one sat by an upstairs window watching for their return. When she saw them coming, far from being laden with goodies, they appeared to be empty-handed. And yet they were doubled up with laughter. Looking closer, she saw that the Yankee commissary, little better off than the Confederate's, had given them its meager all. Each carried, dangling from a string, a dried codfish—"a fragrant and melancholy codfish."

In the best tradition of the Southern lady, they had the practicality to take and use the food and the wit to laugh at themselves and their precious pride's pratfall.

The Southern woman, alone among American women, had the task of helping to rebuild a defeated land. She was in the trenches before the war was over, picking up the rotting bodies of the slain and giving them a decent burial, putting flowers on the graves of the unknown, organizing her Ladies Memorial Associations and her United Daughters of the Confederacy. In a land where the men were beaten and shamed by defeat she was militantly determined to keep alive the glory and the valor of their fight.

As one poor backwoods mother wrote her son: "Don't be shamed by losin. You fit bettern you ever knowed how. And if ol' Abe's folks offer you a mule, take it and come on home. It ain't too late to git a crop in the groun."

A paradox which never fails to arouse the curiosity of the student of the Southern scene is the way thousands of Negroes, principally Negro women, were willing to forego freedom to stand by the families of men fighting to keep them slave.

Apparently oblivious to the enticements of freedom offered them by the Union Army, they toiled on even harder where they were, working shoulder to shoulder with their erstwhile white mistresses for a cause not their own, supplying the Confederate Army, keeping plantations producing, nursing and protecting the families of the absent soldiers.

Why? Some, of course, were ignorant of the advantages of freedom, some unbelieving, and some naturally reluctant to trade the known state of servitude for the strange and precarious chance at freedom. But many more stayed out of simple loyalty and devotion, carrying on after emancipation for the reason which black Katie Bess of Hickory Level plantation, Alabama, expressed in Marie Campbell's story, *A House with Stairs:* "Being friends is a binding thing, stronger than bondage."

Life has never been easy for the dark-skinned Southern woman. Generally she has reared her own children by remote control, an odd hour's attention here and there, while the bulk of her time and energy and strength went into nursing white children across town. That she didn't stint her white charges thousands of Southerners will testify, remembering with genuine affection the love and humor, the warm imagination, and, yes, the discipline, they received at the hands of a Negro cook or nurse. That she also managed at home, in spite of her weariness and lack of time, is evidenced in the careers of many distinguished Negro leaders who owe their education to a mother who was a servant.

Rebuilding was a long-time task, not yet finished. But the dazzling progress that has been made has traveled largely on the dreams, the spiritual convictions, and the iron-clad courage of women, all kinds of women. Negro women who scrubbed floors and washed clothes to get for their children education and a better life than they themselves had known. Women like Florida's Mary McLeod Bethune, daughter of slaves, who baked and sold sweet potato pies to found Bethune-Cookman College for Negroes, placing over the door this admonition: "Enter to learn. Depart to serve." Women like Alabama-born Helen Keller whose fight over total physical blindness and deaf-muteness symbolized the eternal fight against those other handicaps, blind poverty, blank ignorance.

That they were sustained by faith and unselfishness is demonstrated by the example of Martha Berry, daughter of plantation aristocracy, who poured her strength and health and personal fortune into building a school for poor rural children and then charmed Northern and Eastern philanthropists into helping her. Miss Berry was a beauty, reared for a place in society, but she once turned down an invitation to be presented at the Court of St. James because the price of her court gown would finance three years' schooling for a bright mountain boy.

Some people regard as a typical feminine caprice Miss Berry's chicken houses—and it could be that this whim of hers was as typical of a Southern woman as any modern writers will find. She had steeples put on every single chicken house on the Berry campus because she wanted to remind the young people who toiled there for their education that work well done is an act of worship.

3 Gills of Rum for the use of the sick. July 1st, 1771.
P'r order of Doct'r Richards.

NORTH CAROLINA STATE RECORDS

AUBREY D. GATES

The Doctor

ON HORSEBACK, with meager medicine in his saddlebags, his greatest strength was unbounded faith, dedication, and devotion. His medical knowledge was limited, but his knowledge of people was vast. Thus he rode into the frontier wilderness.

This was the Doctor.

From then until now, it has been a long ride—over side roads and swamp trails to cabins and lean-tos, down stately driveways to the mansions of the wealthy, and wherever else sickness or misfortune has struck. He has traveled on horseback and in his buggy, by skiff and steamboat, by rail-handcar, train, and auto. Sometimes he walked the last mile across a muddy field. He graduated to modern medical knowledge as the times advanced it. And often he himself advanced it when alone and face-to-face with dire emergency.

Doc has fought disease, ignorance, fear, superstition, inertia, and quackery. He has died violently on the trail under a falling tree in the storm, or by gun blast from ambush. He has drowned in the bayou, died from infectious diseases of his patients, and been killed in car crashes while rushing to midnight emergencies.

Most of the time he has been noble. Occasionally he has been petty. Some of the time he has grumbled. All of the time he has been human.

From the vantage of modern health standards, the vastness of Doc's present knowledge and skill, the assurance of our vaccines and antibiotics, the asepsis of our hospitals, glance back down the trail of Doc's years.

Risen to statehood only seventeen years before, Kentucky had 400,000 residents by Christmas Day in 1809. Here, on the remote Far West frontier that day, another page of medical history was written. In a humble house in the town of Danville, Dr. Ephraim McDowell performed the first recorded successful removal of an ovarian cyst.

Jane Todd Crawford, forty-five years old and mother of five children, had ridden horseback some sixty miles to reach Dr. McDowell's home. A bedroom was converted into an operating room, the kitchen table served as the operating table. Anesthetics were unknown and no mention is made of using opiates of any kind. Mrs. Crawford sang hymns to dull the pain while the frontier doctor, who had passed up the choice of doing nothing, risked death while trying to save a human life.

In a letter to a medical student years later, Dr. McDowell described this first operation of its kind: "I was sent for in 1809 to deliver a Mrs. Crawford near Greentown of twins; as the two attending physicians supposed. Upon examination per vaginam I soon ascertained that she was not pregnant; but had a large tumor in the abdomen which moved easily from side to side. I told the lady I could do her no good and candidly stated to her her deplorable situation; informed her that John Bell, Hunter, Hey and A. Wood, four of the first and most eminent surgeons in England and Scotland, uniformly declared in their lectures that such was the danger of peritoneal inflammation, that opening the abdomen to extract the tumor was inevitable death. But notwithstanding this, if she thought herself prepared to die, I would take the lump from her if she could come to Danville. She came in a few days after my return home and in six days I opened her side and extracted one of the ovaria which from its disease and enlarged state weighed upwards of twenty pounds. She was perfectly well in 25 days."

The morning of the operation, Dr. McDowell wrote a prayer and put it in his pocket: "Direct me, O God, in performing this operation, for I am but an instrument in Thy hands." Jane Crawford recovered fully and lived another thirty-three years—twelve years longer than her thirty-eight-year-old benefactor.

No surgeon, in America or Europe, would successfully repeat this type of operation for another thirty years. It was not until 1842, that Dr. Crawford W. Long of Danielsville, Georgia, used ether as an anesthetic for the first time. He was four years ahead of Dr. W. T. G. Morton of Pennsylvania, but because Dr. Morton published a report of his work before Long did, he received the credit.

In those early days, the physician's equipment was little better than it had been in the Middle Ages. Surgical incisors were not as good as modern kitchen knives; forceps were wooden tines, padded with leather. Many herbals and drugs were homegrown by "Doc" in a sideyard garden. (Even during the Civil War, historians affirm, only one clinical thermometer existed in the entire Medical Corps of the Confederate armies.)

Dysentery, typhoid and yellow fevers, tetanus, milk-sickness were the commonplace killers of the pioneer South. Many mothers died in childbirth; an appalling number of children died during babyhood.

This was the future confronting any adolescent who resolved to become a physician and undertook the long, arduous apprenticeship of study and observation. Withal, medical science made giant strides in the South's seaboard cities as well as on the frontiers of the Old West.

At the second annual meeting of the American Medical Association in Boston in 1849, the New Orleans delegation reported, in meticulous detail, on its campaign for public health and its determined stand against "inebriety" as an important part of that campaign. During AMA's fourth annual meeting in Charleston in 1851, plans were made for a section of the society to be "exclusively devoted to the reception and discussion of scientific papers;" subjects assigned to special committees for detailed research included "the milk-sickness," "permanent cure for reducible hernia," and "diseases of parasitic origin."

Through the horrors of the War—when medical supplies ran so perilously low that wives and sweethearts were sent to Baltimore, Philadelphia and New York to purchase drugs and smuggle them home sewn in their petticoats–when C.S.A. generals lost far more soldiers to dysentery, typhoid and tetanus than they did to Yankee guns and bayonets—Doc worked tirelessly, ceaselessly on.

In the post-war years, with asepsis and sterilization still medical mysteries and in spite of the lack of sufficient instruments, facilities and knowledge, Southern physicians continued in the tradition of Dr. McDowell. Dr. T. J. Woods, of Batesville, Arkansas, for instance, successfully removed the first appendix in that section of the Ozarks, removed a forty-pound uterine cyst, and did early brain surgery.

The challenge of wartime agonies fired Walter Reed of Gloucester County, Virginia, to enroll as a medical student at the University of Virginia. Still a "callow" eighteen-year-old, he won his M.D. in 1869 and became a U.S. Army surgeon in 1875. It was Reed who, as head of a medical team in Havana in 1899, discovered that the *stegomyia fasciata* mosquito is the carrier of yellow fever. Walter Reed gave his own life to the cause, dying in 1902. But his research ended this dreadful scourge across the South. Mosquito-control enabled American engineers to build the Panama Canal, along the very route where De Lesseps and the French had succumbed to malaria and plague a few years before. It also released doctors from the

The country doctor

heart-breaking chore of an endless procession of malarious people, suffering from chills and fever, doubly susceptible to other illnesses if not dying of the malaria itself.

Pellagra, the penalty of ignorance, caused by the diet of sowbelly, meal, and molasses on which so many Southerners existed, remained a mystery as to cause, cure, and prevention until the discoveries of Dr. Joseph Goldberger in the 1920's. Led by Dr. Tom Spies of Birmingham, now a world-wide authority, it is a rare disease in the modern South.

Even more difficult for the southern doctor than ignorance has been superstition. When Dr. M. C. Wiginton, of Hammond, Louisiana, first started his practice thirty years ago in southern Mississippi, he encountered a widespread superstition that baffled him for months. In cases of malaria, typhoid, diarrhea and other infections causing a high fever, the people believed the patient should have no water. "Potions and brews, but no water." Patients who, with competent medical care, should recover were dying from dehydration. What to do? Heartbreak and frustration prevailed until an elderly Negro woman revealed her secret of "pebble tea," and its mysterious power to heal a fever.

"You gather small, white, round pebbles from a brook," she whispered. "Wash them well. Put them in a bag, and boil 'm a long time in a lot of water. Pebble tea's a real powerful healer."

Pebble tea! The answer to a prayer and the solution to a problem. This device for administering liquids became a part of his practice, not of his belief. And he could smile about it, because the local death rate dropped.

Critically important in the long struggle away from "the magic and mysterious" have been the medical schools. In the seventeenth and eighteenth centuries, most doctors in the South started as apprentices of older doctors. They "read" medicine. After 1840 schools of medicine like those at Louisville and Tulane turned out well-trained physicians, and gave further training to doctors already in practice. Today every southern state has at least one Grade A medical school; twenty-three of the eighty-five medical schools of the nation are located in the South; and two more were being built in late 1958.

There is a new kind of pioneer doctor in the South today—the Dave Millers of Kentucky, the George Bonds of Bat Cave, North Carolina, and countless others "out on the frontier" jeeping in fourth gear over into the remote coves and isolated valleys. They possess most of the knowledge of modern-day medicine, but have to persuade, educate, even "cudgel" reluctant people into understanding that only meager and emergency treatment can be given in the home. Through their pioneering, clinics and small hospitals have been built in remote villages to become a complement to the jeep, the Millers, and the Bonds. Other members of the medical team—the nurse, the aid, the technician—are being trained there.

In no one person in the South is the legend, the tradition, or the inheritance of the doctor better exemplified than in J. Paul Jones, M.D., Camden, Alabama. His father, his uncle, his grandfather, and two great uncles have all practiced in Camden. A Dr. Nettles, friend of the early members of this medical family, did the first Caeserean delivery of a baby in Alabama in 1856. Grandfather Jones began his practice in 1860 after graduating from Tulane. His father followed in 1899 after graduating from the College of Physicians and Surgeons in New York. Dr. "Paul," out of Tulane, began practice in 1919 and carries on the family tradition today with an ultra-modern four-bed clinic. There, or in the hospital at Selma, thirty miles and thirty minutes by ambulance, he provides every care known to medical science.

The Jones family have utilized all the modes of travel, faced all the problems of ignorance, superstition, lack of medical knowledge and equipment, have adopted developments that have taken much of the risk and pain out of living, prolonged lifespans and eased the fear of dying, for white and Negro alike for almost one hundred years.

The lower classes of America, taken altogether, are more cultivated and more rational than in other countries. Even the backwoodsmen read the newspapers, and show considerable information on many subjects.

FRIEDRICH VON RAUMER, 1844

THOMAS D. CLARK

The Communicators

WHEN A SOUTHERNER of an earlier generation thinks about the good old days, he brings into his thoughts the pleasures of going to the store. When he thinks of his earlier community, he recalls reading once a week the news of his county and the bigger world about him.

Progress has brought the Southerner greater comfort and safety in life. The Pure Food and Drug Act has protected him from the patent medicines that injured his system; the chain stores have brought him a wonderland of merchandise and reduced prices; many of the fancy, modern local papers have abandoned their editorial pages; large numbers of editors are all but anonymous.

But modern life lacks the simple color and excitement of those far-off days when the rambling stores, behind their square fronts pasted with advertisements of chill tonics, female regulators, and chewing tobacco, were centers of the world of commerce for millions of people, or when a kind-hearted editor sent a member of a bereaved family to the grave with a gracious word of praise for a life well-spent.

An apprentice of Benjamin Franklin's founded the *South Carolina Gazette* at Charles Towne in 1732. By 1737, the *Virginia Gazette* in Williams Burg was reporting the prize of "a Violin to be played for by 20 fiddlers" at the Hanover County horse races, plus "A pair of handsome silk stockings of One Pistole value [to] be given to the handsomest Young country maid that appears in the Field." Thereafter, the journeyman-printer, the "hell-box," and the hand-press were part of the procession along Wilderness Road.

As settlers pushed up the river to plant tobacco patches and widen cattle ranges, "the store" became the focal point of Southern society. Stores appeared before courthouses; even before churches. A community made its first pretense to permanency through its store. The great roll of the frontier can be paralleled with the expansion of the country merchandising system.

Stores were necessary if the new settlers were to maintain any sort of a life for themselves. Even where the factors attempted to supply goods, they could not anticipate in their big annual orders the day-to-day needs of their patrons. Besides, only a fraction of the frontiersmen moving across the frontier South patronized factors. The country merchant supplied stocks of goods, played barkeeper to his patrons, and accepted their country produce in lieu of cash.

After the Civil War this doughty mercantile pioneer became one of the economic mainstays of a region struggling to recover from the ravages of war. Where native sons in the ante bellum period thought of the ministry and the law, the sons of the New South had to accept more modest callings. All a prospective storekeeper needed with which to begin business was a good crossroads, a pine-board building of tobacco-barn proportions, and a will to attend to business.

When the wreckages of war were cleared away, and railway promoters could once again focus on the South, they needed freight-producing sources. One way to concentrate freight at points along the endless stretches of railroads through the pine barrens was to build sidetracks and develop stores. A likely lad was selected and put in business on the siding. He created a demand for freight by ordering goods; he accepted cotton, crossties, produce of all kind, and lumber in exchange for merchandise.

There was the case of the young lad in Dewey Rose, Georgia, who was working in a gang helping to build a stretch of the Louisville and Nashville Railroad. A promoter spotted him and suggested that he build a store and go into business. The railroad would finance him. Inexperienced and frightened at the idea of being in business, the Georgian protested that he might go broke. He was asked by the railroad promoter if he had anything? When the boy answered he had nothing, the retort was "How in the hell can you go broke if you don't have nothing?" This logic was convincing. In time, the lad grown gray was to retire from a long mercantile career, a wealthy man.

As the stores popped up all over the South, the region was combed by those industrious souls who came out from the big cities in two-horse buggies and spring wagons to sell merchandise. Nowhere in the nation did the profession of drummer become a more profitable one. These agents were generally Confederate soldiers who could mix well-planned salesmanship with rich memories of experiences in the commands of General Forrest or Marse Robert E. Lee, of riding with Jeb Stuart, or of standing firm with "Old Jack" at Chancellorsville or elsewhere on the sprawling Virginia front. It was hard for a rising young Confederate merchant to say "no" to a comrade-at-arms who came selling the wares of wholesale houses in Louisville, St. Louis, Charleston, Nashville, Mobile, and New Orleans.

The drummer, a merry specimen who came from strange and far places, carted heavy trunks and bags. He was a man who had seen over the hill and knew what was going on in the next village, the county seat, or in the big cities. Not only did he come peddling news and making persuasive sales talks; he brought along an abundant supply of naughty stories which tickled the sense of humor even of the strait-laced deacons who sat about the potbellied stoves.

Possibly few institutions in the South have so successfully combined business and social life. From the seventeenth century on, the country store was half mercantile house, half community center. A word of gossip dropped about the stove, or on the porch, went the rounds of the community almost before the sun set. News of an accident spread over the community like wildfire, a death was noted on the currents of the air, and a social scandal was "norated" about instantly. Every ear in the constant circle of loafers was bent for the news, whatever its nature.

The storekeeper himself was the master board through which all the currents of community life passed. He knew almost everybody's secrets. He knew intimately the value of a man's word, his credit rating, his ability to make a living, his religious views, his politics, his enemies and his friends, the date of his birth, the state of his health—and the success or failure of his love affairs and his marriage. He knew where everybody lived, what they did to make money, and where they could be found at almost any hour of the day.

There is no assortment of goods, not even in the highly lighted and refrigerated modern supermarkets, that is more tempting than was the disorder of the Southern country stores. Barrels and boxes were piled in corners and crowded on the floor. Platforms supported heavy barrels of oil, lard, piles of white meat, and heaps of chains and harness. Drawers in the counters were filled with shoes, bolts, screws, guns, pocket knives, tableware and coffin fixtures. Counter tops were heaped with clothing, tools, cracker boxes, hoops of cheese, egg boxes, cases of apples, oranges, and tinware. Shelves were crammed with bottles of patent medicines, bolts of cloth, cans of sardines and salmon, shoe tacks, cartridges and shotgun shells, hardware, and hundreds of other bits of merchandise. Goods, seldom if ever displayed in anything like a modern concept of the term, were flung into place so the customer could dig for what he sought. Merchants made clumsy efforts to departmentalize their stores, but both they and their customers tended to destroy the order of things as time went on.

A good part of the attractiveness of the Southern country store was in the smell. No lad who carried a bucket of eggs to exchange for a box of baking soda, a piece of fat meat, and a gallon of molasses can ever forget the intoxicating aroma of the store. It took a lot of mixing of merchandise, animals, and human beings to develop that peculiar odor which greeted customers as they entered a well-run store: at Christmastime, for instance, it was the combination of apples, oranges, raisins, candy, and firecrackers and gunpowder.

Customers seldom if ever had cash with which to buy goods. They relied on a stipulated amount of credit which was set at the beginning of the year, and merchants undertook to keep their patrons within the agreed limits of their credit. Merchandise was purchased by order. A customer tore off a strip of paper from anything in sight—the calendar on the wall, a margin from a newspaper, a sheet from a patent medicine memorandum book, a corner from the marriage certificate, or a fragment of wallpaper snatched from the wall—and wrote an order to the storekeeper. The storekeeper in turn strung these order-notes on long pieces of wire and hung them on the wall of his store.

The long rattails of paper documented the level of education, the importance of the merchant in the lives of the people, the nature of the Southern diet, the kind of clothes they wore, the type of implements with which they plowed and cultivated their fields, their hopes, frustrations, and senses of humor. A single length of baling-wire sometimes strung together the local story of the Negro wheedling a piece of fat meat and the woes of an ex-Confederate general struggling to rebuild his fortunes on a Southern plantation. Storekeepers' wire files made no class distinctions in recording the affairs of their customers.

The big leather-bound account books took up where the rattail files left off. They recorded in more precise manner the fortunes of customers from year to year. Often their failures are noted in splotches of red ink, splotches which in fact document the failure of Southern agriculture itself.

The storekeeper was banker, representative of the wholesalers, cotton and tobacco buyer, warden of church and school affairs, father confessor to his community, place of first resort for the newborn, and place of last resort for the customer in death. On the larger scale he was an agent for economic interests far removed from the South. What he did at the crossroads in a poor hill county in Alabama was of importance to a wholesale house in

Interior of a typical general store in a country town

Louisville, and ultimately to a banker on Wall Street. In a moment when the South was definitely an economic colony of the rising industrial and capital nation, the storekeeper was an important agent of the system.

But however farflung the economic and social ramification of the old system of country general-merchandising in the South, the store was also a central factor in the region's folk history. Inevitably a mass of folklore would develop about it. There is the ancient story of the illiterate who attempted to keep books by using symbols of the merchandise he sold. At settling-up time in the fall, when the cotton crop was ginned and sold, the merchant undertook to charge a protesting customer with a hoop of cheese. Upon a more precise analysis of the year's account, it was discovered what the customer had really bought was a grindstone. The merchant had forgotten to add the hole to the symbol in his ledger.

Another story (told about half the stores in the South) is that of thieves who undertook to loot the liquor barrel by boring a hole through the floor and tapping the barrel from underneath. But every time the augur touched the barrel, it rolled over. When the merchant opened the store the next morning he discovered a row of holes bored all the way across the floor.

Where the storekeeper enjoyed a place of prestige in his community, the country editor served a county. The editor, like the storekeeper, was often a lad unable to afford the expensive education necessary to become a doctor or a lawyer; he bought a printing press, a jug of printer's ink, and went into business. Publishing a country newspaper in the South was both an interesting and exciting undertaking. The editor first of all had to assure himself that he could either whip most of the bullies in the county or outrun them. Southern people up to 1920 regarded libel as a personal matter. If the editor published something that displeased them, they took it up directly with him instead of dragging him into court to defend a libel suit.

Like the storekeeper, the editor needed assistance in starting his business. Sometimes printing press manufacturers and ready-print services gave him a boost. The average Southern county between 1865 and 1920 seldom generated enough worth-while news to sustain a newspaper. But this mattered little because the editor had the ready-print pages on which to rely. Ready-print houses in St. Louis, Chicago, Baltimore, and New York printed two or four pages and distributed them to country editors to add a couple of pages of his own print.

Ready-print editors were highly sensitive about the matter they published in their pages. They played safe by extracting the editorials of Southern editors like Marse Henry Watterson, Captain F. W. Dawson, or Henry W. Grady and Clark Howell.

In his less rugged moments the Southern country editor was a whimsical chronicler of the passing scene. A farmer dug up a tree root that resembled the face of General Lee; he hastened with it to the editor. First cotton blooms, tall stalks of corn and sugar cane, giant watermelons, two-headed chickens, strange eggs, old guns, and weird bones were all carried to the editor's desk for examination, and to be given publicity. A spider looped a web about the neck of a mouse in a livery stable; the editor recorded a week-by-week account of how far off the floor the tiny spider had drawn the mighty mouse. A local rat-killing revealed the fact that one of the victims had stolen a wedding ring and worked it over his neck. A local hostess fell into a barrel of molasses when she was trying to get a ham from the smokehouse to cook for company; the editor published the story in detail with a warning that people had better be careful where they bought their molasses for a few days.

An alert editor tried to print the names of everybody in the county at least once a year. This was hard to do because many a Southerner did nothing worthy of noting. Many of them, however, were born, got married, grew ill and died. All of this was news. A local wedding of importance tested the mettle of the editor. He felt it his bounden duty to send the young couple into life with a flowery editorial puff that would sustain their ego at least through the birth of their second child. No aspect of Victorian writing revealed the art more clearly than the typical rural newspaper account of the marriage of the county's most attractive lass.

The editor was the conservator of both local fact and fiction. When factual news was hard to gather, he sat down and wrote original stories. Some of these are prime pieces of American yarn-spinning. There was less squeamishness in parts of the South about stories that were stoutly suggestive than prevails today; sometimes an editor got by with the publication of materials that would do Boccaccio credit. They could do this because they could always preface their stories by saying, "It is all in the family."

Part 3
The Building

Preceding page:
View of Richmond from Hollywood

I returned home to my family with a determination to bring them as soon as possible to live in Kentucke, which I esteemed a second paradise.

DANIEL BOONE, 1784

W. D. WORKMAN, JR.

The Trailmakers

FOR ALMOST THREE CENTURIES "the West" beckoned the venturesome, the restless, the land-hungry, and those who felt crowded by their fellow men or by the law. But the first of the many "Wests" which came to enliven the pages of American history began on the far slopes of the Southern Appalachians and stopped short of the Mississippi.

Geography and topography gave their own special meanings to this oldest West of Kentucky, the Natchez Trace and the dark and bloody trails toward fabled "Tejas." The mountains guarding them on the east stretch continuously from Pennsylvania down into the upper regions of what came to be Georgia and Alabama. These are the Blue Ridge, or, more accurately, the Blue Ridges. Tier after tier of heavily forested ranges confronted the pioneers who scaled the easternmost peaks to gaze westward into the Great Smokies.

These were the barriers which early in the eighteenth century deflected into the Carolinas and Virginia the hardy Germans and Scotch-Irish fleeing from the taxes, high land costs, and bias of Pennsylvania, New York, and New England. Ray Allen Billington describes these pioneers as "bold, devout, shrewd men, hating Indians and Easterners with impartial vigor, and determined to 'keep the Sabbath and everything else they could lay their hands on . . . .'" The lure of cheaper farms to the South and the foreboding look of the Western mountains veered them southwest into the hills and valleys of the Piedmont.

It was from these beachheads on the eastern slopes that they mounted assaults, first individually and later collectively, against the Appalachians. From 1700 on, the trailmakers ranged westward and upward, probing for passageway through the homelands of the Cherokee, Shawnee and Creeks. Many a woodsman, scouting on a trader's commission or hypnotized by the blue peaks' challenge, padded ghostlike across the divide, stared out over Kentucky bluegrass—and henceforth was content nowhere else.

These were the ones who broke trail for the settlers of the 1780's. Frederick Jackson Turner immortalized the sequence: "Stand at Cumberland Gap and watch the procession of civilization, marching single file—the buffalo following the trail to the salt springs, the Indian, the fur-trader and hunter, the cattle-raiser, the pioneer farmer—and the frontier has passed by. Stand at South Pass in the Rockies a century later and see the same procession with wider intervals between."

What Turner pictured at Cumberland Gap—probably the most important pass of all—was repeated up and down the Appalachian chain. Climb today to Wagon Road Gap in the shadow of North Carolina's Mount Pisgah and see the western valleys open up. Further south and east, in South Carolina, trace the cart road up to Jones Gap, then down into the valley of the French Broad River that curves through gorges and hemlock forest toward the Gulf of Mexico.

Legends attach to these gaps like cockleburs to buckskin. There is the tale of Solomon Jones, as fictitious as it is fascinating, telling how the old mountain man surveyed the cart road up to his Gap by following a pet hog, which, of course, picked the easiest grades. The truth is that Solomon was an able engineer who knew his business, and who lies buried atop Mount Hebron in North Carolina beneath a headstone which says: "Here Lies Solomon Jones, The Road Maker, A True Patriot. He Labored 50 Years to Leave the World Better Than He Found It."

As one type of pioneer followed another through the Passes, so did one sort of tool follow another—first the peculiarly American "Kentucky rifle," then the ax, the hoe, and finally the plow. Not since the British longbows at Crecy had a weapon been so effectively adapted to need as this long-barreled "Kentucky rifle."

The stubby European muskets which were lugged ashore at Plymouth Rock and elsewhere along the Atlantic seaboard soon lost their identity in the evolving of a firearm adapted to the frontier. Solitary hunters, whether stalking animal or human game, could ill afford a wasted shot—so the barrel was lengthened for accuracy and the bore reduced to save weight of both shot and piece. Sights were redesigned to accommodate the shadowy depths of the forest, and, perhaps most important of all, the use of the grease (tallow) patch for wrapping bullets permitted tamping the shot home with a light wooden ramrod rather than driving it down, noisily, with an iron ramrod.

Most famous of all the Long Rifles, as these explorers of the first West came to be called, was Daniel Boone. Son of an English emigrant to Pennsylvania, reared as a cattle guard in the hills behind Reading, Pennsylvania, he helped drive the family herds to a new home in North Carolina's Yadkin Valley in 1751. His first sniff of the West came as a waggoner on Braddock's disastrous march against Fort Duquesne. He is believed to have been with General Forbes in 1758, when Duquesne surrendered and became Fort Pitt. Five years later he was in Florida, but his new wife refused to live there. Back they trod to destiny in the West.

No other American, including the boisterous Davey Crockett, gained such identification with the lonely wilderness. Who besides Boone would have been found, as he was by a group from North Carolina, lying flat on his back in a Kentucky glade, singing aloud for the sheer joy of it?

It was "Boone's Trace," later expanded into the famous "Wilderness Road," which in 1775 opened the way through Powell's Valley and Cumberland Gap into the bluegrass lands of Kentucky, with "soil as rich as cream."

Not all of the Trailmakers were unschooled and wrote, like Boone, that they had "Cilled A Bar." James Adair, an English trader with the Indians, wrote scholarly tall stories of life across the Blue Ridge. Once captured by the French, he tells: "They were fully resolved to have me sent down to Mobile or New Orleans as a capital criminal to be hanged. . . . But I doubted not of being able to extricate myself some way or other. They appointed double sentries over me for some days before I was to be sent down in the French King's large boat. They were strongly charged against laying down their weapons or suffering any hostile thing to be in the place where I was kept, as they deemed me capable of any mischief. . . . About an hour before we were to set off by water I escaped from them by land. . . . I took through the middle of the low land covered with briers at full speed. I heard the French clattering on horseback along the path . . . and the howling savages pursuing . . . but my usual good fortune enabled me to leave them far enough behind."

There were other scholars less imaginative. Alexander Neely helped while away wintry hours by reading aloud from *Gulliver's Travels* to Daniel Boone, his brother, Squire Boone, and the rest of a band of Kentucky explorers. From this event, according to Constance Skinner, came the naming of Kentucky's Lulbegrud Creek, an understandable corruption of the "Lorbrulgrud" in *Gulliver's Travels.*

A glimpse of Kentucky
from the Cumberland Gap

Although Boone is justifiably remembered as the most spectacular figure of the first West, he was far from being the first pathfinder across the mountains. John Finley (or Findlay), a Pennsylvania trader, was one of the first to set foot on the "dark and bloody ground" of Kentucky. In 1752, as a prisoner of the Shawnees, he learned of Kentucky's accessibility through the Cumberland Gap. He passed on the story, adorned with fascinating but true accounts of the land's wonders, when a guest in the Boone cabin in the Yadkin Valley.

Even earlier, Dr. Thomas Walker reached Cumberland Gap, but failed to lead his small party west to the lush, level lands along the Kentucky River. Instead he moved north, searching for a likely site for the 800,000 acres granted his Loyal Land Company.

The venturesome Judge Richard Henderson of North Carolina was another land speculator who glimpsed prospects of affluence and influence in the virgin tracts beyond the mountains. He envisioned a vast area under the jurisdiction of his Transylvania Company and came heartbreakingly close to its realization. Boone and other backwoods notables worked on occasion for Henderson. But they would not go along with his schemes for a Transylvania government. Opposition both from mountain men and from the government of Virginia punctured the judge's dream.

In 1777, Virginia's House of Burgesses turned from perilous bulletins about Burgoyne's advance against the Continental Army long enough to read requests from the Kentuckians and declare their region "the Kentucky County" of Virginia. Judge Henderson's "treaties," which supposedly vested him with title to a considerable area of erstwhile Indian lands, were not recognized. He had to be content with a grant of some 200,000 acres of land between the Ohio and Green rivers. A similar grant from North Carolina, in the valleys of the Powell and Clinch rivers, made him, nonetheless, one of the West's largest landowners.

Meanwhile, war or no war, Tennessee was being settled by hundreds of hardy families, following hard on the heels of James Robertson, one of Judge Henderson's agents. Nashville, founded by Robertson in 1780, became the northern terminus of the Natchez Trace and was a city by 1806.

Back east beyond the mountains, kinfolk and old neighbors fought not only for political freedom but for the freedom to give full vent to that old Southern lure, the lands of the sunset. Kinfolk was kinfolk. Freedom, viewed in all its glorious majesty from a Kentucky glade or Tennessee clearing, was worth fightin' anybody to keep. Quietly, the Trailmakers began their eastward trek back through the gaps, leaving hawk-eyed sons and wives to fend as best they could against Indian raids.

Only recently have scholars recognized the true significance of the roles the Southerners played in the American Revolution.

Due recognition has long been accorded to Southern statesmen and generals, to frontiersmen such as burly Daniel Morgan, whose riflemen helped turn the tide against the British at Saratoga and elsewhere, and to George Rogers Clark, whose "Long Rifles" from Virginia and Kentucky swept the British out of the Ohio region. But it was in the South itself that the British scheme for subjugating the American rebels began falling apart at the seams.

Between 1778 and 1780, the British, in company with imported mercenaries and indigenous Tories, took virtual control of the Southern theater of operations. Under the able leadership of Clinton, Cornwallis, Rawdon, Tarleton, and Ferguson, the King's Men laid the plans for a massive rolling up of the Southern flank. This would reduce the American area of resistance by half. Aided by the fumbling tactics of the American commander, Horatio Gates, the British seemed well on their way to accomplishment of the goal.

But by October, 1780, frontiersmen from the Watauga settlements of Tennessee had joined old neighbors in the Carolinas. At Kings Mountain, athwart the North Carolina-South Carolina border, they ambushed Major Ferguson and his Tory raiders and virtually annihilated them.

That single encounter may well be described as a turning of the tide in the Revolution. General Nathanael Greene, of Rhode Island, replaced Gates as American commander in the South two months later, and a new and effective pattern of American resistance developed. Guerrilla forces under such valiant but elusive South Carolinians as Thomas (the Gamecock) Sumter, Francis (the Swamp Fox) Marion, and Andrew Pickens co-ordinated their strikes with those of more conventional cavalrymen, especially Lieutenant Colonel Henry (Light-Horse Harry) Lee, in raids against British columns and supply points.

Greene masterfully kept his scattered and sparse forces intact in the face of superior British numbers and supplies. He seldom won a pitched battle, but rarely lost men or matériel. And persistently, through the "irregulars" under Marion, Sumter, and Pickens, he smashed and hacked at the British lines of supply. Major clashes at Cowpens, Guilford Courthouse, Hobkirk's Hill, Ninety-Six, and Eutaw Springs all resulted in virtual standoffs so far as "victories" were concerned. But Greene sought the long-range results: a gradual withdrawal of British troops from the interior, back into Charleston.

Greene's strategies were sustained by Lord Cornwallis' surrender at Yorktown in October, 1781. In 1782 the British relinquished their controls of Charleston and Savannah.

The Treaty of Paris, in 1783, gave the newborn United States of America all the lands west to the Mississippi River, save for Florida's jungled sandspit and the Gulf Coast. Now the sunset magnetism could function freely, over the ridges and through the gaps where the trailmakers' blaze marks still wept pine-gum and sugarsap tears. In 1790, the nation's first census takers counted 73,677 Kentuckians and 35,691 Tennesseeans. Lincoln, Jackson, Crockett, Houston, Bowie, Austin, Davis . . . the names were scrawled into their record books. The babies squawling in cabin corners looked like all other babies. Freedom is a big place. Anything could happen.

In the quick, rash years that followed, the Indians proved to be larger losers than George III. One by one, Creek, Choctaw, Chickasaw were coaxed, goaded, bullied from homelands in west Georgia, Alabama, and

Mississippi. Finally, in stoic pride, the Cherokee walked in long columns down the west slopes and across the Kentucky bottoms on the shameful Trail of Tears toward Oklahoma.

There were spasms of uncertainty, of course, such as the one at Jonesboro in 1784 when New Westerners convened to form The State of Franklin and elect the transplanted Virginian, John Sevier, its governor. North Carolina reasserted her sovereignty over the territory. Franklin quibbled and argued, but was finally absorbed by the new State of Tennessee in 1796.

By that time, a new threat loomed from the east. It would prove to be a revolution, greater even than the war against England and the red men. It was coming, of all places, from a plantation Georgia had given General Greene a few years back.

Monument to General Nathanael Greene
at Guilford Courthouse National Military Park,
near Greensboro, North Carolina

Cotton, with us, is almost human. Cotton is like some member of the family that the folks have had a lot of trouble with, but in whom they still believe.

BEN ROBERTSON—"Red Hills and Cotton"

GEORGE HUBERT AULL

King Cotton

THE INK was hardly dry on Treaty of Paris signatures when Southern planters began designing an agricultural kingdom in which—although they did not know it—cotton would be "king." The Agricultural Society of South Carolina, second of its kind in the United States, came into being in 1785 "for promoting and improving agriculture and other rural concerns." Its high-minded purposes were defined by Thomas Heyward, Jr., its first president, who expounded: "After having gloriously succeeded . . . in terminating a war . . . it is incumbent upon us equally to endeavor to promote and enjoy the blessings of peace. This cannot be effected by any means more interesting and advantageous than by turning our attention to the cultivation and improvement of our fields. . . . Agriculture was one of the first employments of mankind. It is one of the most innocent and at the same time the most pleasing and beneficial of any. By its variety it keeps the mind amused; . . . by its exercise and regularity it conduces to give vigor and health to the body; and in the end it is productive of every other necessary and convenience of life. . . . It becomes the duty, therefore, as well as the interest of every citizen to encourage and promote it."

Promote it they did! Meeting regularly in Charleston ("admission money, entrance one guinea; annual contribution, two guineas"), they sponsored cattle shows and industrial exhibits, awarded prizes to "fortunate competitors" and "meritorious overseers," and established an experimental farm where various "exotics" were to be tried out under the supervision of a "scientific horticulturalist" imported by the Society from France.

This interest in diversified agriculture was further evidence that the institution of slavery—a national rather than a sectional cancer—was well on the way to extinction before the American Revolution. Jefferson was strongly opposed to it; his original draft of the Declaration of Independence contained a denunciation of it. Early attempts along this line were thwarted by the British crown. To Virginia goes the honor and distinction of being the first American state to prohibit the importation of slaves, having passed a law to this effect during the very first session of its existence under the republican government (1778). Maryland followed suit in 1783. The tobacco planters, slavery's principal eighteenth-century exponents, were learning slavery's economic folly and coupling it with old guilts of moral shame. So firm was the resolve and so positive was the action that there can be no doubt as to the demise of the slave during the early years of the nineteenth century, had it not been for the "sudden apparition of the great cotton crop, conjured by the genius of Whitney" and dwarfing all other Southern resources by the "instant employment of the half-idle slaves, whose presence had begun to be felt as a burden."

Without an economical means to separate the lint from the seed, cotton could not have become the ruthless king that it did. Without King Cotton, slavery would have withered and died. Without the emotionally packed issue of slavery, the newly formed states would have arrived at a peaceable solution to their other differences, because their quarrels centered around cotton and the tariff.

Eli Whitney's part in this reversal of what had seemed an irrevocable trend has the "plot" of a Grimm Brothers' fairy tale. Farm boy with a mechanical turn, Whitney graduated from Yale and accepted an offer to teach school in South Carolina. Sailing from New York in the autumn of 1792, he met and, during the ten-day voyage, charmed the widow of the great Revolutionary general, Nathanael Greene. Mrs. Greene had spent the summer in the North and was returning to the Georgia plantation, "Mulberry Grove," near Savannah, presented to her husband by the new state in gratitude for his critical 1780–83 campaign. She invited Whitney to visit in her home before going on to his school. Whitney began to make himself useful by mending things about the house and making toys for the plantation children. Meanwhile he watched the cabin Negroes as they picked the fuzzy, stubborn seeds from "vegetable wool," at an average rate of two pounds per day, and heard his hostess and her plantation manager, Phineas Miller, wish for a machine to speed the chore.

When Whitney learned that his South Carolina school would pay him not one hundred but fifty guineas a year, he determined to give up his job provided he could perfect the machine Mrs. Greene and her friends desired. Within ten days he had the "engine," a combination of squirrel cage and the "churka" long used in Asia to pop seeds from silky, long-staple cottons. He entered into a partnership arrangement with Miller, designed to insure them a complete monopoly on the cotton industry. Refusing to sell any gins, the firm demanded a rental fee of one pound of free lint out of every three combed from the seeds by the spikes in the invention's wooden cylinder.

The model for the engine (soon slurred to "gin") was so simple, and so readily reproducible, that it was impossible either to protect the patents or to collect the rentals. One legend is that Whitney's "gin" was first put on exhibition "for women only." However, "an ingenious young mechanic" introduced himself into the room "in woman's apparel" and by a minute examination of the gin satisfied himself that he could not only imitate but improve on its construction. Another version of the same story suggests that it was the other way around: Whitney got *his* ideas from the "ingenious young mechanic." At any rate, three Southern states—North Carolina, South Carolina and Tennessee—were sufficiently convinced of the merits of Whitney's claims and the value of his invention (*or* disgusted with his attempts to create a monopoly) that state appropriations were made to reward him. The records show that Whitney received approximately fifty thousand dollars in royalties from South Carolina, thirty thousand from North Carolina, and ten thousand dollars from Tennessee. Had Whitney made himself less obnoxious, Georgia, whose governor first proposed this method of compensation, would have at least matched South Carolina's contribution.

Whitney was so angered that the cotton states had interfered with his plans to lease the gins, and so vexed by lawsuits relating to his patents, that he could never thereafter be objective about the South. Writing a friend in 1803 he said, "I have a set of the most Depraved villians to combat and I might as well go to *Hell* in search of *Happiness* as apply to a Georgia court for *Justice*."

Cotton production soared from about 10,000 bales in 1793 and 21,000 in 1796 to more than 100,000 in 1801 and nearly 180,000 in 1810. Although perceptibly reduced as a consequence of the Embargo and Non-Intercourse Acts and, subsequently, the War of 1812, it kept on climbing to 209,000 bales in 1815, to 439,000 in 1822, and 532,000 in 1825. And the prices held, having averaged less than nine cents a pound during only one year (1811) and reaching more than twenty cents in at least six years.

Thus by 1815, making his "Valedictory Address" as first president of the Pendleton Farmers' Society in northwest South Carolina, Thomas Pinckney, Jr., spoke for a "Lost Cause" of the South when he urged:

"I implore your attention to an object, without which, there can be no good farming; an object which will double our comforts and quadruple the value of our lands; that will enable us to raise four fat oxen where we now barely sustain one. . . . This important object is meadow. . . . I hope and persuade myself that the views of the Society will encourage individual attempts to introduce grass fields as a regular rotation. . . . The last words of your first President are, 'Gentlemen, make hay.'"

Other agricultural enterprises quickly fell before Cotton's despotism. Urban and industrial development stagnated as factors, planters, merchants, and statesmen gave full energies to rapidly expanding cotton culture.

Small wonder Henry Grady, eminent editor, could later orate:

"Not the fleece that Jason sought can rival the richness of this plant as it unfurls its banners in our fields. It is gold from the instant it puts forth its tiny shoot. The shower that whispers to it is heard round the world. The trespass of a worm on its green leaf means more to England than the advance of the Russians on her Asiatic outposts. . . . The uttermost missionary woos the heathen with a cotton shirt in one hand and a Bible in the other, and no savage, I believe, has ever been converted to the one without adopting the other. . . . It peeps from the satchel of every business and religious evangelist that trots the globe. . . . The Dominion of our King is established,

Loading cotton on the Alabama River. The bales of cotton were sent down from the bluffs above the river by means of a long wooden chute

this princely revenue assured not for a year, but for all time. It is the heritage that God gave us when he arched our skies, established our mountains, girt us about with the oceans, tempered the sunshine, and measured the rain —ours and our children's forever."

Looking back, it seems incredible that any plant, even any person, should have elicited such devotion. But as Henry Savage points out in his recent book, *River of the Carolinas: The Santee*, the rich rewards of this new allegiance brought a veritable multitude flocking to a fleecy standard, which for a century and a half would fly over an ever-growing domain— "even above the Stars and Stripes."

Meanwhile, in Great Britain the ingenuity of other mechanics had contrived to produce machines capable of speedily converting cotton fibers into yarn and cloth. What could be more natural than for the South, with its rich soils, its mild climate, and its abundant supply of cheap, slave labor to furnish the raw product for the spindles and looms of the Mother Country and take her manufactured goods in return? And what could stir up so much sectional strife as a tariff act designed to curb these imports, raise the price of British goods, and perhaps restrict the market for King Cotton himself!

The South, long conditioned by the tobacco and rice trade with Europe and livestock shipments to the West Indies, had never favored tariff legislation. In the 1789 Congress, South Carolina's Senator Pierce Butler denounced the import law, charged Congress with oppressing the South, and threatened dissolution of the Union with regard to his state. When the Tariff Act of 1824 came up, the cotton states were almost unanimous in opposition; only three of their sixty-seven representatives in the House voted for the measure.

Southern opposition to the Tariff Act of 1828 (the "Tariff of Abominations") was equally violent. South Carolina, with exports exceeding $8,000,000 (second only to New York and Louisiana), was naturally in the forefront. Her governor, in response to numerous petitions, appointed a day of "fasting, humiliation, and defeat." John C. Calhoun, her spokesman in the Senate, advanced the argument known as the "South Carolina Exposition," declaring the tariff laws of 1828 to be unconstitutional, oppressive, and unequal and calling for a state convention to decide in what manner they ought to be declared null and void. This same document set forth the declaration that there was a permanent dissimilarity between the South and the rest of the Union, since the Southern states were "staple states" exclusively devoted to agriculture and destined always to remain so "because of their soil, climate, habits and peculiar labor." The South by that time had few manufacturers to protect.

The roles played now by John C. Calhoun, representing the South, and Daniel Webster, representing New England, provide one of the most interesting chapters in American economic history. Calhoun entered Congress from South Carolina just prior to the War of 1812, and was one of the "War Hawks" who urged the conquest of Canada. He not only voted *for* but strongly supported the Tariff Act of 1816. But, a good listener back home and a sharp analyst of straw polls, he switched sides when the Act came up for revision in 1824, then four years later led the movement to declare the "Tariff of Abominations" unconstitutional, oppressive, null and void.

Webster, on the other hand, had voted *against* both the Act of 1816 and that of 1824, defending "freedom of trade" as a great principle. But by 1828, he, too, had changed sides, and the Senate's two powerful debaters were again in opposition; each now standing in the other's "old shoes." The reason for the turnabout is not hard to find. New England had expanded industrial output; her interest in foreign trade subsided as the South's grew.

As cotton moved west across Kentucky, then jumped "ol' Miss," so did the Negroes *and the tensions*. Since Negroes were thought to be essential to cotton cultivation, every Congressional discussion about "new land" developed into a controversy over slavery. It has been estimated that between 1830 and 1850 the slave population of Louisiana more than doubled; that of Alabama approximately trebled; and Mississippi's nearly quintupled. The increase in cotton production was almost as spectacular. Total output rose from about one million bales in 1835 and two million in 1842 to three million in 1852 and more than 4.3 million in 1859. That year (1859) the Southern states produced for export agricultural products valued at nearly $200,000,000; more than 80 per cent is credited to cotton.

Yet the higher cotton rode, the higher rose its production costs. Like tobacco, it was a greedy land-eater. Plantation soils were "used up" in less than a generation. Erosion gullied abandoned fields. Western land prices soared. Edmund Ruffin, arguing bitterly against the hell-bent pace of cotton planters—yet himself destined to fire one of the first guns against Fort Sumter—demonstrated the advantages of marl and manure fertilizers on his own Virginia acres. All attempts to obtain relief from the increasing costs were vetoed in Congress. The only feasible alternative, to many, was separation from the Union! To this cause, and for these reasons, leading statesmen of the South committed themselves as early as 1858. There was talk of the possibility of British aid in case the separation should lead to a war.

Some have claimed that "The War" was fought over slavery; others took the view that freedom of trade was the real issue. But more than trade and more than slavery, cotton triggered the tragic conflict. To the South it

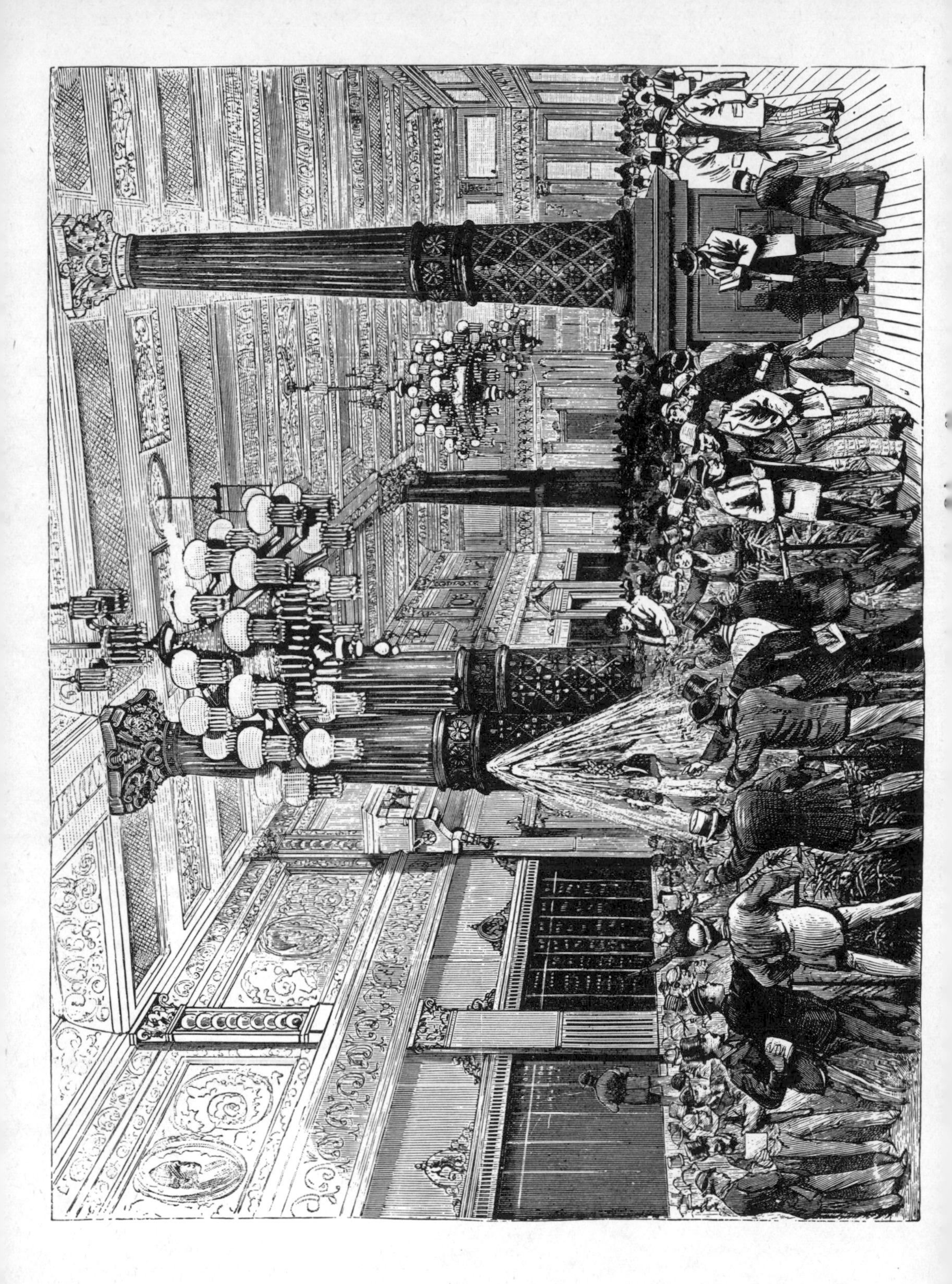

had become the royal plant—highly desirable, basically necessary, and wholly invincible. Many nodded agreement with U.S. Senator James H. Hammond of South Carolina when on March 4, 1858, he challenged: "Would any sane nation make war on cotton? Without firing a gun, without drawing a sword, should they make war on us we could bring the whole world to our feet. The South is perfectly competent to go on, one, two, or three years without planting a seed of cotton. . . . What would happen if no cotton were furnished for three years? I will not stop to depict what every one can imagine, but this is certain: England would topple headlong and carry the whole civilized world with her, save the South. *No, you do not dare to make war on cotton. No power on earth dares to make war upon it. Cotton is King*."

In 1859 the South provided nearly 90 per cent of the cotton reaching the European market. England alone took over a billion pounds a year; one-fifth of her population was said to be dependent upon cotton manufacture. By January 1861 Southern exports had all but stopped. Production that year reached an all-time high of 4.5 million bales, but only ten *thousand* bales were exported— down from *3.5 million* in 1859 and *0.6 million* in 1860. Production itself declined drastically after 1861 to 1.5 million bales in 1862, 0.4 million in 1863 and 0.3 million in 1864. Total exports during the War averaged only about seventy-five *thousand* bales a year, and most of this moved out in 1864.

Thus, in much less time than the three years envisioned by Senator Hammond, Europe's cotton famine was on—the devastating product of the Union Navy's blockade of Southern ports. The British attempted to relieve their situation by importing some "Surat" or Indian cotton; the quality was poor and exceedingly unpopular with the spinners. It has been reported that on one occasion during the height of the famine a Yorkshire minister included a petition for more cotton in his prayer. A pious mill hand chimed in with "Amen, O Lord!" and hastily added, "But, please, not Surat!"

Realistic Southern diplomats made petitions to Napoleon III in Paris. In return for French help in breaking the blockade, the Confederacy was prepared to give France not less than one hundred thousand bales of American cotton (not Surat!). The idea received a ready response from the Emperor, who suggested that he enlist the co-operation of the British in the undertaking.

There are Southerners who insist to this day that Anglo-French aid would have materialized except for a personal appeal by Mr. Lincoln "To the Workingmen of Manchester" *on the issue of slavery*, coupled with the great emotional appeal of Harriet Beecher Stowe's *Uncle Tom's Cabin*, which seems to have become required reading for every spinner and weaver in England after 1860. So effective was the Lincoln-Stowe propaganda that the London *Index* was moved to say: "The emancipation of the Negro from the slavery of Mrs. Beecher Stowe's heroes—has become the one idea of millions of British who know no better and do not care to know."

Nonetheless, British shipyards were constructing two ironclad men-of-war for the Confederacy. To counteract their potential, the federal government sent strong military and naval expeditions to occupy Southern ports and seize cotton which could then be doled out to the British in sufficient quantity to "hold them out of the war." The C.S.A.'s British agents learned what was afoot. So when Port Royal was taken by the Federals, the planters burned their entire harvest rather than let it fall into enemy hands.

The Charleston *Courier* described the incident:

"At eleven o'clock last night the heavens toward the Southwest were brilliantly illuminated with the patriotic flames ascending from burning cotton. As the spectators witnessed it they involuntarily burst forth with cheer after cheer and each heart was warmed as with a new pulse. . . . We learn with gratification that the planters on the seaboard are hourly applying the torch to their cotton."

How much cotton was actually destroyed in this way will probably never be known. However, about this time (July, 1862) U.S. Secretary Seward reported to his Minister (Adams) in London that as many as 3.5 million bales remained in the South, "though large quantities of it are yet unginned."

Enough cotton apparently got through to ease the problem of unemployment in British mills and to convince the British Parliament of the ultimate defeat of the Confederacy. At any rate, when the two ironclads slid down the ways they carried the flag not of the Confederacy but of England! The British had yielded to the voices of Lincoln and Stowe.

The total of Southern dead by 1865 is estimated at nearly half the entire Confederate army. Almost one-third of the white households in the South experienced the loss of a member. With these losses came the havoc of organized destruction, capped in scarlet wrath by General Sherman's "March to the Sea" across Georgia and final lunge into South Carolina. It was Christmas 1864 when he wrote that his army (sixty-five thousand men) burned with "an insatiable desire to wreak vengence upon South Carolina."

How well it succeeded was told by one of his officers in 1865:

"Over a region forty miles in width, stretching from Savannah . . . agriculture and commerce, even if peace come speedily, cannot be fully revived in our day. . . . Day by day our legions of armed men surged over the land, destroying its substance. . . . In all the length and breadth of that broad pathway the burning hand of war pressed heavily, blasting and withering where it fell. It was the penalty of rebellion."

Thus war's end found thousands of former slaves lost, bewildered, frustrated, without food and with no means to earn a livelihood. The Southern landlords who survived were left with little more than the bare earth. There were rumors that this, too, might be taken from them and parceled out to the hordes of former slaves. Born out of the urgency created by this combination of circumstances grew the system of farming "on the halves." The landowners furnished the land, work stock, and equipment. Negroes and landless whites provided the labor. Cash expenses and receipts were to be shared on a fifty-fifty basis after the harvest. Along with the land ostensibly came the cabins, enclosures for cows, hogs, and hens, and a "patch" for the vegetable garden.

Most important of all was the "furnish." Food and clothes were furnished on credit at the plantation store. Obviously, the share-crop system required a crop which could absorb a large amount of unskilled labor; was adaptable to a wide range of soils and weather; was not too sensitive to ill-treatment; was relatively imperishable; and could not readily be eaten or carried away. Again, cotton was the "natural."

Share-crop burgeoned during the years of Reconstruction. With it, in the grim procession of carpetbaggers, crackpot schemes, and the sadism of "Radical" leaders who backed Thaddeus Stephens' convictions, leered the spectre of racial distrust. Illiterate Negroes vying with illiterate whites in ante-bellum cotton fields fanned the smoldering flame of CSA's defeat; emancipation came to take the brunt of blame for the War itself. Then, the records indicate, the racial segregation laws of "Jim Crow" swept the South.

Before the War, Savannah had Negro units in the local militia and Negro volunteer fire departments. Negro ministers preached from the pulpits of city, as well as rural, churches. Frederick Law Olmsted's concise *Journey in the Seaboard Slave States* reported Negro passengers in the coaches of railroad trains across Virginia and "Negro passengers admitted to southern stage coaches without demur." An Englishwoman, the Hon. Miss Murray, touring prewar Alabama, wrote, "From what we hear in England, I imagined Negroes were kept at a distance. That is the case in the Northern States, but in the South they are at your elbow everywhere and always seek conversation."

Where, then, did "Jim Crow" come from? Describing a train ride from Boston to Lowell, Massachusetts, in 1842, Charles Dickens wrote:

"There are no first and second class carriages as with us; but there is a gentlemen's car and a ladies' car; the main distinction between which is that, in the first, everybody smokes; and in the second, nobody does. As a black man never travels with a white one, there is also a Negro car, which is a great blundering clumsy chest such as Gulliver put to sea in from the Kingdom of Brobdignag."

That was thirteen years after Garrison founded *The Liberator*, a few blocks from Boston's North Station, and eight years before Mrs. Stowe would ride the same Jim Crow'd trains to Brunswick, Maine, to start work on *Uncle Tom's Cabin*. Eli Whitney had died in 1825. But the assembly-line firearms he perfected "back home" in New Haven would eventually become standard equipment for Federal armies during the War. Now, in the sordid years of Reconstruction, "Jim Crow" finally migrated from Boston, too, down past Whitney's grave, to become a final bar sinister on King Cotton's coat of arms. Slave ships—gin—"Uncle Tom"—Whitney & Ames rifles—Jim Crow. The Yankee cycle was complete.

Nonetheless, in less time than it takes to say "damyankee," ante-bellum cotton production baled back to new records. When World War I broke, it stood at the all-time high of sixteen million bales, even though the bottom fell out of prices in 1914 and farmers received less than eight cents a pound. Then, like everything else, it shot to seventeen, to twenty-seven and, in 1919, to thirty-five cents.

The urgent need for cotton in the production of smokeless gunpowder was one large reason. The German army alone required 400,000 bales a year for its ammunition. On the average, for all classes of ordnance in that war, a bale of cotton was consumed every one hundred and fifty shots, and each company of three hundred soldiers carried three bales in its cartridge belts! When guns on one battleship were firing at full blast, they consumed ten bales of cotton every minute. For four murderous years cotton again became a king.

But a challenger in the shape of a tiny insect had crossed the Rio Grande and was making its slow, deadly way across the Cotton Belt. Merely by depositing a microscopic egg in the tender squares of the cotton plant, the Mexican boll weevil achieved what men had failed to achieve through 110 years of "common sense," great oratory, high tariffs, the continent's grimmest war, and the impoverished hatreds of Reconstruction.

Cotton production fell from nearly fourteen million bales in 1920 to less than eight million in 1921. Yield per acre, which previously had averaged two hundred pounds of lint, fell to 132 pounds—the lowest since 1866. Value of production dropped from more than two billion dollars in 1919 to less than 0.7 billion in 1921. The contrasts were more pronounced, and the consequences more grave, in the states where cotton's reign had been most secure. Not even Sherman's army could have wrought more havoc than was wrought by this $\frac{1}{8}$ x $\frac{1}{4}$ inch beetle to King Cotton and the hosts of humanity—white and black—who depended on his greatness.

Cotton was not really dead. But the old King was forced to abdicate. Barren fields, empty cabins, ragged and hungry sharecroppers were now the desolate heirs of the Cotton Gin dynasty. Men looking back on glory saw anew the vision of their forefathers—the towering trees, the blankets of green, and the cattle on a thousand hills. They heard the hum of industry and the roar of commerce. They dreamed of a New South—a good land and fertile, diversified in its crops and industries—a land of better homes, with peace and plenty.

Bales of cotton being loaded on a river steamer

Too little is understood about social momentum as a force in human affairs; I really think we have it down here.

DAVID E. LILIENTHAL, when director of TVA

ALEXANDER NUNN

The New South

THE "NEW SOUTH" had become a familiar and much-used term when the guns of World War I began booming in Western Europe in the summer of 1914. For forty years dreamers, planners, editors, hardheaded businessmen, politico-economic evangelists, and simon-pure schemers alike had made it their rallying cry.

In the 1880's, as a flaming and unheralded comet captures the imaginations of mankind, Henry W. Grady had captured the hearts and minds of his fellow Southerners and of the nation with his gospel of a New South. With all the fervor of a camp-meeting evangelist, he epitomized the spirit of Ben Hill's declaration: "There was a South of secession and slavery—that South is dead; there is a South of union and freedom—that South, thank God, is living, growing every hour." "It was Hill," said Grady, "who named the New South."

But these planners and prophets of a New South needed long lives to see their dreams become reality. Henry Grady was in his grave before he was forty. The period of World War I, a quarter-century later, clearly marked the break from the Old South to the New. For the first time since 1860, the war years and the boom-prosperity year of 1919 put real money into everybody's pockets in the fifteen states that make up the New South.* Five years of good farm prices for a region that continued to be largely rural had triggered the change.

*In compiling the statistical material for this chapter, Maryland, Oklahoma, and West Texas were included.

Yet it was not money alone that had brought revolution. Change was in the air. To all the kaleidoscopic changes of a world technological revolution the South added its own.

The cotton boll weevil began remaking the South from the time it crossed the Rio Grande into Texas in 1892. It reached the Atlantic Ocean by 1921 and 1922.

A traveling salesman in his Model T got stuck in the mud of a Mississippi Delta road. While he fretted and sweated trying to get it out, a weevil crawled up on a fender to ask, "Mister, what's your trouble?"

"You see what's the trouble," the salesman told him. "I'm stuck."

"If that's all," said the weevil, "I'll pull you out."

"How can you pull me out?" said the salesman.

"Mister," said the weevil positively, "I pulled all the Cadillacs out of the Delta. I won't have any trouble pulling your flivver out of this mud."

Into the campaign for an agriculture that could survive under boll weevil conditions Uncle Sam sent Seaman A. Knapp in 1903 as "special agent." Dr. Knapp was seventy. A native of New York who had lived most of his life in Iowa, he had moved to Louisiana when he was fifty-two. As special agent to fight weevil ravages, he quickly turned to farm demonstrations of new methods for his chief weapon. Thus began "co-operative demonstration work." It rapidly spread across the South, gained permanent status in the Smith-Lever Act of 1914, then became fully nationwide when World War I's demands for food became insatiable.

Dr. Knapp's contributions to agricultural progress in a few short years have led many to rank him as the greatest agricultural leader the South has produced.

Railroad lines spread over the South in the forty years after 1865 as they had over the entire nation; Atlanta's Five Points was becoming the hub of a great city of diversified industries and commerce; Birmingham began to light her night skies with blast furnaces; Texas and Oklahoma were growing increasingly important in petroleum. It was also a matter of special pride to nearly every town of any size in the Southeast that it had a textile plant, often financed with local capital. With considerably less pride did these towns view the many early "mill villages" that followed, or the working conditions that harked back to sharecropper days on the farm.

By 1915, eradication of the Texas cattle fever tick, nemesis of Southern livestock expansion, was well under way. Here, as in so many other facets of agro-industry, groundwork was being laid for the resurgence of Tall Grass and 1959's booming cattle industry.

The inauguration of Woodrow Wilson in early 1913 brought and kept in key positions in Washington in the next eight years more Southerners

A modern cotton picker at the Delta and Pineland Company, Scott, Mississippi

than had held public office at any other time since 1860.

Effective public school systems began to develop all across the South after 1900. In North Carolina, Governor Charles B. Aycock (1901–1905) could boast of a new public school built for every day he was in office. From 1881 to 1915, Booker T. Washington labored unceasingly through Tuskegee Institute, Alabama, to lift the level of the Negro race and to gain recognition for their potential as American citizens.

A South living in "high cotton" that fateful spring of 1920 saw prices plunge from as high as forty-three cents when it planted a new crop, to as low as ten cents in December. Solid, substantial landowning families were wiped out by the tens of thousands. The level of banking capital and bank deposits per capita in early 1920 would not again reach so high a percentage of the national average for more than twenty years.

What the price crash left undone in 1920, the boll weevil finished by 1923. King Cotton's days were numbered. Doggedly he held on until the late thirties. Empire cotton state of the Old South, Georgia produced 2,769,-000 bales in 1911, in 1923, 588,000, in 1930, a final peak of 1,592,000. In 1958, with acre yields almost double those of 1911, it ginned only 355,000 bales.

Nevertheless, the march went on. In early 1926 the then-leading national monthly, *The American Review of Reviews*, devoted an issue to a series of analyses about the New South, "for their national significance." A group of distinguished editors, educators, and business leaders participated. Clarence Poe, president and editor of *The Progressive Farmer*, built a platform on which all others undoubtedly stood.

"We have come up," he wrote, "through great tribulation, but we have come. . . . And though we have made much progress these last twenty years, we propose to show 'that which we have done but earnest of the things we yet shall do.' The next half-century belongs to the South as the last half has belonged to the West."

The great gains of the twenties and early thirties would not become obvious for a generation. A higher percentage of all boys and girls, white and colored, got more and better schooling. Automobiles and better roads fostered consolidation of struggling one- and two-teacher schools into units large enough to serve education effectively. School bus routes began reaching out to serve the children of the most isolated families. College enrollments climbed rapidly. Youth and adults slowly acquired new skills and found wider opportunities to develop leadership. Circulation of newspapers, farm magazines, and general magazines multiplied. Radio began to take the rest of the world to distant mountain coves and the loneliest range families. "Book farming" and "book farmers" acquired status they had never enjoyed. Industrially, we grew both in know-how and in our concepts of sound regional development.

It was in renewed faith and confidence, new energy, and new determination that the thirties after 1932 counted for the South. Franklin Roosevelt did bring a New Deal to the region—in Southern leadership of national and world affairs; in his personal interest in conservation; in his support of rural electrification and new approaches to farm problems; in seeing the wisdom of expanding and adding to banking and farm credit legislation begun twenty years earlier under Wilson; in eliminating discriminatory freight rates against the South. When in 1938 Roosevelt branded the South "The Nation's Economic Problem No. 1," its people quickly accepted his implied challenge. Like Robert Lee Bullard in World War I, a great American born on an Alabama farm, they were tired of being on the defensive. Their reaction was what his had been twenty years earlier. Many remembered that last desperate German drive on Paris in 1918. Day after day Allied field commanders followed instructions higher up to pull back to new lines. Finally, tired of retreat, General Bullard sent back the message: "We are going to counterattack." The offensive he set off in July 1918 ended in the collapse of the German Army on November 11. Snapped back the South in 1938: "We are not The Nation's Economic Problem No. 1. We are The Nation's Economic Opportunity No. 1."

The late 1930's saw the beginning of technological agricultural revolution. In 1925, cotton still brought in 40 per cent of the region's cash farm income; the figure dropped only to 37 per cent by 1935. But in 1957 it was down to 15 per cent. Cash income from livestock (including poultry) climbed from 17 per cent in 1925 to 45 per cent in 1957. Mechanization began to gain momentum. As tractors moved onto farms, mules "headed for the dogs." Two-thirds disappeared that way in twenty years.

In 1930, three out of every five farmers were croppers or renters. (At one time in many areas of the Old South the ratio of tenants to owners was virtually two-to-one.) In 1959, that ratio is almost two owners to one tenant. "Croppers" (i.e., "halvers" or "sharecroppers") have almost disappeared.

In 1924, 19,200 farms in the South enjoyed highline electricity; in 1935, but 105,741. Now, in 1959, electricity is available to virtually every farm family that wants it. The South, with over two million electrified farms and farm homes, has almost as many as all the rest of the country combined. Multiplication of available electric power by the private power companies, by TVA, and by REA has greatly accelerated industrial growth as well as rural progress.

With religious fervor, through those same giant-striding years, the South has pushed soil conservation. Galled, gullied, and eroding lands have rapidly disappeared in green blankets of either pines or grasses. We've learned that to save more souls we must save more soil. Yet conservationists today face an equally great challenge to save the South's water resources. Whether for agriculture, or industry, or the tourist, good water will be a trump card.

Within the memory of many living men and women, the enormous timber resources of the South were pillaged and gutted. Little of the value got back to owners. Far too little stayed in the South. Here again, the thirties began to bring drastic changes. Migration from farms, higher per-acre crop yields, crop adjustment programs, and stepped-up interest in conservation all helped to boost timber as a crop and insurance against erosion for abandoned acres. In 1931, Dr. Charles H. Herty proved that Southern pine could be made into excellent newsprint. The year before, we produced one and one-half million cords of pine pulpwood. The rate in 1959 is about twenty million cords annually; 85 per cent is pine. H. J. Malsberger, of the Southern Pulpwood Conservation Association, stated in late 1958 that the forecast for national pulpwood and paper needs called for an increase from thirty-six million cords now to fifty-six million cords by 1967—and that most of the increase must come from the South. Including Texas and Oklahoma, 200,-185,000 acres of the region's total of 335,605,000 are in timber. Timber grows two to four times as fast in the South as in the Northwest—and even faster compared with that in Canada.

Southern governors, bankers, farm leaders, urban businessmen were all teaming up to "balance agriculture with industry"—BAWI, to use Mississippi's phrase—by the time the United States entered World War II. During the war years the South benefited tremendously from the unprecedented mobility of the nation, from new skills and techniques Southern people acquired, and from the stepped-up importance of the South as buyer of goods.

The industrial boom that began after 1945 continues to gain momentum. So enthusiastic are Southern industrial leaders today that they don't hesitate to echo Dr. Poe's 1926 claim, "The next half century belongs to the South." In 1955, the Southern Association of Science and Industry predicted that the South would add ten thousand important new industries between 1956 and 1965 (industries employing twenty-five or more people or with an investment of $250,000 or more)—better than three for every working day. The record so far shows: 1956—1,056; 1957—1,314; 1958—1,419. President T. F. ("Tom") Patton of the Republic Steel Corporation, whose company is investing heavily in the South, predicted in November, 1958, that the South should have at least 30 per cent of the country's total manufacturing capacity by 1965.

The last forty years have also brought drastic population changes to the

South. Half its people in 1920 belonged to farm families; in 1955, that ratio was one in six. But only 9,000,000 out of 33,000,000 were classified as "urban" in 1920; by 1955, the South was by census definition more "urban" than "rural." The South's white population increased by 14,000,000 from 1920 to 1955; nonwhite, less than 2,000,000.

Checks of population movements in recent years indicate that the region is gaining better-trained, better-educated people than it is losing through migration. The climate, the resources, the growth opportunities, and the recreational facilities all play a role. I listed forty-one boys and girls in our home beat (township) who married during World War II or later. Nine had found their partners outside the South; seven in other Southern states. Of the other twenty-five, almost none had found mates in our home community. Strikingly and rather typically, too, most of these young families, better educated than average, have located somewhere in the South.

Wherever these newcomers or these native sons and daughters settle in this New South they find the challenge of continuing change. Having overthrown King Cotton, we now fight to keep from losing it as an invaluable cash crop. With our past rooted in agriculture, we now face the North's grave problem of how to raise good citizens in an urban environment.

Having helped the Negro to make more rapid material progress in a hundred years than any other race has ever made before, we now must deal with the extremists in both races who think they can secure their goals by legislative fiat.

In forty years we have wiped out hookworm, pellagra, typhoid fever, malaria, and infectious diarrhea; now we have urban stomach ulcers and urban heart disease.

We have virtually rehoused ourselves since 1935, either by building new homes or remodeling and modernizing the old. The air traveler over Dallas, Texas, sees thirty-five to forty thousand acres of new homes; all this was farmland in 1946. Similarly, the South has built continuous communities almost unbroken for hundreds of miles along ribboned highways of concrete and asphalt. Yet we must face realistically the fact that our lowest income groups still need to be moved out of their cabins.

The game that disappeared from excessive clearing and overcropping is coming back amazingly—deer, mink, coon, quail; hundreds of thousands of ponds for fishing, irrigation, livestock water, and recreation can be found. Whereas a favorite weekend pastime forty years ago was to "watch the cars go by," an equally stimulating pastime today is to "count the boats behind the cars." Our great challenge, then, is to conserve our water resources and avoid polluted streams and rivers.

Florida, ruined by boom-and-bust plus hurricanes in the twenties, now

Logs are now being harvested in Mississippi where cotton grew only fifty years ago. The old cotton house is still standing

has to concern itself with the pains of the fastest-growing state (of a million or more people) in the nation.

The city slicker who once made fun of his country cousin now seeks to get a farm or a ranch to bolster his social standing.

Educators and other civic leaders who concerned themselves for so many years about getting all children into school for nine months now worry about buildings to put all the children in and teachers to instruct them. College overflow has become the most serious school problem of all. Southern 4-H clubs and vo-ag and home economics classes now proudly enroll well over half the nation's total. The big problem is to hold a fair percentage of the finest for future farm leadership.

Withal, our New South has many of the marks of the Old. For every "Tobacco Road" there are a thousand neighborhood and community churches lifting and strengthening the everyday lives of the people; for every Jeeter Lester there are multiplied thousands of informed, substantial citizens seeking to improve their homes, their communities, and their country. One Southern leader put it pointedly in saying,

> "We are still ladies and gentlemen;
> We still believe in paying our debts;
> We are still the Bible Belt—and proud of it."

The South has too often been pictured as a land of magnolias and mint juleps, or of barefooted poverty and frustration and degradation. Far more thrilling and truthful is the story of the sincere men and women, the families and communities who held the South together in its years of tragedy and are now leading it forward as we gain back the years that the locust and the palmer worm have eaten. These are the folks who will settle the important issues of today and tomorrow. They will continue to set the pace of the New South that lies ahead.

Part 4

Preceding page:
Land travelers in Virginia in Colonial days

I am not sure that we ought to change all our names. During the regal government, sometimes, indeed, they were given through adulation; but often also as a reward of merit of the times, sometimes for services rendered the colony.

THOMAS JEFFERSON, 1800

JOHN CHASE

The Streets

A LAND of contrasts is the Southland. It has the highest mountains east of the Rockies, and the most swamps. Along the Gulf Coast we drill four miles into the earth for oil, but across Florida, at Cape Canaveral, we shoot rockets at the moon and Mars.

Our cities are just as contradictory. You can't sigh over the name of a single one of them—Memphis, New Orleans, Charleston, Savannah—without nostalgizing about the street that made it famous. For some reason, we seem to have built distinctive streets and then grown cities around them. Except, of course, where we built streets five hundred miles long that remain more famous than any of the communities hitched to them.

Think about it. Canal Street . . . New Orleans, of course . . . was named for a canal that was never dug. The Battery in Charleston has been formidable only on the society pages for almost a century, and no large catfish could hope to push past those air conditioners jutting out into Catfish Row. There are no bulls on Bull Street, no peaches on Peachtree Street, and along Beale Street, where rock-'n'-roll has succeeded the blues, they've long forgotten who Beale was.

Take Canal Street as an example. In 1805, an act of Congress authorized New Orleans to grant permission to a company to dig a canal that would connect an old waterway behind the colonial town with the Mississippi River in front of it. This waterway gave the city communication with Lake

Pontchartrain, an inlet of the Gulf of Mexico. Connecting the lake and river would be a tremendous economic asset. With a burst of enthusiasm, the city proceeded to have streets planned from the turning basin of the existing waterway, and around the side of the colonial town—which is the Vieux Carré now—to the river. Each street was 171 feet wide to accommodate the fifty-foot canal that was to be dug down its center. The street near the basin was named Basin Street. After it turned around the corner of the city, it was named Canal Street.

But the canal company began to speculate in real estate, and went broke. The new waterway was never built. The streets named Basin and Canal had to look around for other things to distinguish themselves. Basin's early association with jazz music—some say American jazz originated there—brought it fame; and everybody knows about the spectacular parades on Canal Street each year at Mardi Gras time. Fewer know how Canal Street promoted the name of Dixie for all the Southland, or how it came to be named heir in a will, inheriting $150,000.

But this was long after the story of the lavish bequests of Charles I and II, of the first antinicotine campaigner, and of the French fears which were all involved in the initial spread of such streets across the South.

It all began in 1622 when Charles I issued a royal grant bestowing forever upon Sir Robert Heath certain lands carved from Virginia, extending southward to Spanish Florida, and also "extending from sea to sea." At this time the province was named "Carolana." Sir Robert was the king's attorney general, but not a good enough lawyer to save him from Cromwell. The "Carolana" grant passed through several ownerships and was ultimately acquired by Daniel Coxe, physician to King Charles II.

An odd man in Southern history is Coxe. He had received a measure of professional distinction through some pioneer experiments which prophetically proved that nicotine was harmful to dogs. But his passionate love was North American real estate. At one time he owned most of New Jersey and claimed part of Virginia, as well as demanding that the government of Charles II put him in possession of his property, "Carolana," extending from sea to sea and including Charleston.

This created a problem, for the king had given this same province to eight noblemen for their aid in restoring his throne. These newly created Lords Proprietors of Carolina had each put up $2250, loaded a hundred and fifty colonists into three ships, and pointed them in the direction of the new province. "Hurry up and found a city and name it Charles Town for the king," they told Joseph West, who was in charge. So the Charles Town that came to be Charleston was founded in 1670 on its narrow peninsula, situated, as a Charleston schoolboy has described it, ". . . . where the Ashley and

Cooper rivers meet to form the Atlantic Ocean."

Under the leadership of a colorful and visionary man, Dr. Henry Woodward, venturesome Carolinians pushed into the woods, some of them going as far westward as the Mississippi. Returning traders, their pack horses loaded with valuable pelts, were a familiar sight on Charleston streets.

The Merry Monarch, with or without the advice of Nell Gwynn, solved the tricky claim business by giving Coxe the Mississippi Valley, Rocky Mountains, and Pacific Coast parts of the province, with provisions that he would have to colonize them. Coxe actually had some plans for settling these remote lands with French Huguenots. Everybody considered him a little balmy except the French, whose interest in the Mississippi Valley province, which La Salle had discovered and named Louisiana, had lain dormant. When it was learned that Coxe was actually outfitting ships for Louisiana, the Count of Pontchartrain, for whom the lake was named, minister of marine and in charge of French colonization, hastily authorized an expedition led by two Canadian brothers, d'Iberville and de Bienville. In 1699, d'Iberville, the elder of the brothers, secured a French beachhead on the Gulf Coast by building the fort at Biloxi, and Mobile and New Orleans followed.

French occupancy in Louisiana put an end to Dr. Coxe and his schemes. Now Charleston jittered when it learned about d'Iberville. They considered the French trespassers on their land, just as the Spaniards at St. Augustine had always looked upon the Carolinians as trespassers on Spanish lands. So, in 1733, there was joy down King Street when news came that Oglethorpe would establish the colony of Georgia between Carolina and Florida. "Go over and help Oglethorpe get started," Governor Johnson instructed Lieutenant Governor William Bull. "And," he added, "give them this two thousand pounds in Carolina money which can only be spent in Charleston. That'll help us both."

For a month Bull and his men labored, helping Oglethorpe establish his town. That is why Savannah's beautiful Bull Street bears his name as a mark of appreciation from Oglethorpe, just as Johnson Square says "thank you" to the Charleston governor.

In another way, Governor Johnson can be remembered. He built Fort Johnson on James Island in Charleston Harbor. In 1861, it fired the shots toward Fort Sumter that started the Civil War.

North Carolina, too, has many lovely cities, such as Asheville in Buncombe County. Its representative in the Sixteenth Congress didn't put Buncombe County on the map any more than it already was, but he did land it in the dictionary because of his bombastic speechmaking. It is no buncombe (the semantic daddy, of course, of "bunk") that the state university's char-

ter stipulated it had to be at least five miles away from politicians. For good measure, Raleigh was established to be the state capital a good hundred miles from Chapel Hill. In its beginning, Raleigh was for some years a city of streets without houses, a situation which a 1958 population of 65,679 has corrected.

Greensboro, on the road from Raleigh to Winston-Salem, is named for General Nathanael Greene, even if those responsible did spell his name without an "e." Both the Carolinas and Georgia sought to honor this general after the Revolution, but perhaps Georgia was more personal about it. Georgia adopted Greene as a favorite son, and gave him a plantation twelve miles up the Savannah River from that city, where the general died of sunstroke in 1786. There, too, of course, Eli Whitney invented the cotton gin.

The final scene of this historical sequence took place in Greensboro, North Carolina, on April 9, 1865. President Jefferson Davis arrived there for a final meeting with his generals. Lee had surrendered. What was the future

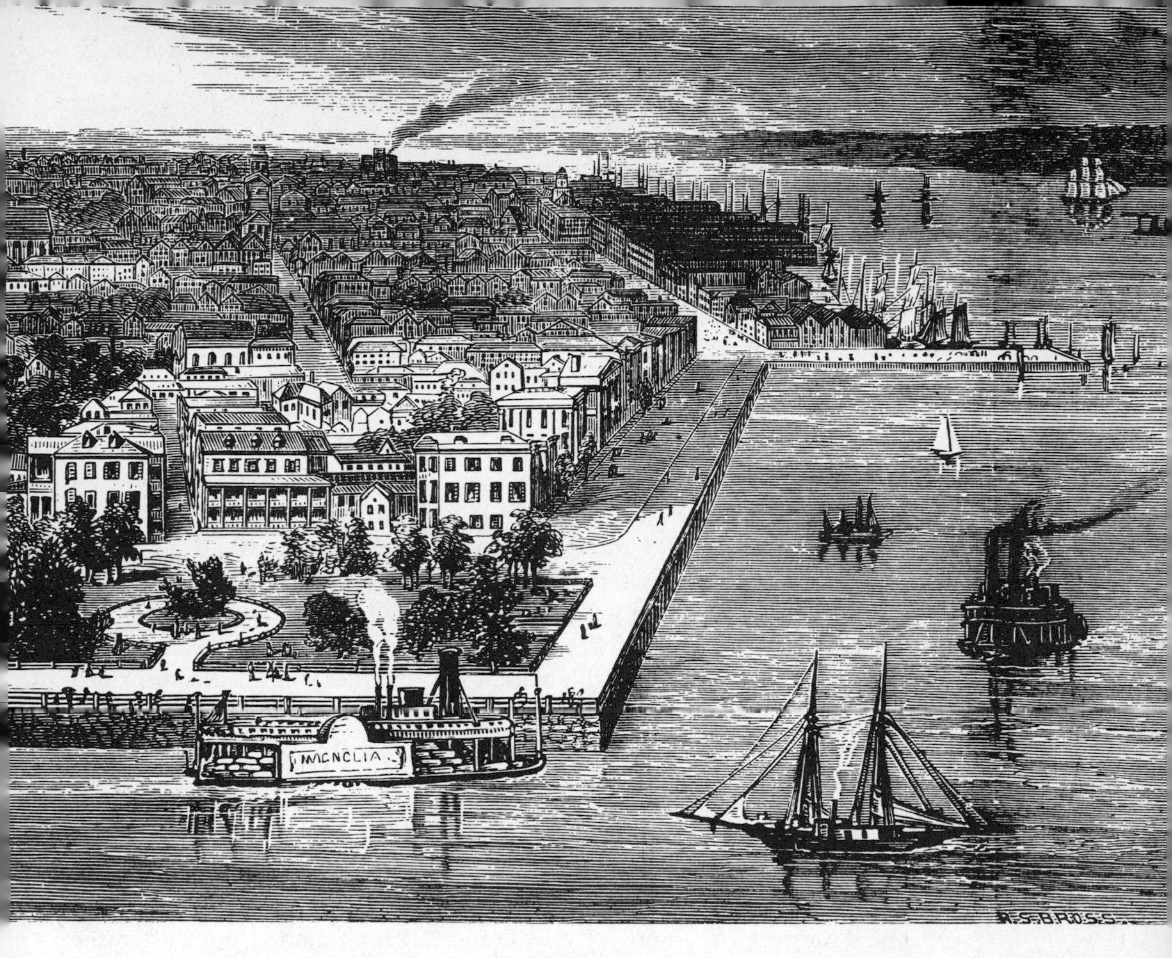

A panoramic view of Charleston about 1855

of the Confederacy? There wasn't any future, was the conclusion of the meeting. In the town named for General Greene, the slave-labor cotton economy of the South officially succumbed.

In the Richmond Davis had just fled, as in all Virginia cities, the streets bear names of its long list of distinguished sons, and read like pages of American history books. Different, however, are the streets called Francis and Nicholson in historic Williamsburg. Visitors to this colonial capital, so realistically restored, will recall these two streets are separated by wide Duke of Gloucester Street. Both are named for the same man. Francis Nicholson was certainly a man apart. The only professional colonial governor of his time, he held the post in five colonies, including Virginia. He established Virginia's capital at Williamsburg, Maryland's at Annapolis, and was one of the founders of William and Mary College. A man of great ability and awful temper, Francis Nicholson never married. But once he did propose. The girl turned him down; thereupon, he stormed at her: "If you ever marry anyone else, I'll cut his throat. Also, I'll cut the throat of the preacher who marries you, and the justice of the peace who issues the marriage license!" Historians are exasperatingly silent about whether the lady had any more dates.

In the classic meaning of streets, Wilderness Road is one of the main streets of the South. The Romans made roads into streets when they built their roads with *stratumens*, or stratas, of rocky foundations. Our word "street" comes from *strata.* Not all streets in all cities were paved, though; not a hundred years ago in the South, that's for sure. There was the street in that Southern city in 1843 that was so *un*paved that not only did an oxcart get stuck but the ox that was pulling it drowned. Much of the two hundred miles of the Wilderness Road was like that, yet along no classic Roman street marched greater conquerors. These people won the South; they won Texas, and most of the West too. Their secret weapon was Women; they begat families, who built cities and lived in them—on streets!

Another classic street was the Natchez Trace that stumbled and groped its way through the virgin forests and thickets of Tennessee and Mississippi, to become a vital line of communication that tied the vast Louisiana Purchase into the United States.

Similarly, another such street tied Texas into the Southland. This was the San Antonio Trace, colonial trail from Natchitoches on the Red River in Louisiana that wandered westward, via Nacogdoches, to San Antonio. Along with its Alamo, San Antonio was founded the same year as New Orleans. Houston, just south of the Trace, wasn't founded until after the Texans won independence from Mexico at San Jacinto, twenty-one miles from downtown Main Street. Houston's a main-street town, but what a Main Street! One writer has speculated nervously that if they don't stop building it out, it'll run smack into the Gulf of Mexico.

September 8, 1565, only seventy-three years after the discovery of the New World, is the birthday of St. Augustine, oldest of all cities in North America. Always a fortress and mission, no street names tell St. Augustine's history. It's the same with Pensacola. Established as a fort in 1696, Pensacola city was not laid out until forty-seven years later.

Mobile, Pensacola's neighbor, began French and has been both Spanish and British. Everybody knows its long, long Government Street. Strangely, Government Street has had its location changed several times in an effort to remain the street the government was on. Now it's still one block away from the corner of Church and Royal, the address of Mobile's present city hall.

Ponce de Leon may have discovered Florida, but it was Henry M. Flagler who rediscovered it. Second only to John D. Rockefeller in founding the Standard Oil Company, wealthy Mr. Flagler was fifty-three when

The old Georgetown Road, known in Colonial times as
the "King's highway" between Georgetown and Charleston

he first visited Florida. He fell in love—with the entire state! "But, honey," Flagler told his beloved, "you need railroads and hotels the worst way. I'll build them for you." During the next twenty-seven years, Flagler lavished a total of forty million dollars on transforming desolate beaches and swamplands into luxurious playgrounds.

Miami was a village of fifteen hundred people when Flagler's East Coast Railroad passed it a-building to Key West. In 1958, it was a metropolitan area of a half-million, not counting tourists. There are Flagler Streets in cities all over Florida, even one in Miami. But the great street in Florida's greatest city is Biscayne Boulevard, named—we are told—as is the bay, for Don Pedro Biscaino, Keeper of the Swans at the Spanish Court. Unlike the original Flagler, the original Biscayne was for the birds.

Many of the South's inland cities began as crossroads and grew into hubs of communication. None has grown further from crossroad beginnings than Atlanta. It is great enough, and old enough, to revere Five Points as a civic shrine. Atlantans are proud of it. They're proud of Whitehall Street, too, named for the first painted building in the country. They're proudest of all of Peachtree Street. Only thing is that Atlanta historians can't be sure whether it was named for a peachtree or a pitchtree; everybody is sure there's nary a peach tree anywhere along any of the sixteen miles of its way.

Continuing the contradictory pattern of things is Montgomery in Montgomery County, Alabama. The city is named for Major General Richard Montgomery, killed the night he and Benedict Arnold got within a half block of adding Quebec and probably Canada to the U.S.A. A bold Irishman who married into New York's Livingston family, he never set foot in Alabama. But Montgomery County is named for the Major Lemuel Montgomery who fought Indians with Andy Jackson.

Speaking of Andy Jackson, more big cities and little towns, more counties, more streets, roads, creeks, hills, and everything in the South are named for Old Hickory than for anybody else. Andy was the darling of the Southern frontier; and Jackson is ideally suited for a place name, easily pronounced and spelled.

Like Montgomery County, Birmingham's Jones Valley was named for an Indian fighter. The Indians who required all this fighting were the Creeks. They took on the United States Army and gave a good account of themselves. It was the Creeks who named the 2225-foot mountain near the Moccasin Bend of the Tennessee River. They called it "Rock-rising-to-a-point"; or, in their language, Chattanooga.

According to Eldon Roark, the columnist and author, Memphis' famous Beale Street hasn't changed a lot since the days the blues were born there—

when W. C. Handy wrote *The St. Louis Blues*, *The Memphis Blues*, and a lot of other blues that ushered in a new era of American music. Of course, the beat of the music has quickened on Beale. The store that had its bargain basement upstairs has retrenched some; it doesn't have a bargain basement anywhere now. There are changes like that; but Beale is still the street to which American Negroes can justifiably point with pride—after all, their race achieved musical immortality there.

The blues are really no more dead than the national anthem. They're just drowned out by rock 'n' roll, a kind of substitute for music seemingly designed to drown out jet engines.

Vicksburg was founded by the Reverend Newitt Vick. Newly arrived from Virginia in 1818, he figured the best way to build up a congregation was to build up a town. Of course, the Reverend could have gone just a few miles downstream to Natchez-under-the-Hill and tried to rescue the riverfront from its hell-raising way of life. Maybe he would have, but he died of yellow fever while Vicksburg was a-building. Even so, maybe the good doctor reported Natchez-under-the-Hill to some heavenly department. Anyway, Natchez has been washed clean of its rowdy riverfront. Old Man River has swept it away.

Old Man River washes past Canal Street in New Orleans, too. Canal was always more than just a street. It divided the Creole city (today's French quarter) from the newer uptown American city. Judah Touro was among the merchants who sought to make Canal a neutral ground, to which both French- and English-speaking customers would come and shop. It was Canal Street's Citizens Bank that issued those ten-dollar bills that were printed *ten* in English on one side and *dix* in French on the other. Citizens was a strong bank. Its banknotes—called "dixies"—were trusted. These dixies provided the best-documented story of the origin of the South's nickname. And it was the merchant Touro who died naming Canal Street his heir, bequeathing $150,000 for improvements.

Besides never having a canal, Canal Street is contradictory in one other way. Of a morning one can go down to the foot of Canal on the east bank of the river, and watch the sun rise in the east over the west bank!

The Mississippi is contradictory, too. Maybe that's why the streets of Southern cities are like that. After all, Old Man River is the "main street" of North America.

The receipts of cookery are swelled to a volume; but a good stomach excels them all.

WILLIAM PENN, 1693

SALLIE HILL

Kissing Don't Last: Cookery Do

THE LAND shaped the cookery of the South, seeping the magic of mist-ringed headlands, emerald savannah, and shadowed glade into the very names of Malvern Pudding, Brunswick and Pine Bark and Burgoo stews, Barbecue, Shrimp Mull, Chess Pie, Hopping John, and corn pone. As homespun as calico, as serenely regal as a Charleston Ball, the "receipts" eddied for 350 years from the brick kitchens beyond the dog-trot, from the iron pots glooming cabin fireplaces, from mansion and hut and bungalow. They were dreams of mistress and slave "mammy" alike, spun to fragrant magic from crude things the local earth provided. And through her magic, the Southern woman pointed up, with humble satisfaction, those ingredients of initiative, imagination, and individualism essential to the challenge of "building God's kingdom on earth" from tortured wilderness.

Since "receipts" played such an important role in the development of the South, and focused the ingenuities and meticulous detail of its homemakers, cookery research has been a passionate hobby throughout my adult life. Too many of our priceless pioneer foods are by way of being lost.

Southern dishes, generally, differ from those of other American regions because flavorings are distinctive, often varying from county to county. Some of my most treasured recipes come by word of mouth from

Southern homemakers, or on scraps of paper specifying "a fist full of flour, 6 gullups of molasses, a pinch of salt, or a wine glass full of cream." Obviously they must be modified to meet present-day situations.

Corn, the Indian's gift, still has a secure place in Southern diets. Corndodgers (made with scalded meal), hoecakes (once cooked on a hoe in a bed of coals, now cooked in a skillet), egg bread, spoon bread (resembling a soufflé), mush bread, the ubiquitous "hush puppy" (one-third flour, two-thirds corn meal, and ground onion), all have a maize base. In Georgia, Alabama, and much of east Texas hominy grits, a direct gift from the Algonquin Indians, are as essential a part of breakfast as the eggs. Waitresses call the dish "Georgia ice cream."

Corn light bread, the homely but uniquely flavored dish that nourished our early settlers, featured scalded meal with molasses to attract the wild yeast. County-fair barkers used to hulloo a delicious sandwich made with corn light bread and baked ham. (Ham, to many Southerners, isn't fit to eat unless cured for two years after the sugar and pepper rubdown and lazy hickory smoke.)

Cracklin' bread is a winter delicacy that comes with hog killing. To make, add one cup of cracklings (residue from rendered hog fat) to your corn bread mixture. No other shortening is needed. As an ambrosial fillip to turnip greens, drop in corn-meal dumplings.

Most corn bread, Southern style, doesn't need wheat flour. The economic history behind this is as clear-cut as the Mormons' development of the sugar beet. The South raised very little wheat. As a breakfast delicacy, lacy corncakes still are superb. Many families still make bread and hot cakes from fresh grated corn.

Hot biscuit is a favorite bread for any meal, snack, or tea, made with either buttermilk or sweet milk. A plate of hot biscuits, rich, brown and crusty on the outside, and tender and flaky inside, brings forth the old refrain, "Take two and butter 'em while they're hot."

Do you want an easy-to-come-by supper dish for Sunday night? Well, any night, perhaps? Here's an old Southern one handed down. Heat molasses and butter in a skillet. Drop in biscuits split in half. Brown on both sides and serve hot with coffee, tea, or cocoa. The dish is usually known as "stickies," but See Rice, a Mississippi friend, insists that her family has always used the term "Monkey Biscuits." Take your choice, but don't miss them.

"My mother delighted us with 'britches patches,'" declares Mrs. W. E. Vanderford of Jefferson County, Alabama. "She cut oblong pieces of biscuit dough, fried them in butter and served them hot with jelly."

Butter rolls are from our Anglo-Saxon heritage. To make, simply spread

At the market, Richmond, Virginia

strips of rich biscuit dough four by four inches square with butter, sugar, and cinnamon. Roll up. Place side by side and bake in a medium hot oven. Result: a rich, crusty roll with butterscotch flavor.

Buttermilk, a necessity in the days before modern refrigeration, has lost none of its popularity in the South, and can be used in almost any way that sweet milk can: yeast breads, dumplings, candies, pies, ice creams, and sherbets. Mrs. B. F. Hilbun, wife of the president of the University of Mississippi, recently served me a delicious buttermilk poundcake.

Black-eyed peas and hog jowl are served on New Year's Day as a bid to good luck. Hopping John, a fried combination of cowpeas and rice, is high on the list of requested dishes.

Most families consider "creamed Irish potatoes" rather special. To prepare, cook peeled potatoes, mash, and season while hot with hot milk and cream. The result is a light, fluffy, airy product, served hot if you please. "Of course, it is 'creamed potatoes,' " my grandmother explained. "You add *hot* cream. Never let anyone call this dish 'mashed potatoes.' "

Every section has its favorite pudding. Serve grated raw sweet potato pudding with damson preserves or blackberry jam or sweet cream. Woodford Pudding, a Kentucky favorite, contains blackberry jam and is served with an orange sauce. Boiled plum pudding has its quota of devotees chiefly in the Carolinas, Virginias, Maryland, Tennessee, and Kentucky. Banana and lemon puddings enjoy great popularity over the entire South.

To see a pudding in the grand manner, try the Queen of Puddings as Mrs. Paul K. Bowman serves it at her plantation home in Sumter County, South Carolina. It is so distinctively Old South that I have included it among my favorites at the end of this chapter.

Malvern Pudding, sometimes called "Salem," is a delightful inheritance from pioneer years. Slice stale bread, cut off the crusts, and line a bowl. Fill with well-cooked blackberries, and add another layer of bread. Cover with a saucer and press down with a weight. Leave about eight hours until the bread has soaked up the berry juice, and the pudding will hold its shape. Turn it out; serve with boiled custard or whipped cream.

Boiled custard, as served from the Rio Grande to the Rappahannock at Christmastime especially, really is *not* boiled. Use one cup of milk, two tablespoons of sugar, and one egg for each serving. Cook in the top of a double boiler (water must not boil) for ten to twelve minutes. No flour is needed. Flavor with grated nutmeg, vanilla, etc.

Ambrosia, long a part of Christmas, is made only of alternate layers of peeled, thinly sliced oranges that are tree-ripe and grated or flaked coconut.

Southern states differ in their methods of barbecuing meats. Almost every community has its "barbecue king," a being possessed of infinite patience. Above all else, a barbecue must proceed slowly. Allow seven to nine hours cooking time for even a thirty-five pound pig. One North Carolina method calls for frequent basting of the meat with this "soption": one-half gallon heated vinegar, one pound butter, one tablespoon black pepper, two teaspoons mustard, and four to five pods diced red pepper. In South Carolina, the pork is ground up after barbecuing and served a-swim in the sauce. Pork hash is often made from barbecued pork.

Barbecue, Bengal style, at Louisiana State University, is something to grow lyrical about. R. M. Crown and J. B. Francioni of the LSU Animal Husbandry department ride herd on the barbecue and have concocted a hot sauce that blends Bengalene cookery with Creole. Since "Bos Indicus," the Brahman cow, plays such an important role in the modern South, why not a Bengal Bayou Sauce for our four hundred-year-old ritual of barbecue? These Louisiana friends served me sweet potatoes, tender and delicately browned, pickles, ginger cakes, and soft drinks with this barbecue. It was perfect.

A note of sadness, too, about our wonderful barbecues. Stern measures should be taken against those who serve cold roast meat with an indifferent vinegar sauce and call it "barbecue"! There ought to be a law!

Deep South or Upper South, one expects a generous bowl of Brunswick Stew at an honest-to-goodness barbecue. Use equal parts of young corn, lima beans, and tomatoes. Add water and cook slowly with finely chopped squirrel meat and/or chicken. Season, then cook until too thick to pour. Serve it with cole slaw, potato salad, raw onions, tomatoes, pickles, and corn pone and/or hot rolls.

Southern fried chicken has been and still is an honored dish. For special Sunday morning breakfast, probably nothing tops fried chicken, cream gravy, blackberry jelly, and hot biscuits. From the Sea Isles to Dallas I have talked with women about favorite methods of frying chicken. Most vote for the crunchy, crisp product, tender but well-done to the bone. No pink meat, please! The chicken pieces, chilled overnight, are shaken in a paper bag with flour, salt, and pepper and put in hot fat in a heavy skillet. The skillet is covered for five to seven minutes, then uncovered, and the chicken turned to brown on the other side. Some excellent cooks add one or more of the following to the flour mixture: monosodium glutamate, paprika, chili powder, or curry powder. Others insist that the chicken soak in sweet milk for an hour or more before cooking, or simply dip the pieces in buttermilk before dredging in flour.

Vinegar, molasses, and buttermilk pies, popular in the days before refrigeration, are still favorite fare. Special meals in North Carolina often call for Brown Sugar Pie. Virginia festive occasions consider Damson Pie a matter of course. Chess (a corruption of cheese) Pies came down from our English ancestors, from all I can learn. Jeff Davis Pie is another favorite. Transparent Custard (Chess Pie with blackberry jelly) is a hand-me-down in Virginia and Kentucky families, and often found in Tennessee.

Only an encyclopedia could hold the array of "receipts" that nameless wives and mammies, from Jamestown to High Plain, over the centuries have built into a unique Southern heritage. I shall whet your appetites with only a few of them. Swing South on a tastebud adventure to learn some of the others, from Key Lime Pie to Texas Pecan Cake, barbecued pig to Kentucky Burgoo.

Grandison's Mush Bread

- 2 cups corn meal
- 2 cups boiling water
- 1 cup sweet milk
- 1 egg
- salt
- 2 tablespoons butter or margarine
- 2 cups sifted flour

Cook corn meal and water to make a good mush. Blend in the other ingredients and turn into a well-greased skillet that has corn meal sprinkled in it. Let it stay on top of the range until bread is brown on the bottom. Put in hot oven and bake until bread is brown all over. Turn out on large platter and cut in wedge-shaped pieces.

Short'nin' Bread

4 cups flour
1 cup light brown sugar
1 cup butter

Mix flour and sugar; add the butter. Place on floured surface and pat to ½ inch thickness. Cut into desired shapes and bake in a moderate oven, 325 to 350 degrees F., for 20 to 25 minutes.

Mississippi Stuffed Ham

Bake ham half done. Skin, remove excess fat, leaving only one-half inch of fat on ham. Turn ham over, insert small vegetable knife at the hock, and split, following the bone carefully. Cut the meat from the bone, leaving as little meat as possible. When bone is removed, fill cavity with a highly seasoned dressing made of bread crumbs, onions, and sage, pressing it well into all cut places. Pour in a little melted butter or sherry wine. Sew up the ham with a cord. Make highly seasoned dressing (enough to cover the ham ½ inch thick) of bread crumbs, moistened with the juice of the ham. Wrap in a cheesecloth. Bake in an oven set at 275 degrees F. until done. Leave cheesecloth on until ham is cold. Serve slices of ham and dressing.

Easy-do Shrimp Mull (Sea Island, Georgia)

3 tablespoons butter or margarine
¼ cup diced onion
1 small clove garlic
1½ teaspoons salt
1 No. 2 can tomatoes
2 cups water
½ cup ketchup
½ teaspoon celery seed
dash of Tabasco sauce
¼ teaspoon Worcestershire sauce
⅛ teaspoon pepper
1 to 2 teaspoons lemon juice
1 pound raw shrimp (peeled, black vein removed, and cut in two lengthwise)
½ cup fine cracker crumbs
1 package (1⅓ cups) precooked rice

Melt butter or margarine in a saucepan or large deep skillet. Add onion and cook over low heat a few minutes. Meanwhile, peel garlic and crush in ½ teaspoon of the salt until garlic is in fine shreds. Add to onion with remaining salt, tomatoes, water, ketchup, celery seed, Tabasco, Worcestershire, and pepper. Cover and simmer one hour. Add lemon juice and shrimp and cook five minutes, or until shrimps are done through. Add cracker crumbs and bring to a boil, stirring constantly. Prepare rice according to directions on the package. Serve shrimp over rice. Makes 4 to 6 servings. Note: One box of quick-frozen shrimp may be used if desired.

Queen of Puddings

- 1 quart milk
- 2 cups broken or coarse bread crumbs
- ⅛ pound butter (½ stick) salt to taste
- 6 eggs, separated
- ½ cup sugar for custard
- 1 teaspoon vanilla for custard
- ⅔ cup sugar for meringue

Scald milk. Add bread crumbs, butter, and salt. Cream egg yolks with the ½ cup sugar and vanilla. Pour milk mixture slowly over the egg yolk mixture, stirring constantly. Place in casserole or pan, filling to about ⅔ full. Place in pan of hot water and cook in a 350 degrees F. oven until custard is the consistency of heavy cream in center when tested with a spoon. Remove from oven. Cover with favorite jelly or preserves (cherry or strawberry is good). Make a meringue of egg whites with ⅔ cup sugar. Flavor with a few drops almond extract or 2 tablespoons sherry or brandy or 1 tablespoon grenadine. Spread over custard. Return to oven and cook until meringue sets. Cool. Serve with unsweetened whipped cream. Note: The custard part of the pudding may be made a day ahead, and the meringue added the day of serving.

The educated Southerner has no use for an r, *except at the beginning of a word.*

MARK TWAIN—"Life on the Mississippi"

OREN ARNOLD

Laughter Is to Live

ALMOST LITERALLY everything the Southerner says or does has a spicing of humor in it. His stories point up an inherited, and wonderful, attitude. Southerners have had to have an abiding sense of humor . . . or perish.

We need that humor as an antidote for adversity. Climate, geography, and other environmental factors have saddled us with many unique burdens. If the Southerner of the past hundred years may have just one star in his crown, let it be for facing up to difficulties, for triumphing over all ignorance and misunderstanding of him, and for working out a successful, even enviable pattern of life. He has done so by tacitly insisting that each day, even each hour, somehow have its modicum of fun.

Even a superficial look at Southern humor reveals two great areas of cultivation, that of the colored people and that of the white. One suggests tobacco—weedy, earthy, rough. The other is like cotton—brighter, softer, more refined. Yet all of it is spontaneous and honest.

Inevitably the two great races have made an impact on one another. And if one has profited more, it's the whites. Some critics will tell you that the white humorist down South ridicules the black man in order to maintain a feeling of "superiority." This is as asinine as are most other social criticisms from reformers. The truth is, in our world the white man *imitates* the black —which is altogether different from ridiculing him. Moreover, the black man carries no chip on his shoulder about this. He mimics right back, making hilarious meat of the mores and manners shown by us whites. Consider the Negro Baptist congregation which invited the eminent Rev. Dr. Wilson from the fashionable white church to be guest preacher one Sunday. Kindly Dr. Wilson was beloved by all. In introducing him, the Negro pastor subtly added, "Though his skin is white, mah bretherens, his heart is jes' as black as ouahs."

What the critics miss is that the echoing, both ways, is almost always done with a warmth of affection. There's a current trend toward not printing or even telling (via radio or TV) any joke that includes Negro dialect, lest this be "prejudice" against the Negro. Such a feeling is pure poppycock. Were Al Jolson and Eddie Cantor showing prejudice when they did their famous blackface acts? Of all people who might be sensitive to prejudice, these two distinguished Jews would rank high, would be last to encourage it. Fact is, they sensed the grandeur of the Negro's humor. They knew that no showman, since time began, has equaled the appeal of the Negro comedian.

The black man's contribution to humor arose from sheer necessity. He faced (and still faces) even greater adversity than the white. He had to see the funny side of almost every episode, event and incident, or his very soul would die. His doing so is to his eternal credit. For the ultimate in human achievement and philosophy is making life pleasant, *come what may*. Happily, over the decades, a considerable amount of this adaptability has rubbed off on the whites. This, not his cotton pickin', bale totin' muscles, has made the Negro a priceless American citizen. It almost justifies his enforced importation.

The first manifestations of humor are in the way we talk. It is astonishing to hear how Southerners have taken the "pure" English language and refined it—like sugar from cane syrup—into the most charming method of communication the human animal ever devised. I do not understand it any more than you do. But my sweet niece Nancy Preston in the piney woods of Texas regularly takes a simple one-syllable Yankee word and converts it into four inspired syllables. Her "Yes" comes out, quite unconsciously, a liquid "E-yea-e-yus."

A college graduate, well traveled, highly literate, humble and kind, given to no posing whatsoever, Nancy is not any Southern Belle show-off. She does not affect the phony "You all" or "Y'all" which Yankees *think* all Southerners misuse. ("You all" down South is, in truth, the essence of courtesy. We never use it to mean "you," singular, unless we are kidding. We may use it to one person, but he understands that we mean it in the plural, that we are inviting or including him and all his kin and friends. This subtle heart-outreach eludes our critics.)

Now, is that famous Southern drawl funny? It is if you live up North! Down here, we take it in stride; we just say, "Welcome to ouah front po'ch, suh." Somehow in the spoken word we have become allergic to the letter "r." If we sound it at all, it usually comes out "ah" or "uh." This startles Yankees so that they burst out laughing, then set in to make fun of us. We don't mind. We know they don't realize how unmusical—how truly awful—their regional accents sound. We can't conceive of waxing romantic under a moonlit magnolia by using their labials. We think *they* are funny.

Our less educated neighbors go much further. If you are a barefoot citizen of Mississippi, a swamp-loving Louisianan, a hill-hopping Arkansan or simply an unschooled citizen anywhere down here, you will have revised the American vocabulary. You'll say "shore" for sure, "mout" for might, "keer" for care, "sartin" for certain, "ax" for ask. You'll greet a stranger cordially, then ask, "Whereabouts do you'uns live at?" In short, the dialect and the idiom of the typical downscale Southerner are so thick that comedians have mimicked them the world over. Inevitably a portion has moved, by a kind of phonetic osmosis, right into the halls of our universities and colleges, our clubs and drawing rooms. It is amusing, and quaint, and very useful. Any story told in Dixie language is likely to be twice as effective.

Why does the Southerner talk the way he does? Is it because of Negro influence? If so, then why does the Negro do it?

The truthful answer is—Ah just don' rightly know. A lot of theorists have popped up with analyses, including the boys and girls who write long documents for Ph.D. degrees; somehow or other, they usually struggle onto a common ground. They say—and I am forced to agree with them—that it takes more energy to talk "Yankee fashion" than us Southerners usually can summon. You listen to a money-minded Yankee some time! That gentleman will be expending more ergs on more decibels to make one sale than four plantation field hands can expend in explaining why they were asleep under a persimmon tree. The Yankee is inherently a go-getter; the Southerner is inherently a porch-sitter. The one scarcely pauses to make a wisecrack; the other takes half an hour to weave one simple joke. You simply can't produce humor in the Bob Hope machine-gun pattern when there's sweat on your brow and a tall cool one in your hand.

It may be that our slurs and elisions, our dropped consonants and liquefied vowels, stem from away back yonder in Africa. One sharp observer, Col. Robert Joseph Allen of the U.S. Marines, who has traveled deep into the Dark Continent, says that African Negroes today use many of the same liquid sounds that we Southerners make. He suggests that these came right on down through the centuries of slavery into the now. Reasonably enough, he adds, they are funny, by reason of contrast. And any person is funny, per se, if he speaks your language somewhat differently from the way you speak it.

In many of us, the deep Dixie talk undoubtedly is an affectation. As such it is more pitiful than funny, so generates a sardonic, or even sarcastic, reaction in the outsider. The "professional Southerner" is simply perpetuating a bid for attention. He sensed the appeal of the genuine drawl, so began putting lace on it. (More often than not, this person is a she.) Such individuals are without stature even in their own homeland, indeed are socially rejected, just as the over-bragging Texan is rejected by genuine Texans who brag with gentle geniality. You can tell when an alleged Southerner is "puttin' on." He'll be so syrupy that he's startling; then his attention is distracted, and he drops his guard. He's the one who doesn't get invited to the next plantation ball.

But in the long run it's not merely how we say it that's funny down South, it's what we say. And heavens-to-Betsy, ma'am, we do say the darndest things! Over the centuries we have often been too far out of town to have much exterior entertainment. Since we can't eat and drink and breed all the time, we have had to think up other ways of pleasurin' ourselves. We became yarn spinners, jokesmiths.

We leaned on that fine old Southern mammy, Mother Nature, for much of our inspiration. Thus the Uncle Remus tales and all in that category. They hold adventure, yes, but they are heavily laced with humor, too, like molasses stirred into hominy grits. It is congenitally impossible for a Southern darky to tell an adventure story, even a true one, without somehow making it funny. His white neighbor has acquired much of the skill. Humor is not the froth of life and literature that many a dour Yankee considers it to be; it is, rather, the meat.

We could list a thousand or more fine Southern humorists, and you are urged to go to the library and enjoy them, or better yet, come down here and spend some time in personal contact. This will be good for your soul even though you be strict about things of the spirit: John Wesley himself told us that "Sour godliness is the devil's religion." It was down here, incidentally, that the newly ordained minister got himself fouled up. He went far into the backwoods to do some missionary teaching, and gathered about twenty young "hillbilly" adults for his first Sunday lesson. He decided he'd best start by examining them. Bible in hand, he turned to a barefoot but comely miss of nineteen and said, "Tell me, Mirandy, who was the first man?"

Mirandy glared at him, shook her head, and replied, "I'd druther die fust!"

An astonishing amount of the humor down here is indeed "religious": I have a collection of some ten thousand church-related jokes, and more than two-thirds came from Dixieland sources. This does not imply that Southerners are irreverent. It suggests a happy emotional balance. "God made us in His image," a great pastor in Houston once told me. "Because a leveling, healing, inspiring ability to laugh is a part of our heritage, we can only conclude that God has this sense of humor, too."

He is the same man who told me about the demise of Mrs. Minnie Jones. It seems that Miss Minnie (you understand that we often say "Miss" when we mean "Mrs.") was a booming, drivin' female who bossed her little town unmercifully and vociferously. The folks always said, "She'll make a big noise reorganizin' Heaven itself." Finally, she up and died. Just as the preacher closed his prayer at her grave, a big clap of thunder burst through the skies. So one mourner turned to another and said, "Well, I see she got there."

If you think that mere jokes are too trivial and unimportant (as many folks erroneously do) then start with our wonderful, funny folk tales. Texas especially, via J. Frank Dobie and others, has published some fascinating volumes of folklore, much of it hilarious. Almost every Southern state has its quota. One standard pattern is for some villain or other to get his comeuppance. Here is one from Arkansas:

A chronic blabbermouth gossip ran around his village telling everybody everything he saw, or imagined, concerning his neighbors. One day he met a big turtle in the road. "Man," said the turtle, "you talk too damn much." Astounded, the gossip hurried to the town tavern and proclaimed he had found a talking turtle. The gentry scoffed. Indignantly, he said, "C'mon, I'll show you." They traipsed out with him, and found the turtle. But the hardshell beast wouldn't say a word. The gentry got mad at the gossip for luring them out into the hot sun. They kicked him into the ditch beside the turtle and hurried back to the tavern.

As the gossip groggily sat back up, the turtle turned its head and eyed him from bruised lip to torn breeches. It said, "See what I mean? You talk too damn much."

Up Old Man a piece from Arkansas is the home-place of two young fellows we like to think on as 99 per cent Southern boys . . . Huck Finn and Tom Sawyer, of course. Sam Clemens was a product of our end of the Mississippi. Most of the things he wrote go right to the top of our list of Best Books to Read on Southern Humor. Kitty-corner across Old Man, the ghost of Irvin S. Cobb still chaws a cheroot from a rockin' chair on a Paducah verandah; his "Judge Priest" possessed such wonderful Southern attributes that he became all-American.

A lady named Lamb spawned a book called *Miss Minerva and William Green Hill* back in the pre-World War I era. It became so popular that the same characters were further developed by Emma Speed Sampson, in books that recorded our white people's humorous mores and manners as few others ever have.

Of Negro humor there is much in print. Yet the best of it is likely to be in files of magazines, or in obscure little volumes published by some small printer and thus not readily available to the world at large. I find these in friends' homes, but I can rarely buy copies of them; libraries seldom have them. There ought to be a superanthology of Negro humor, edited perhaps by a Negro himself.

He could start with a gent named Russell who back in the 1870's collected some fine exhibits of "slavery-time" humor, got them published, then managed to drink himself to death before their popularity soared. Surely, too, our boy would have to include Uncle Remus, perhaps the greatest and kindest and funniest of fictional Negro characters, especially for children and mild-mannered adults. Then, for us lusty, gusty readers, stories by Roark Bradford would make a good tee-off point. A lot of folk think Roark's *How Come Christmas* and *John Henry* are classics of Southern humor. Clever poetry in Negro dialect is one of the richest fields. Some of the stuff out of *The Talking Turtle*, a grand book loaded with folksy yarns collected by Vance Randolph, ought to be included. Also I'd recommend *The Lawd Sayin' the Same* by Hewitt Leonard Ballowe, especially for Negro stories and dialect.

But if I had to choose one American writer who had done most to capture the down-to-earth humor of the funniest people in the South, I'd vote for the late Octavus Roy Cohen. He made an impact on literature via *The Saturday Evening Post*, by portraying the antics of the most hilariously funny fictional Negroes since time began. Their very names dredge up beloved memories—Florian Slappery, Escrow Banes.

In recent years almost no magazines and few book publishers have issued "Negro humor" for fear of being tactless toward a minority group. To a degree, the same "tactful" or political omission has kept white Southern humor out of print; publishers feel they can't afford to offend the Southerner by mimicking us in a portrayal of our accent and quaint manners.

They wouldn't be insulting us at all. Only a picayunish minority would ever take offense. Rather would they be paying all of us the highest compliment possible. We look for a New Day when editors will show the world why all across the South, for Negro and for white, *laughter is to live.*

The Southerner talks music.

MARK TWAIN—
"Life on the Mississippi"

HUGH H. MCGARITY

Music's March

THE JOY of a fiddlin' tune: *Roll, Jennie Jenkins, Roll!* Shapers and rounders; the banjo and the dulcimer.

Camp meetings: "And Pharoah's daughter went down to the-e wa-terr." A mightier surge of rhythm: "Were you *there* when they crucified my Lord?"

In the Charleston wing, Puritan missionaries chant *Old Hundredth.* Out of the New Orleans grills, battered C.S.A. cornets rag *When the Saints Go Marching In.*

This was music's march across the South . . . 275 years from Ainsworth's Psalter to Buddy Bolden's jazz band. What happened? Where did they go, a-singing?

England's farmers and craftsmen came to Jamestown with rollicking choruses of *Greensleeves*, of *Barbara Allen*, of sea chanteys and morris dances. Set them down, in fancy, beside moss oaks or tawny hickory behind a greenbark stockade. Give them fiddle music, a wailing hunting oboe, a marching drum, perhaps a trumpet and flute. In the pauses, no louder than surf at the ebb, whisper in the shipload of slaves humming, to muted banjo, something like that "Mangwani Mpulele" chant the Zulus still sing—with almost a Bourbon Street soft-shoe beat— in Natal, Union of South Africa.

Tremolo, finally . . . far up the sands but coming closer, with the masterful clank of Cromwell's halberds, the Puritans dirge-chanting from their Psalter hymnbook.

This was the beginning—the start of the march. It doesn't make much difference: 1619, 1645, 1700. It went on from there.

In 1620 when the Mayflower Pilgrims landed at Plymouth they brought with them a little psalmbook prepared in Holland for their use by Henry Ainsworth. Thirty-nine tunes were printed. By 1680 much of this music was rejected by the congregations of Boston churches as being too "irregular"; it encouraged singing "by ear" to the detriment of "regular singing" (singing by note).

A striking characteristic of the "common way" of singing was the practice of "lining-out." The leader simply sang the verses of a psalm tune, a line or two at a time. The congregation, often without hymnbooks, repeated after him.

Lydia Parrish has adduced that the psalm-hymns were first introduced into South Carolina and Georgia coastal regions by Puritan missionaries who left Dorchester, Massachusetts, in 1695 to work among the Indians of South Carolina. Later these Puritans moved to St. John's Parish in Georgia and built a Congregational Church that they named Midway. For a generation, then, Civil War tore across England between the Puritan Roundheads and the Stuarts' Cavaliers. While Cromwell lived, Puritans had their way in the South. Negroes were encouraged to attend church services. Thus, Parrish believes, the slave had a first contact with songbooks, lining-out, and surge-singing.

The tunes Ainsworth collected in his songbook were from England, Scotland, France, and the Netherlands. They sound so much alike that it causes one to wonder if there actually is such a thing as "pure" French music or pure American music or pure English music, or, for that matter, pure Southern music. Music is so basic to the life of man that he has consciously, and more often unconsciously, "borrowed" tunes from others as readily as he has borrowed customs. It is much easier to borrow a tune: it doesn't have to be translated from one language to another.

The Puritans were not always stern. They enjoyed singing psalm tunes so much, in and out of church, that they were often ridiculed. Sometimes in forgetting the tunes they would make changes here and there. Moreover, the out-of-church tunes of both Puritans and Southerners were so merry that they were looked upon as "devilish." Church authorities were not long in insisting that the congregations "dignify" the worship service by singing more slowly, and by singing strictly in accordance with the way the notes were written or "prick'd down."

But at home and at social gatherings everyone continued their mirthful singing; if the clergy didn't care for "this trashy country way of singing" there were plenty who did. It was fun to sing together, and it became even more so when amateur musicians—singing masters—began to hold classes.

This was the beginning of the Music Teacher and the Singing School. As the Southern planters began their drive for Culture, music appreciation was a desirable "grace." Singing teachers were imported via Charleston and Williamsburg. Planters' children underwent painful lessons in harmony, dancing, and instrumentation. Out yonder, in the cabins, the slaves and poor whites translated these arts into rowdier tunes and verses. The guitar migrated in from Spanish Florida. Somehow the dulcimer, too, rang into existence. (Did it come from England? Is it a Southern invention? Nobody knows! Ancestored doubtlessly by the lute, the harp, the fiddle, it lilts best with a turkey feather or hickory sliver "picking stick" or a sugar-cane "frettin' bar.")

The Singing Schools prospered. Singing masters began to publish their own hymnals. They continued this practice as they joined the southwestward movement into Virginia's Shenandoah Valley. By the 1850's there were nearly fifty of these books in use, each claiming to solve many problems in music teaching. The usual title read something like this: "A Plain and Easy Introduction to the Rudiments or Grounds of Music" or "A Choice Collection of Tunes for Church Use."

The tunes of the singing masters were in three-part harmony. The men carried the melody, singing a part called the "air." The "gravest" or lowest male voices sang bass, while the women sang a "counter" part or "tribble." Notice it was the men who were assigned the melody! The notes were in three different shapes, making them very easy to sing. Some called the shaped notes "buckwheat" notes, and laughingly referred to the singers as "shapers." The shapers retaliated by labeling the Puritan-hymn devotees "rounders" and "roundheads." One prominent Virginia singing master obtained a patent for his note shapes, and today many shapers speak of "patent" notes.

In addition to the roughhewn hymnody of the singing master there were more than a hundred ballads from the Old World. *Pretty Polly*, whose heroine pushed her false-hearted lover into the sea, is one. Families and neighbors sang such fun songs as *Roll, Jennie Jenkins, Roll*, with each man asking his "Jennie" which color she likes best. In no hurry to decide, she replies, "I won't wear red for it's the color on my head." She doesn't choose green, "for t'ain't fit to be seen." She finally concedes, "Don't know what I'll wear, but I won't go bare," and taunts, "I'll buy me a foldy-roldy-tildy-toldy-seek-a-double-use-a-cause-a-rolly-bindy." Then everybody sings a brief refrain, "Roll, Jennie Jenkins, roll."

Other rollicking play-party songs were: *Flop-Eared Mule*, *Black-Eyed Susie*, *Sourwood Mountain* (in which the swain complains, "I got a gal in Letcher, she won't come and I won't fetch 'er. He de ing-ding, dilly-ally day"). *Swing Sally Good'n, Bile Dem Cabbage, Soldier's Joy, Leather Breeches, Zip Coon*—all were enthusiastically rendered by "off-the-shoulder" fiddlers, and danced from dusk 'til dawn. There was also plenty of time for "adding-on" songs—*Green Grow the Rushes, Ho, She'll Be Comin' Around the Mountain.* Many were a curious mixture of sacred and secular.

The tippler, too, sang of his devotion to rye whisky: "Darlin' Cory" was last seen on the bank of a stream with a jug of "likker" in her arm and a "forty-five" across her knee. The roving gamblers were present and lilting, too.

But what about the Negro? How did he come to share in the Southern folk-music scene? In West Africa music was used for communication as much as for speech, and the marvelously complex rhythms came to America. You can be sure that his bearing up under hardships in a strange land is mirrored in the eloquence of the Negro's music.

Some students of Negro music say that he "just naturally sang." Others assert that he merely copied the white man's music. Both are extreme statements; there is probably some truth in both.

In the South the Negro learned melody and harmony from the white man. This does not mean that he did not sing or harmonize in his native land. But now we may be getting close to his real contribution to Southern (and American) music—the unique blending of his complex rhythms with the white man's melody and harmony. Some of this rhythm would gain new complexities when many Negroes came into New Orleans from Central America after 1865.

During the Great Revival period (1795–1825), plantation families took slaves with them to the camp meetings. Again, the singing was contagious. Here was a "revival of spirit." Thousands sang together, lifting their voices to *Amazing Grace* and *Alas, and Did My Savior Bleed*, *On Jordan's Stormy Banks*, and many others.

The camp-meeting spirituals inspired the slaves to sing some of them back home. One example shown by George Pullen Jackson is the Negro spiritual, *Roll, Jordan, Roll*, taken from the camp-meeting spiritual of the same name. The latter was in turn adapted from a line in a Charles Wesley hymn, "His lightnings flash, His thunders roll."

Sing a few of the Negro spirituals—*Steal Away; My Lord, What a Mornin'; Swing Low, Sweet Chariot*—and you will be more impressed by their beauty than by the possibility that they were "borrowed."

In West African music the primary emphasis is on rhythm, although harmony is achieved through the overlapping of melodic-rhythmic patterns. The principal trait of West African singing is the alternation between solo and chorus. Here the Negro sang his melodies diatonically but frequently would lower or "flat" the third and seventh degrees of the scale, resulting in the so-called "blues" scale. The predominance of a diatonic melodic construction in both African and European music provided a strong link between the music of these two cultures, and facilitated their acculturation. John Wesley's method of selecting random popular melodies during his travels in England and South Carolina, then setting hymns to them, seems to have initiated the homespun folk hymns. These are frequently set to well-known English and Old South ballads: *Barbara Allen*, *The Wife of Usher's Well* and *Three Ravens*.

During the Great Revival, with no denominational control, a free and easy style of singing emerged, typical of the pioneers as a whole rather than of any particular group. The boisterousness of the camp meeting led to the creation of a hymnody so simple that the urge to join in the singing was irresistible. The simple tunes were in part responsible for this joyful, uninhibited singing; but the verses of Isaac Watts and the Wesleys were often difficult enough to make memorization a problem. The imaginative song leaders solved this by simplifying them so that lines were frequently repeated with little or no change of words:

An old banjo player in Georgia, 1907

My home is over Jordan,
My home is over Jordan,
My home is over Jordan,
Where pleasures never die.

Thus simplicity played a huge role—again—in enabling the development of some of Protestantism's most cherished hymns, as well as the Negro's spirituals.

The first collection of the Negro's music in America did not appear until after he had gained his freedom. This collection entitled *Slave Songs in the United States*, and released in 1867, consisted of songs of the Negroes on the Port Royal Islands. Their manner of singing was perplexing to the compilers. What they were hearing was part singing; yet no two seemed to be singing the same thing.

Because of its form, variety in melodic construction, and emotional expressiveness, the spiritual is properly regarded as the most highly developed Negro folk-song type. Spirituals are now classified as: call and response chant (*I Got Shoes*); the slow, lyric, sustained melody (*My Lord, What a Mornin'*), and the fast-moving, syncopated melody (*Little David, Play on Your Harp*).

The "blues" contrast sharply with the spirituals. The latter are distinct choral and communal; the blues are usually performed by a soloist. The spirituals are centered around heaven and the hope of getting there; the blues take an opposite view of things, with the singer assuming a rather hopeless outlook on everyday life and an utter lack of interest in heaven. The spirituals, created in the church, contain verses which dignify the most exalted pulpit; the blues often contain unprintable verses.

Listen to a real "blues" as a Negro on a Texas chain gang sings, "White boss, I due to be in Seminole, Oklahoma." The gang heaves together on the third syllable of Ok-la-*hom*-a. This "call and response" is found in all kinds of folk song—white and Negro. The camp-meeting song leader asks, "What can wash away my sins?" The worshipers answer, "Nothing but the blood of Jesus."

The Negro was the source of material for the music of the minstrel show that originated in New York in 1843. One of its troupers was Daniel Decatur Emmett, whose "walk-around" song, *I Wish I Was in Dixie's Land*, was claimed by both North and South. The South used it as a rallying tune and shortened the title to "Dixie." After Appomattox, President Lincoln officially "restored" it to the North. Another composer of minstrel music, Stephen Foster, born near Pittsburgh, wrote a "hit" song called *Oh! Susanna* that was taken to California by the "forty-niners." Later it was translated into nearly every language in the world. Sing Foster's *Old Folks at Home*, and you will glimpse more than just one side of plantation life.

Not many months after America entered World War I another pioneer was uprooted. This time the movement was from the South to the North and West. Up the Mississippi River came the builder of a new kind of folk music—jazz. It was not as tarnished as it might appear. Jazz was born when Negro brass bands, using discarded Confederate Army band instruments, marched off the streets of New Orleans into the dance halls. Now there was dancing to the tunes that had been "ragged" by the brass bands as they marched along the streets in funeral and wedding parades. The replacement of the string ensembles by the brass bands, both all-Negro, took place in the 1890's. The first jazz band was that of one Charles ("Buddy") Bolden, and consisted of a cornet, clarinet, trombone, guitar, bass, and drums. White musicians, quick to follow the Negro, organized "Dixieland Bands."

Leaving New Orleans in 1917, the jazz musician migrated up the Mississippi, with stop-offs at Memphis and St. Louis. Some went on to Kansas City. But it was in Chicago that jazz was to really "catch on" in the 1920's. It spread then to New York and to Hollywood, where in the 1930's a certain part of its "folksiness" was engulfed by "better music" advocates—the arrangers, schooled in European traditions. Of course, the "original" jazz is labeled today as "classic" jazz.

Thus almost three hundred years after the Pilgrims marched ashore in 1620 singing *Old Hundredth*, the jazz musicians marched back playing *When the Saints Go Marching In!*

What happened to the "shapers" and the "rounders"? Part of the answer lies in the fact that as the South became more and more urban there seemed to be less and less room for the shapers. Nevertheless, if you go to a Sacred Harp singing convention in Atlanta, or witness a folk festival like the one that takes place every year at Grandfather Mountain near Asheville, North Carolina, you will wish that you could forever join their ranks and sing with the "tribbles," or "base out" with the men.

You can!

After breakfast visitors consult their pleasure—if they wish to ride, horses are ready at their command—read, there are books enough in the Library—write, fire and writing materials are ready in his room. The Master and Mistress of the House are not expected to entertain visitors till an hour or two before dinner which is usually at 3.

HENRY BARNARD, 1833

PHILIP G. DAVIDSON, JR.

Plantation Life

THE DAY began mighty early on a Southern plantation for most people. Houseboys, yard boys, stableboys, cooks, housemaids, riding boss, Big Boss—all were up and stirring at "the crack," with even Ole Miss herself soon to start the long day ahead. Only the inevitable house guest lay abed, waiting for that welcome sound of Willy with the coffee.

Sometimes Willy would bring up something a little stronger than coffee. One such guest was greeted with a "Julap" which, with some surprise and pleasure, he drank. Pretty soon Willy was up with another. This the guest also drank after some polite protest and with some reluctance: it was a new experience and he wasn't quite sure what all the effects might be. But back came Willy with a third. The guest flatly announced he couldn't take it. Willy ruled, "You'd better drink it, kase Ole Marster says this is positively the last Julap he gw'ine to make this mornin'!"

Except for the "Julap," this could be any Southern plantation home, large or small, from Virginia to Texas—tobacco, rice, or cotton; eighteenth or nineteenth century. The number of servants would vary; the house would range from good log to magnificent mansion, the living from simplicity to wasteful luxury, the manners from boorishness to elegance. But the pattern of life was the same, for its ingredients were the same.

The plantation was the unique product of the English colonies in America. By the end of the seventeenth century the plantation way of life had developed such compulsive, almost explosive, qualities that it spread like redbud over the entire South and became the model and ideal for generations of Southerners.

It is fashionable now to decry the good old days of moonlight and magnolias and white-pillared mansions, to emphasize the myriad small farmers, the poor white trash, the log house, and the meanness of life, and to think of the plantation ideal as the fiction of Margaret Mitchell. But the plantation ideal was real; if there were more yeomen than planters, more ignorance than cultivation, there were in truth magnolias and jessamines and fireflies in the long summer evenings, and there were big houses and fine homes, and people of wealth and cultivation.

Westover, the most beautifully situated plantation on the James River, Shirley, Melrose, The Hermitage, and dozens of others throughout the South are magnificent testimony to the quality of life at its best in the ante-bellum South. Once there were many more. A disappointed Northern visitor asked her South Carolina hostess, "But where are the lovely homes I've heard about?"

"Don't you remember, my dear?" came the reply. "You burned them."

When Sambo rang that early morning bell, the plantation went to work. Before breakfast in the big house, the planter and his manager or overseer started the field hands on the tasks that had been worked out the day before in the planter's office at the back of the house. When the main crop did not need attention, the hands were put to work clearing new land, ditching, draining, building rail or stone fences, repairing, or building cabins. The chores were innumerable, the work unending.

The hands worked in the fields until their appointed task was done—usually by two or three in the afternoon. The midday meal of bacon, corn bread, and molasses was eaten in the field. Back at the cabins or slave quarters (on a big plantation, a mile or more from the main house) the hands tended their own little garden plots and looked after their chickens, for each family had a cabin and a small plot of ground allotted to it and was supposed to raise its own vegetables.

A visit to the slave quarters was a "must" for all Northern visitors and a frequent event for the owner's family. The Negroes throughout the plantation South were in the main good workers and were as well treated under the circumstances as one might expect. They were fed and clothed and cared for in sickness and old age. But the institution was not designed for the benefit of the slave, but of the owner. Runaways were not infrequent: "Gilbert left home. . . . I have serct the neighborhood and Cannot hear of him.

A scene of domestic life on a South Carolina plantation

i do not no what took him of. . . . i have not struck him one lick in a year nor yet thretend him." And from John C. Calhoun, known as a firm, kind master: "Aleck, our house servant, gave us the slip yesterday . . . if he should be taken . . . have him severely whipped. . . . He had offended your sister, and she threatened him, with a severe whipping. He ran away to avoid it."

Slave uprisings were almost unheard of, but were always feared and, like Nat Turner's in 1831, horrifying. "Every Southern *woman* to whom I have spoken on the subject has admitted to me that they live in terror of their slaves," wrote Fanny Kemble. This was undoubtedly an exaggeration. But if she did not live in terror, the mistress of many a mansion felt keenly the responsibility of so many lives and sighed with Letitia Burwell, "Will the time *ever* come for us to be free of them?"

Yet on plantation after plantation life went on steadily, quietly, and happily. At its best, it was a benevolent paternalism in which real affection developed between servant and master and a mutual sense of responsibility and obligation, together with a high degree of easy familiarity and personal intimacy.

The wealth the slaves produced went into more land, more Negroes, bigger houses. Some of them along the Eastern seaboard were magnificent Georgian brick with boxwood walks and formal gardens. They are found on the banks of every Maryland and Virginia river. In these large homes the rooms were numerous but small, for the winters were cold and large rooms hard to heat; for the same reason, beds were heavily curtained, and the chairs and settees high-backed to keep the drafts off the back of one's neck.

In the nineteenth-century Lower South, the fine homes showed the influence of Roman and Greek Revival periods, with the familiar white columns, high porches, and tall windows. Here was developed the typical Deep South plantation home, built high off the ground both for coolness and as a protection against floods. Wide verandas, large rooms, high ceilings, and wide hallways running through the house, open at both ends, created the spacious coolness that alone made the long hot summers bearable. (But if they were lovely and cool in the summer, they were also lovely and cold in the winter!)

Before nails became readily available, the overwhelming majority of Southern homes, plantation or farm, were log, notched, chinked, and sometimes covered with siding. The better homes were brick, rarely stone. Set in large grounds, the big house was surrounded by a cluster of buildings—kitchen, shop, barns, necessary houses, stables. Beyond the whitewashed paling or rail fences grazed and fed sheep, horses, goats, and every variety of domestic fowl—including guineas and peacocks.

The big house was the business and social center of the plantation. Here the owner had his office where he kept his accounts, wrote his plantation journal or diary, and carried on his correspondence. Here Ole Miss had her responsibilities, too, and they were extensive. Breakfast was a big meal because it had to keep you going till two or three in the afternoon when dinner was served. There was bacon (bacon was best south of the Potomac, beef, north of it), ham, eggs, fried chicken, quail, dove, wild duck, hominy grits (large and small), hotcakes, waffles, hot biscuits (hot biscuits *every* morning), light bread, corn bread, coffee, tea, sweet milk, fruit; and, in Virginia, shad roe, broiled tomatoes, fried apples, and Sally Lunn. (Incidentally, in the old South, "milk" was buttermilk, "bread" was corn bread, and "potatoes" were sweet potatoes. Guests had to ask for "sweet" milk, "light" bread, and "Irish" potatoes.)

After breakfast, the mistress with her chain of keys gave out the day's supplies. On Monday it was the week's rations for the hands, usually given out by the manager: three or four pounds of bacon per person, a peck of meal, a quart of molasses. There was plenty to eat, for who wanted a weak and ailing hand? The daily supplies were issued to the cook: flour from a barrel, sugar from a hardwood chest, meal, meats and so on, all under lock; and the kindly, understanding mistress usually turned her back at some point so the cook could slip out a few items in her capacious apron.

Then there was sewing to be done, and clothes to cut out. On some of the larger plantations the coarse cloth for the Negroes was woven, on others it was purchased—a sort of linsey-woolsey—as was the calico for Sunday wear. The pieces were cut out by the mistress or a seamstress and given to the Negro women who then made them up. Sewing was a big part of every Southern woman's life. All of them could do everything from fast straight sewing "with a red hot needle and a burning thread" to the daintiest needlework.

While Ole Miss did her own work and supervised the servants (from many points of view, she was the real slave on a plantation!) the rest of the family and the guests scattered, engaged in the endless enjoyments and activities of a big country place. The children took off with the tutor or to a nearby one-room school ("Old Field Schools," they called them in Virginia), or, when free, to play with the myriad little pickaninnies around the place. Riding, hunting, and socializing were the principal amusements. Everybody rode, and rode well. Fox hunting was a formal sort of sport. Far more common was riding out with the dogs after 'coon or 'possum, or just riding for the sheer fun of it. What a gay time they had! Game abounded—deer, wild hog, squirrel, rabbit, bob cat, 'possum, 'coon, quail, dove, turkey, duck, and geese. And Southern waters swarmed with bass, perch, sunfish, bluegill, plus plenty of buffalo, croaker, and "good ol' catfish."

Other times there were letters to write, or books to read with a hammock to read them in—Scott, Thackeray, perhaps a Southern novel like Simms' *The Yemassee* or a magazine like *The Southern Literary Messenger* or *The Cultivator*. While you read there was a servant to fan you with a peacock-feather fan, if you could stay awake.

Letter writing meant a great deal to the families of that day. Many of the letters were long, detailed, intimate, and full of the daily activities: the news of family and friends, moral and religious reflections, and political ob-

A planter's home along the Mississippi

servations. Among our finest sources of information for the period, they range from brief business notes to long descriptions of the last illness and death of loved ones, often harrowing in detail, but always tender and sweet.

Neighbors rode back and forth informally. Visitors from far and near were almost a daily occurrence. The Plantation South was a source of constant interest and curiosity to Northern and Old World travelers. Southern hospitality was real. Inns or hotels were few—most of them impossible—and distances great, so the benighted traveler was at the mercy of the elements, or a plantation home. Rarely was he denied or charged.

The event of the day was dinner. Usually at two or three in the afternoon, it began with whisky or brandy from the sideboard and proceeded through numerous courses for two hours or more. What an occasion it was! Even in the simpler homes it was a time of bountiful plenty and good spirits. In the wealthier it could be truly elegant. In some of the more formal dinners the table was set with a fresh cloth for each course. The table was bare for the final course of fruit and nuts.

"The table was furnished with a profusion of the delicacies afforded by the country," wrote John Pendleton Kennedy of a Virginia residence. "At the head was deposited a goodly ham of bacon. . . . The opposite end of the table smoked with a huge roasted saddle of mutton. (A turkey was more common.) Between these two extremes was scattered an enticing diversity of poultry . . . and especially that topical luxury . . . fried chicken. . . . The intervening spaces displayed a profusion of the products of the garden; nor were oysters and crabs wanting . . . and where nothing else could be deposited, as if scrupulous of showing a bare spot of table cloth the bountiful forethought of Mistress Winkler had provided a choice selection of pickles of every color and kind. . . . The courses disappeared; a rich dessert came and went. . . . The wine, iced almost to the freezing point, moved in a busy sphere. . . . Finally, we were left alone and before us glittered the dark sea of the table, studded over with 'curracks,' 'argosies,' and 'barks' and with the wealth of the Azores, Spain, Portugal, and France."

Roast pig barbecued was a favorite, and even a greasy old 'possum would be made palatable by being roasted like a pig. A barrel of oysters shipped in was a great treat; neighbors hurriedly were gathered to enjoy them. On one such occasion a certain lady was dining. "Her dress was none too high in the neck and by no means tight fitting around her lovely, highborne F F V bosom. The oysters were red hot. One fell! She screamed! B——— dived for it with a fork, fished it up in a trice. There was much confusion of face, and an instantaneous drawing up of her light shawl. With a fork! Imagine! The muff! I should certainly have risked burning my fingers that time!"

There was hardly a dinner without a guest, or two or three. What with the regular members of the family and the bachelor uncles, old-maid aunts, cousins, and grandparents who were the permanent residents of every Southern home, the table needed to be long and food plentiful. One planter's diary records going out to dine or having guests for dinner nearly every day for a month, and he broke the sequence then only because he took a trip to New Orleans. The conversation was a lively feature of the dinner—politics, slavery, the abolitionists, literature, music, and the arts, with the visitor the center of attention.

After the evening meal, there was a light supper or tea. During the long evenings there were visits to the slave quarters to join the singing, then back to watch the dancing or card games at home. Card playing was a large part of a Southerner's life; all loved gambling and would bet on anything. Southern belles loved to dance. The balls were gay and flirtatious, with minuets, gigs, reels, waltzes, even country dances.

Everything went on in the big house—birth, death, and marriages—even preaching on the grounds, although churchgoing on a Sunday was an important event. Births were unattended in the slave quarters, unless by a midwife. A kettle of boiling water, a solicitous aunty, and a patient, but almost unnecessary, physician were the accompaniments of births in the big house. Children had a hard time of it, what with croup, diphtheria, malaria, dysentery. The second summer was a crucial one, and the most pitiful sight in the old family burying grounds are the little headstones of the babies and children.

Marriages and funerals were major social events. Relations and friends came from miles around and stayed for days. With marriages the partying went on for two or three days after the ceremony, and the bride and groom stayed around for the fun. A bride's "second day" dress was almost as important as her wedding dress, and as beautifully made.

The War and Reconstruction drastically altered the South and left a residue of bitterness which time has not yet fully sweetened. The relation of planter and sharecropper (or renter) was a basically different one from that of master and slave, but it was a long time before the Negro's new-found freedom really came to mean anything to the great majority of them.

Today, things are different down South. There aren't the servants there used to be. There are tractors down by the barn instead of mules, and harvesters instead of field hands. The plantation is bigger, but the house is smaller. There are electricity and air conditioning and running water and store-bought clothes and a lot of changes of the kind you would expect. There are government regulations galore; a farm economy is emerging which will revolutionize the pattern of plantation management. It is a South new in a thousand ways, but old in a thousand more. If its greatest and most perplexing problems came from its tragic exploitation of people and land, so its greatest contribution to American life came from the ideals of the abundant life established on the eighteenth and mid-nineteenth-century plantation. It is these qualities which have given distinction to Southern life and which will live.

The commerce of the Upper Country that concentrates at New Orleans is amazing, and every year is rapidly increasing. Sixteen hundred arrivals of steam-boats took place in 1832 and the estimated number in 1835 is 2300.

J. M. PECK

HARNETT T. KANE

River People, River Ways

THE RIVER FOLKS were a special variety of Southerners, whose lives—sleeping and waking, from birth to the grave—were shaped and directed by Old Man Mississippi at their door, or by the tributaries which were his grandchildren. Let it be noted quickly that the great river of the South, and of America as well, was always "he." Anyone who called the Mississippi "she" received the stare he deserved as a fool from some other part of the country or, worse, from the South itself.

Now and then a native of New Orleans, greatest of the river cities, will murmur as one did recently to me: "You hear all this talk about the Mississippi, but me, I haven't set eyes on it in a year or two. As far as I'm concerned, it could be over in Pasadena." Because the Old One flows beyond the green-brown mound of the levees, the riverside dweller may forget him. The fact is, however, that the man would not be there to speak if it were not for the Mississippi; there would be no New Orleans, as there would be no Memphis, no Natchez, no Baton Rouge, no St. Louis.

For millions of Southerners the river has been the friend and benefactor but also the enemy—the force that created the frame of his life, but sometimes threatened, as in floodtime, to destroy him in a day or two. Above all, the Mississippi and its side streams have supported him. Today in New Orleans, for instance, some 60 per cent of the town's income comes through the river and the world that lies upstream, downstream, and beyond.

THE FOLKS

The Old Man brought the long river-edge its many-hued, many-dispositioned folk. During most of the South's history the waterways were the main (often, the only) highways; a man traveled by stream or not at all. From the Mississippi, from creaking ocean vessels or from barges and canoes and other frail craft, there stepped the people who would hunt their fortunes on the fertile banks: Englishmen and Scotsmen and Irishmen, Frenchmen and Spaniards and Germans, or men of the long-settled Virginia coast and the Carolinas. Then, as the years passed and the American frontier advanced, the lower reaches of the Mississippi received Kentuckians and Tennesseeans and men of present-day Alabama and Georgia, in their search for opportunity in the heartland of a continent.

Here was the great liquid roadway of the emerging nation, the passage to the burgeoning South and an earlier West. Along it spread a string of settlements like beads on a wide ribbon, with towns that grew and declined with varying influences and, as the years passed, some of the major estates and slave plantations of the New World.

It was not all of one piece, this River South—rather, a succession of diverse areas. Earliest in settlement was the Creole, French-Spanish vicinity of New Orleans, built out of a semiswamp, and in certain seasons more liquid than land. Below it waited the Deep Delta of the South, sinking slowly from the Creole City toward the Gulf, a long stretch of somnolent earth extending to the upreaching fingers of the Gulf of Mexico, a land of thick sugar-cane stalks, of orange groves and pale, lily growths—and, today, of oil wells at the Gulf and Bayou borders.

Above New Orleans the land rose, again slowly, toward Baton Rouge, with still greater crops of emerald stalks. Next came the start of the Land of Cotton, which thrived in the drier soil toward St. Francisville and Natchez and other river settlements with names like a soft caress. Over thousands of acres, the cotton bolls provided a potential treasure for some owners, less rewarding labor for others, and bondage for those of darker skin, captured and stolen from their native lands.

Now rose the high river bluffs of Vicksburg and the towns beyond, giving another look, another air. At many places stood swampy expanses, with low islands that faced inundation yet nevertheless supported ripe crops —typical among them the property of a self-made planter, Joe Davis, who had a stern, hollow-jawed younger brother named Jefferson.

And into the Mississippi poured other streams which were wide and deep, tapping the earth for thousands of miles in three directions: the Red, the Arkansas, the Yazoo, the Quachita, each sharing the great river's civilization.

Here was a region of shifting population, of shifting classes. Many a once buckskin-clad backwoodsman rose to be a planter, enlarging his status as he moved from a small wooden house to a towering establishment. For generations the river land remained on the American frontier or close to it, and for a thousand miles the Mississippi's borders had the manners of the West rather than those of, say, Virginia or Maryland.

From the wide-hatted planter of the veranda along the river to the black man who worked in the steaming fields and the small merchant whose enterprises grew out of the shifting trade . . . each became one of the "children of the river." Even more directly of the Mississippi were the roaring flatboatmen and keelboatmen, who, before the steamboat came and for decades afterward, followed a steady course down the stream.

The rawboned, unshaven, hard-drinking frontiersmen, "Kaintucks" or Kentuckians, Tennesseeans, and others, swaggered along the levees, gouged out eyes, bit off noses, and kicked an opponent where it would do the most good. They called themselves "sons of alligators," "off-spring of snapping turtles," and similar creatures. America had never seen anything like them, and never saw their like again in the less vivid days that followed their passing.

It was a robust civilization, a place of high ambition, lusty deeds, and strong humors, a region of ungenteel jokes and gusty spirits. Among the plainer folk, horseplay was the rule; a man had to know how to take a jibing or fight to ward off the jiber. Among the better-to-do, the planters guffawed together over their wines and whiskies and told stories that might not have been greatly different from those recounted in the saloons and shanties of the riverbanks.

The river plantation had a half-tropic appearance, with houses that lifted themselves in the style of West Indian dwellings, elevated against the danger of flood; with wide doorways and windows to admit every available wind, a framing of junglelike trees, a glint of distant swamps. In New Orleans and its surroundings there developed early residences with a particular Creole look: brick piers below, slender columns above, or simple brick town houses flush with their *banquettes* (or sidewalks) and patios, fanlighted, with fountains splashing in the sunlight.

Eventually the Greek Revival spread over Louisiana and Mississippi and Tennessee and the states beyond, with riverside versions of the classic white columns and sweeping galleries, hand-painted porcelain doorknobs and a White Ballroom, complete down to enameled floor. Belle Grove, a pink pile with four florid Corinthian columns, dwarfed everything along the river; its rounded wing was like that of a medieval tower, its chatelaine sometimes described as an American Duchess.

This "lady" was noted along the Louisiana river coast for a story. Once

GROCERY

she dropped a diamond earring at dinner. When two male guests leaned over to hunt for it, she restrained them. "Don't bother, please. The servants will probably sweep it up in the morning."

Eventually Belle Grove became a pink elephant for the owners; abandoned, it housed cows for a time, crumbled away until the last remnant burned down a few years ago.

Meanwhile, of course, there were the smaller growers or townsmen or plain farmers, who lived quietly in the shadows of the more fervent river life.

They and the other people of the river and its tributaries shared an existence that surged or sagged with the course of crops and their traffic. In the warm season, cotton bolls stood against the forest backgrounds; in the fall the sugar stalks swayed lightly in the wind. With colder weather, the vessels piled high with produce headed for Memphis or New Orleans or other points. A steamboat sometimes looked like a collection of cotton bales flowing south "on their own." But in bad years, years of panic or poor crops or levee breaks, the waterfronts could be bare, with men begging for handouts at the warehouses.

In their offices the cotton factors and sugar brokers gauged the scale of their existence by that shifting line of trade before them. They and their wives might enjoy a season of shining balls and cotillions—or they might have to move, temporarily or permanently, to a smaller residence in the back section of town. Meanwhile, more or less steadily, there continued a furious social activity, many-faceted, at which men and women of other states shook their heads in disapproval.

For these were no Puritan places, these Southern river towns. "Hell on earth," shocked observers called New Orleans: witch town of the river, wild and depraved. . . . Such terms, often applied to one or another of the Mississippi river settlements, were, of course, largely exaggerations. While the days and nights along the stream had an ease, a careless air that hardly matched that of a New England town meeting, the cities were not the Sodoms that their critics pictured.

Nevertheless, strangers came to gape and went home to talk. From the Creole capital Andrew Jackson's wife Rachel wrote: "Great Babylon is come up before me. Oh, the wickedness, the idolatry of this place! . . . Pray for your sister in a heathen land." Others frowned at the famous quadroon balls of the Crescent town, where well-to-do men of New Orleans and other cities danced with the tawny-skinned quadroon women and perhaps set them up eventually as their "protégées" in the no-less-famous "little houses along the ramparts" at the edge of town.

Others looked on at riverside dives of a dozen grades and styles and varieties. Not always was there mere folklore in the stories of a river planter who gambled a plantation on the turn of a card; who lost his life's earnings and then, walking slowly to the levee, sent a bullet into his head. Nor was there mere romanticism in the yarns about the seamen who were fed whiskey until unconscious, then shanghaied into distant service. Police records verify these and other river-front doings of the last century or two.

This was, beyond denial, a scene of many violences, those of man and nature as well. The river beheld countless tragedies, when steamboats exploded and burned, with scores of men, women, and children drowning in the powerful current or burning to death as they clung to decks in the lurid glare. Many such catastrophes occurred as a result of the racing spirit, the wish of one captain to outdo another, a reckless impulse to outstrip a rival on a run up the river—or a play for greater celebrity and trade.

Other kinds of violence flourished, too; gun fights, knife fights, stranglings in the alleys along the rivers. Many were the murders that resulted from jealousies, clashes over cards or women, or plain ambition. River gamblers thrived at Natchez and Memphis, at Port Gibson and Baton Rogue and all the other towns. And many were murders of another kind, the once-celebrated "affairs of honor" which flourished with a peculiar virulence in the river settlements.

Men killed over fancied insults, a casual look, a rumor. Pistols for two, breakfast for one. . . . An Orleanian of Gallic heritage once said he had been a principal in twenty-four duels, and listed them all. An American, anxious to establish his own standing, struggled with his memory and recounted a mere twenty. One Jean de Buys fought three duels with the same man.

In New Orleans, a Spanish master of the sword and gun established his own cemetery, leading inevitably to the claim that he would kill you and bury you at a cut rate. One kind-hearted fellow would blast down an opponent, and then, if he lived, call solicitously night after night to help the family nurse the man back to health.

And one new arrival expressed a slightly unfavorable opinion of Creole coffee. That, sir, was an insult not to be borne by a real riverside citizen. A challenge resulted, and the scoundrel ended with a sword in his side. Most often-told of the dueling tales, however, is that of the outlander who, gazing at the Mississippi, said he had seen larger.

Ma foi, that was an aspersion not to be endured. . . . Another challenge, a meeting under the oaks, and death for the rash one!

Most of it—the grand scale, the high gesture—has disappeared. The crops continue to pour forth, with changes in method and appearance, with oil wells at the edge of the cotton and sugar-cane fields, chemical plants behind the levee. The white-columned old houses stand in many places, stranded in the middle of their former acres, some cracking apart, others maintained as weekend residences or show places for visitors. Remnants of the more or less wicked old river front—a crumbling building, the marks of an old road or street—can be located by earnest seekers. Largely, however, there is another kind of Mississippi life, more efficient, with bigger, more functional vessels pushed along the stream by tugs and tows. And the great stream supports a larger volume of traffic than it ever did.

Then what remains? An attitude, perhaps! a man's casual way of regarding the scene around him. And memories, memories of steamboats that once slid in and out of the landing at Memphis; echoes of ancient Natchez-under-the-Hill, of bands of raucous roisterers, of a half-dozen ghost towns, with ghost figures of men who carried the cotton back and forth.

And also a river speech, a river lore, and, not least, a river-edge music. . . . For the Negroes, who received least and endured most under the system of bondage, have given the South and America the songs, the blues and spirituals and deep throated jazz, that millions applaud. The kings and the captains have departed; ironically, the chants of these least of men have hung on, to be honored by the world.

A New Orleans scissor-grinder before the turn of the century

It is not lawfull for us to carry a pipe stave or a barrel of corn to any place in Europe out of the king's dominions . . . this is the cause why no small or great vessells are built here; for we are most obedient to all laws whilst the New England men break through and trade to any place that their interest lead them.

SIR WILLIAM BERKELEY, 1671

ROBERT G. ALBION

Sea Lure

ALONG the three thousand miles of coast south of Chesapeake Bay, the Southerners were slow in taking to the high seas. In 1860 the single Maine customs district of Bath on the Kennebec built almost three times as much tonnage as the whole coast from North Carolina around to Texas. That Bath district, together with the adjacent Portland district on Casco Bay, owned or operated almost as much shipping registered for foreign trade as did the eight coastal Southern states combined.

It was not until the twentieth century that the Southerners, under the impact of Florida cattle, Texas oil, and Gulf shrimps, began to make up for lost time. By 1950, New England's 2400 "sailors and deckhands" were quite outnumbered by the 8700 from those same Southern coastal states, while the 10,500 Yankee fishermen were less than half as numerous as the 23,000 on those waters. Chesapeake Bay does not belong in this story because it did not follow the backward patterns of the coasts to the southward in maritime matters.

There had been, to be sure, some colorful Southern maritime specialists even in those earlier days on the North Carolina–Texas range. Edward Teach, a temporary North Carolinian, better known in pirate history as "Blackbeard," terrorized the Carolina coasts until 1718, when a lieutenant of the Royal Navy cut him down in a sanguinary sea encounter near Hatteras.

Tampa still celebrates annually the exploits of José Gaspar, or "Gasparilla," who reputedly was collecting gold and girls from captured Gulf shipping a century later. Historians are skeptical about some of the Gasparilla details, but there is ample data about his contemporary, Jean Lafitte (Laffite), impudent, debonair, and able, whom some have called a pirate and others simply a privateersman and smuggler. He operated from Barataria Bay on the Louisiana coast as leader of a choice band of rascals, and fought under Andrew Jackson at New Orleans. After that, as the law was closing in, he shifted his base to what was then foreign territory at Galveston Bay.

Certain other Southern specialists became associated with shipwrecks in a variety of ways, some helpful. Before adequate lighthouses were erected, the Florida Keys claimed many victims among vessels trying to work southward inside the Gulf Stream. Grounding on the coral reefs was apt to be the end of the vessel, but there was usually time to get much of the cargo off intact. So "wrecking" developed into big business at Key West where, around 1840, twenty or thirty schooners or sloops found salvage work lucrative. Whenever the cry of "Wreck a-s-h-o-r-e!" resounded through the town, crews would speed to the moorings. It paid to get to the wreck first, for the captain and crew who did were entitled to take charge and to claim extra salvage.

One wrecking master, Squire Eagan, was also a Methodist lay preacher. One Sunday morning, while preaching about "the race for the prize of salvation," he could see that a brig was piling up on a reef. Striding down the aisle, still preaching, he shouted at the door, "Wreck ashore!" With this head start, he got his schooner *Godspeed* to the wreck first.

A thousand miles up the coast, shipwreck called for a grimmer and less profitable activity. Vessels piling up at Cape Hatteras, the "Graveyard of the Atlantic," usually pounded to pieces before much of their cargo could be salvaged. It often called for valiant efforts to save their crews from drowning. Lifesaving became a leading occupation for hardy Hatterasmen of the bleak Outer Banks, many of them descended from men who had been shipwrecked there in earlier days.

Eventually their efforts were co-ordinated by the Life Saving Service, and finally taken over by the Coast Guard. Serving as surfmen or keepers at the various stations, some won the coveted Medal of Honor for Lifesaving. Rasmus L. Midgett, from a family long prominent in such activity, received a medal for his singlehanded rescue in 1899 of crew and passengers from the schooner *Priscilla* during a hurricane. Patrolling the beach on horseback, he heard a woman's scream out of the darkness. Riding out into the surf, he found the three-master about to break up and, one by one, stirrup-rode the ten survivors ashore.

The harbor of New Orleans in 1873

The Southern cotton ports, to be sure, saw plenty of maritime activity in ante-bellum days. But, although Charleston, Savannah, Mobile, and New Orleans ran up great export totals, the craft crowding their water fronts usually had "New York," "Portland," "Liverpool," "Havre," or some other distant harbor painted on their sterns, and their crews contained few Southerners. The South was pretty much content to concentrate on raising cotton and then to say to the outside world, "Come and get it!" The North took such thorough advantage of this that one Senator angrily exclaimed that of every dollar paid for Southern cotton, the Yankee got forty cents.

The comings and goings of those cotton ships, however, did develop a group of Southern specialists who for a while would be in a position to make their maritime know-how a factor of historical importance. But for those pilots, long experienced in taking vessels into and out of the ports, the Northern naval blockade of the coast from 1861 to 1865 would have had a still more serious effect upon the South. England provided many of the swift blockade-runners, their cargoes, and, for a long time, most of their officers and crews; prominent officers on leave from Queen Victoria's Navy often commanded the craft on runs to and from Nassau, Bermuda, and Havana. But the trained Southern pilots, with their knowledge of the sandbars and other intricacies of harbor approaches, were the really indispensable ones aboard a blockade-runner.

For instance, at Wilmington, North Carolina, the port which remained open almost to the end of the war, the Cape Fear River could be reached by two different approaches, each closely guarded by Federal inshore patrols. In the final dash, with hails of "Heave to, or I'll blow you out of the water," and grapeshot whining all around, it took "the sixth sense of a dolphin" to cross the bar in the darkness into the shelter of Fort Fisher's guns.

In 1863 John William Anderson, one of the ablest of the Cape Fear pilots, took a blockade-runner out over New Inlet bar to Nassau. There he fell victim to a yellow fever epidemic and was close to death when the ship started back for Wilmington. Just before dawn, a Federal blockader started in pursuit; her shots began to come uncomfortably close. Down below, the dying Anderson heard the firing and gasped the order to be carried up to the wheelhouse. With his face as yellow as gold, he sighted the vague landmarks, murmured commands to the helmsman until the ship was over the bar, and slumped to the floor, dead.

Far down on the west coast of Florida, blockade running far less impressive in scale than Wilmington's was much more closely related to the South's twentieth-century maritime boom. It involved the "run out" to Cuba of Florida's cattle, already growing fat and numerous in the lush grass of the region. Jacob Summerlin, a leading cattleman, provisioned beef to the

Confederacy for a while. In 1863 he and neighbors decided to attempt cattle shipments through the blockade into Havana to trade for outside products desperately scarce in the beleagured South. They turned to Captain Donald McKay (not to be confused with the builder of clipper ships), who with his brother, Captain James, was among the leading mariners of the Tampa region. Early in 1863, six hundred of Summerlin's fat steers were loaded aboard Donald's side-wheeler, the *Scottish Chief*, on the Caloosahatchee River just below Fort Myers for the run to Havana. Before long, she was back at the river with sugar, flour, salt, quinine, and other scarce commodities. These were swapped for more cattle with the Floridians who had gathered from all directions. To avoid the ubiquitous Union blockaders, McKay had knowledge and nerve enough to risk pitch-dark night passages through the dangerous keys and reefs above Key West. Altogether, he made six such risky and highly profitable voyages to Havana and back.

That same combination—shipping cattle to Cuba with McKay participation—soon paved the way for what would eventually become the nation's largest fleet of freighters. In 1874 young Dr. Howell Tyson Lykes, fresh from medical school, married Almeria McKay, daughter of Captain James and niece of Captain Donald. Their seven sons and one daughter would all participate in managing the future Lykes economic empire. Presumably finding West Florida too healthy to support a good medical practice, Dr. Lykes branched into other fields, particularly cattle raising. Ultimately the family would hold first place in Florida's cattle industry

Dr. Lykes, like Summerlin, decided to market many of his steers in Cuba, so bought a seventy-five-ton, three-masted schooner and chartered other vessels. His sons spread out from Tampa to handle the expanding business to Cuba and to other Gulf ports. Eventually the family began to acquire more ships of their own. When in 1933 the Shipping Board was selling off freighters at bargain rates, the Lykes brothers made a package deal. They bought fifty-two freighters at five dollars a ton, on condition that they agree to continue regular line services on five of what the government calls "essential trade routes" from New Orleans and other Gulf ports to Britain, the Continent, the Mediterranean, the Caribbean, and the Orient. Later they also made runs to South and East Africa. Receiving subsidies to offset the cost of foreign construction and operation, they gradually replaced their old ships with efficient new vessels. Today one might say that the sun never sets on the blue-and-white Lykes house flag.

While Lykes is the largest of the new Southern lines, it is by no means alone. The Mississippi Shipping Company, also based on New Orleans, operates its Delta Lines not only to Rio, Buenos Aires, and other east coast ports of South America, but also to West Africa. The Waterman Line long operated ships out of Mobile to various parts of the world. The Bloomfield fleet, based on Houston, is smaller and newer. There are said to be Houston dollars, along with many Southern mariners, in the far-flung operations of the States Marine fleet.

These services helped to lure the Southerners to sea with wages too tempting to resist. The maritime unions won pay raises to levels more generous than most shoreside jobs. A seaman with only moderate experience, if regularly employed, gets six thousand dollars or more in base pay, overtime, and fringe benefits; that is several times the rate in most foreign merchant marines. Cotton picking was never like that, and it is small wonder that the Southerner has been taking to the sea with enthusiasm.

The rapid development of Gulf oil production after 1901 called for transportation on a vast scale. The answer was the economical tanker, which would lure more Southerners to sea.

Ship channel and turning basin at Houston, Texas, which connects with the Gulf of Mexico through Galveston Bay (*Ewing Galloway*)

The various oil companies soon developed huge tanker fleets. Some carry the oil abroad, but the major movement is around Florida and up the east coast to Philadelphia, New York, and other ports "north of Hatteras." New ports quickly sprang up to handle this traffic, notably Beaumont, Port Arthur, and Lake Charles on the Texas-Louisiana border. After 1915, a fifty-mile canal permitted tankers and freighters to penetrate inland from Galveston Bay to Houston, which would eventually have heavier coastwise outward shipments than any other "seaport" in the United States, with Beaumont and Port Arthur as runners-up.

Since a tanker generally sails from the same Gulf port but may go to any one of several ports north of Hatteras, most of the crews settle along the Gulf. The tanker crews have a different way of life from the men on "dry cargo" freighters, who normally spend several days wherever they load or unload. The tanker's oil cargo can be pumped in or out in a matter of hours. Consequently, in lieu of the lost shore leave, the tanker officer or seaman usually gets every third or fourth month off, at full pay. There always has been the danger of fire aboard a tanker, but it is rare except in war time. The tanker quarters are usually clean and comfortable, and the food excellent.

In the mid-1950's, a lilting tune that made the "hit parade" week after week suddenly alerted the nation to another major Southern maritime activity. Its refrain announced that "Shrimp boats is a-comin'; there'll be dancin' tonight." It gave an idea of the comings and goings of the "pink gold" fleet in the Gulf. The distant Northerner, hearing that song, recalled that the "shrimp cocktail" and "fried jumbo shrimp" were appearing on menus more and more frequently.

Shrimping, in fact, has attained superlative status, overtaking in value all rival fish or shellfish catches from Maine around to Alaska. In 1956 the national shrimp catch paid the fisherman $70,000,000, followed in order by salmon ($46,000,000), tuna ($43,000,000), oysters ($30,000,000), menhaden or pogies ($28,000,000), and lobsters ($13,000,000). Cod, long the mainstay of American fisheries, was way down the line at $2,600,000. Of the huge shrimp catch, less than 12 per cent came off the South Atlantic coast from North Carolina down to the tip of Florida; virtually all the rest came from the Gulf's curving shore, Key West around to the Mexican coast. This was primarily responsible for putting Florida, Louisiana, and Texas directly after California, Alaska, and Massachusetts in the "most valuable fisheries" line-up.

Shrimping had a slow, modest start, centering on the squashy Louisiana coast and the adjacent Biloxi region of Mississippi. It began as the informal inshore operation of dragging nets from small boats close in and "hand-dipping" from piers and bridges, as many Florida tourists still love to do. As early as the 1880's a few canneries packed the small "white" shrimp for distant markets. Between the World Wars, the trade began to boom. This was partly due to the development of freezing, which preserved the shrimp flavor better than canning. Probably more important, though, was the discovery of three great new offshore beds. In 1938, jumbo "white" shrimp were found in profusion off the mouth of the Mississippi. Shortly afterwards, rich stocks of "brown" shrimp were located off Campeche and other parts of Yucatan in Mexico. Finally, in 1949, the Salvador brothers of St. Augustine acted on a hunch and found a tremendous supply of "pink" shrimp off the Dry Tortugas. This converted Key West into a boom town as shrimp boats by the hundreds flocked to the scene.

The old beach seines gave way to diesel-powered craft in which two or three men operate big "otter trawls" with ten-foot wooden doors to keep the mouth of the trawl open as it scoops up shrimps and other marine life. The Tortugas and Campeche grounds mean long trips, sometimes stretching into weeks. In contrast to the wages of mariners aboard freighters or tankers, shrimper trips are a gamble. Sometimes, with hundreds of pounds of shrimp at every haul, a good trip pays off the mortgage or makes the down payment on a new car. A meager catch might not pay the ice or diesel fuel bill. A shark can tear up a costly trawl. In the past, off the Campeche grounds, capture by a Mexican gunboat has meant confiscation of catch and gear, plus a heavy fine. But there have been plenty ready to take the gamble.

Those fishermen are doing their part in the South's long-delayed response to sea lure. So, too, are the thousands of Southern officers and men aboard liners and tankers on more distant runs. A century ago, the nasal Yankee twang could be heard in ports around the world, Callao to Canton, Trieste to Tahiti. Now they are outnumbered along the sea lanes by soft, slow Southern accents, aboard ships hailing from New Orleans, Mobile, and elsewhere along the South's lengthy coastline.

Into the woods my Master went,
Clean forspent, forspent.
Into the woods my Master came,
Forspent with love and shame . . .

SIDNEY LANIER—
"A Ballad of the Trees
and the Master"

G. ROSS FREEMAN

Camp Meeting

FIVE MILES up the valley, the roar echoed from the cliff walls of a gap, a muffled discord of shrieks and basso rumbles. Suddenly above it all, clear as the lodestar on a frosty night, soared a baritone challenge, "Who will come and go with me?" The roar hurtled again, joyous in unison: "I am bound for the promised land."

At the camp meeting's clearing, pine knots set on mud-and-stick platforms high in the trees blazed their smoky light on a thousand weather-creased faces—faces staring at the young giant who had jumped up to a stump pulpit beside a preacher, then "swung the meetin' " to this choral of surge-singing. Now he lifted his arms in blessing, roared "Hallelujah," and danced back into the crowd. From their stumps and puncheon benches, the preachers resumed the shrill, staccato warnings of the torments of hell.

Screams of "Amen" again punctuated the fiery phrases. A youth shouted and hunched into a stumbling run around and around a pulpit, arms flailing. A middle-aged woman fell to the ground, screamed, dug the red earth with her fingers, moaned "Lost, lost." The "spirit" spread.

A bearded father and two grown sons decided they had treed the Devil and hopped around a white pine on hands and knees, baying like hounds. In shadow, beside the creek, a half-dozen men passed a jug of "squeezin's," belched, and dared one another to "whip a preacher." A flush-faced girl, who moments before had been pulled up from a leafy bower on the embankment by two boys, eased back into the crowd and shivered to the ground with the wail, "Jeeeee-sus!! I done wrong! You know I didn't mean ter. But hit's soooo easy, Jesus. And I sinned. Jesus, don't let my sweet mama in heaven know what I done. Save me from ma sin. You know I don't want to go to hell! O save me. . . ." The boys cursed, scuttled back into the woods.

This, in the forest clearings and mountain pastures of the early 1800's, was the purgatory of the Southern frontier, the Camp Meeting. It could be, and often was, as carnal as a Roman Bacchanalia or a Cretan bull-worship. Yet this Great Revival, launched by Tennessee and Kentucky preachers and circuit riders, swept, with forest-fire speed and fury, out of the mountains and across all the United States a generation after the American Revolution. It was, without question, the cradle for the Negro's spirituals and many of Protestantism's beloved gospel hymns. From it, the cities would take the pattern for their revival meetings; Moody and Sankey, Billy Sunday and Rodeheaver and Billy Graham would become names in its lineage. The Chautauquas of the North and West, the county fairs, the torchlight parades, ox-roasts, and orations of the political rally—all would imitate it. And, greatest of all, it developed the country churches, the sincere dedication to God's Work, the convictions of His Kingdom on Earth that were to permanently shape family life and community leadership for the entire South.

Life was vicious on the Southern frontier in the last decades of the eighteenth century. Families, pushing further up the creeks and into the mountains in search of new land, had resigned themselves to privation and toil. Social contacts were few. Pleasures were fewer. Almost the only social escape was through corn "likker." Practically everybody made it. And drank it. Children grew up fighting hunger, animals, and Indians in a tooth-and-toenail struggle to survive. As the Georgia poet Sidney Lanier would write, "Most of living consisted of not dying."

There were those who remembered, and prayed. The first of the Methodist circuit riders rode up to the cabins. Baptist farmer-preachers and self-sacrificing Presbyterian teacher-preachers took up the battle for a Christian faith. Then, with dramatic suddenness, came the Great Revival. Historians have not yet agreed on its beginning date. But they uniformly testify that it enflamed the Cumberland region, swept back to the Atlantic coast, and for fifty years fanned out across each new frontier in the West. That invincible pioneer preacher, Peter Cartwright, himself a product of it, wrote, "From 1801 for years a blessed revival of religion spread through almost the entire inhabited parts of the west: Kentucky, Tennessee, the Carolinas, and especially through the Cumberland country. In this revival originated our camp meetings. It promoted sobriety, respect for the law, education, and a purified social life, and created a dazzling new opportunity for the church.

Religion's revival was sparked, apparently, by an incident in Lincoln County, North Carolina, in 1794. Dan Asbury, Methodist circuit rider, had scheduled a visit by the celebrated preacher William McKendree, anticipating the completion of the New Church at Rehoboth. Weather slowed its construction. The ingenious pastor announced services under the trees. More came than could have been accommodated in the church. Conviction blazed; three hundred were converted. Convinced by this demonstration, Dan Asbury projected two more forest "revivals" with a Presbyterian coworker. These elicited similar results. Another Presbyterian, James McGready, visited and was impressed. John McGee, a Methodist, rode over, too. Both of these men moved to the West with vivid memories.

McGready carried the flame to Logan County, Kentucky, known then as "Rogues Harbor." It was a haven for moonshiners, gougers, counterfeiters, robbers, and murderers. By visiting diligently, preaching vigorously, and banding his members together in prayer-covenants, this fiery man of God labored to create a revival atmosphere. In June, 1800, he announced the Red River Sacramental Services. The two McGee brothers, William the Presbyterian and John the Methodist, had labored in Summer and Smith counties, Tennessee. Late in 1799 they left on a tour of the "Barrens" toward Ohio Territory. Hearing of the Red River meeting, they stopped off to help their old North Carolina friend. The unusual sermons, surgesings, and "falling" drew enormous crowds. McGready moved on to Muddy River and Desha's Creek near the Cumberland River, with the same type of outdoor meeting. John Alexander Granade, a back-country poet who would write many of the camp-meeting songs, was converted here. The Cabbin Creek meeting, held a little later in 1801, attracted twenty thousand people. The same year, Bishop Francis Asbury appointed William McKendree to supervise Methodist work in Kentucky. Recalling Rehoboth and sensing the potential, McKendree plunged immediately into a campaign for this new movement.

The fervencies could not be contained long in Tennessee and Kentucky. They ignited in Oglethorpe County, Georgia, in 1802; moved to Lancaster County, South Carolina; were in Brunswick County, Virginia, by 1803; then swept up the coast to Maryland, Delaware, Pennsylvania, New York, Massachusetts, Connecticut, Vermont, and New Hampshire, and went into Ohio's Western Reserve. Nathan Bangs describes vividly a camp meeting on the Bay of Quintie in upper Canada in 1805, where hundreds were converted. Bangs also reports an unusual one in New York at Cowharbor, Long Island, when between six and eight thousand people sailed out from New York City and New Jersey in 1818. Newspapers reported "miraculous visitations," and ran columns of colorful description.

Actually camp-meeting roots go back to the wilderness preaching of John the Baptist, and beyond. Most of Jesus' preaching was done in the open. John Wesley, coaxed at last to the coal fields, preached to vast throngs outdoors. George Whitfield crossed the Atlantic and attracted thousands to hear him in the streets. During the first year of the Revolutionary War, John Waller, a Baptist, conducted what he called "camp meetings" in Virginia. Worshipers, however, did not camp. They were guests in the homes of the community.

Developed a quarter-century before the first American county fair, the camp meetings provided a festival as well as a time of devotion for the pioneers. There was a lot of visiting. In the open, people thought it no disrespect to talk or to walk. In the early days, there were no seats. Children ran playfully. Many came, with no interest in religion, to be entertained or startled. Whiskey was sold at the clearing's edge. Peddlers noisily hawked their wares in competition with the preachers. Actually there were so many people and the confusion was so great that no preacher, no matter how leather-lunged, could be heard by all. Consequently, several ministers would preach at the same time in different sections of the clearing.

Crowd reactions were the most shocking to strangers. Falling, "jerking," rolling, running, shouting, singing, barking, and dancing were all manifestations of camp-meeting fervor. Gideon Blackburn of Maryville, Tennessee, wrote to a friend in Philadelphia on January 20, 1804, "The subjects of these exercises are in all classes, ranks, and degrees. There is the person of eighty and the child of four, the master in affluence and the slave in bondage, the clergy in the pulpit and the laymen in the pew, the man of long religious standing, the one of recent date, and many who have no religion at all."

Falling seemed to be characteristic. Sometimes the person who fell would be unable to speak, his pulse would get weak, and his breathing would be difficult. In some instances the extremities would get cold and all signs of life would cease for about an hour. Yet all testified that they felt no bodily pain; they were able to recount what had been said or done near them. George Baxter reasoned in his *Western Sketch Book*, "From this it appears that falling is neither a fainting nor a nervous affliction. Indeed this strange phenomenon appears to have taken every possible turn to baffle the conjecture of those who are not willing to consider it supernatural."

A boy crept through a crowd with the string of frogs he intended to loop over the preacher's neck during prayer. From a crouching position he

An old-time Methodist camp meeting

suddenly leaped over the mourner's bench, fell at full length, roared like a bull in a net, and cried aloud for mercy.

Peter Cartwright reported an even more remarkable incident in one of William McGee's meetings. A company of drunks came to break up the meeting. Their leader, a very large man, began by loudly cursing "the jerks" and all religion. Then, he found himself jerking. Embarrassed, he tried to run. He couldn't. Supporting himself by holding on to a sapling, he took out his whiskey bottle and swore that he would "drink the damn jerks to death." Try as he would, he could not get the bottle to his lips. A sudden seizure dashed him against the tree, broke the bottle, and spilled the whiskey. This enraged him. Cursing and swearing profanely, unable to control himself at all, his head jerked this way and that. Finally, his neck broke and he died.

Nonetheless great and lasting good resulted. People looked up from the wilderness hardships and found faith and new courage. Church-going became the topic of conversation, of inquiry, of investigation. James Gallaher reported that a spirit of prayer was granted to the converts that was truly marvellous. "Men who had never prayed in public would pour forth supplications with a liberty and a propriety of expression that astounded their acquaintances . . . the compass of their petitions and the force of their language was wonderful."

The membership of the "Free Will" Baptist church in Kentucky soared from seven thousand to thirty-one thousand between 1785 and 1812, and more than doubled in Virginia in the same generation. Methodism surpassed these figures.

Equally spectacular, and of soulful importance to all America, were the roles the camp meetings played as developers of folk music, as literally the birthplace for the Negro's spirituals, and as a bright new ray of hope to the slave. New hymns were written to the tempos of English ballads and sea chanteys; typically, Rev. Alex Means, Methodist minister of Oxford, Georgia, wrote the haunting words for *Wondrous Love* and adapted them to the music of the old ballad beginning, "Oh, my name was Captain Kidd as I sailed, as I sailed."

Similarly, the Negro slave found new Christian expression here. He heard a message of universal hope, of redemption and freedom. And with it came music that surged the loneliness and hunger up from his heart into the glorious part-singing and subtly pert rhymes of the first spirituals. The colored man's genius for homely succinctness revealed itself, as George Pullen Jackson points out, in such deft revising as the change from—

"To hide yourself in the mountaintop,
To hide yourself from God,"

in the white man's gospel hymn, to the Negro's—

> "Went down to the rocks to hide my face,
> The rocks cried out no hiding place."

By 1820, there were forty thousand Methodist and sixty thousand Baptist converts among the South's black people. The spirituals, with the gospel hymns, marched toward glory.

Great Revival? The name the camp meetings gave to the 1795–1820 period of the South's history is not exaggerated.

By 1820 more than a thousand Methodist camp meetings were established. After 1825, the camp meeting was predominately, though not officially, Methodist. Order had to come. Handbooks were written. Sometimes constables and sheriffs were deputized to maintain a respectful assembly. The following rules, adopted in 1831, were typical:

> "The people will be notified of the commencement of Public Worship from time to time by the sound of the trumpet.
> The seats and the grove of timber on the right hand of the stand are for the use and retirement of females: the seats and the grove on the left hand are for the use and retirement of men.
> The trumpet will sound in the morning at 5:00 as a signal to rise and have prayer in the tents.
> All persons committing any act, or making any disturbance, in, or about this meeting, such as are prohibited by the state laws, will be dealt with according to law."

Four-day camp meetings became the pattern. Commencing Friday afternoon, there would be three and four services a day until Monday noon. Camp-meeting associations formed and selected permanent sites for their meetings. The grounds were laid out in three sections. The outer area was for horses, cows brought along for milk, and chickens brought along for food. Closer in were the wagons, loaded with provisions. Family tents went up near the wagons. Within this circle of living quarters and campfires the meetings took place. Additional illumination was provided by candles in the trees and fire platforms, above the heads of the people, covered with dirt. Rows of split-log benches stretched out before the preachers, with wide aisies to separate the sexes.

Basically this pattern has continued to the present. The open-sided auditoriums are modern, with seats that have comfortable, form-fitting backs. The family "tents" are wood or stone bungalows with electricity, refrigeration, and probably a TV set. In 1958, Georgia alone had twenty-six Methodist camp grounds. Several of them had attractive summer-long youth programs. In recent years the various branches of the Church of God, the Nazarenes, the Assemblies of God, and others have adopted the camp meeting, too.

Three things have not changed much: Hospitality still abounds. Good food is on every table. The stranger is always welcome.

Some of the strongest preaching in America is still heard at camp meetings.

And young people still have a wonderful way of courting. Rules governing this aspect have always been strict. Every effort is made to keep their minds on spiritual things. But they find a way. Walks to the spring are permitted, and some of them seem to stay thirsty. One old-timer remarked that the Rock Springs Camp Ground in Lincoln County, North Carolina, had been "the mating ground for our state for fifty years."

Camp meeting, in the rush of modern life, still provides a nostalgic escape, a social outlet, and an opportunity for people to develop a sense of God. And still, "many hardened sinners are arrested by the grace of God there."

"Why, sir, on the north we are bounded by the Aurora Borealis, on the east we are bounded by the rising sun, on the south we are bounded by the procession of the Equinoxes, and on the west by the Day of Judgment."

"The American Joe Miller"—a Kentuckian's alleged reply
to the question, "What are the boundaries
of the United States of America?"

JESSE STUART

Up the Branch

THEY WERE NOT prisoners, debtors, ne'er-do-wells, or castoffs from the seaboard settlements, as some rumors have reported them to be. They were the most aggressive of the aggressive pioneers, brave with dreams and visions, who had come from the Old World of the British Isles to establish new homes and a new country in a wilderness.

When our English, Scotch, and Scots-Irish ancestors settled on the virgin soil of the Appalachian highlands there was plenty of timber, fresh, unpolluted streams, and wild game. Land was the most plentiful of all, selling for as little as twenty-five cents an acre. And our young Republic's first president, General George Washington, was generous to Revolutionary soldiers who had fought under his leadership. He and Congress paid them for their services with large bounties of these highlands that lay westward.

In these inaccessible rugged lands, without roads and with tumbling nonnavigable mountain rivers, with neighbors too often miles away, our ancestors had to become self-reliant. Self-reliance brought independence. The father, like his father before him, was head of the household. The oldest male descendant passed his way of life and law-of-life down to his sons, who passed the traditions on down to their sons. There was usually a bearded patriarch at the head of all families, such as was found in the Bible; and the

Good Book was found in every pioneer cabin whether anyone was able to read it or not.

The father with the help of his sons—if they lived—cut logs and built a house on his newly acquired land. If he didn't have sons, his neighbors helped him.

He rove virgin oak into clapboard shingles to cover his log shack, his stable, and other buildings. He used wild-animal skins, soaked in bear grease, to cover the sawed-out holes for windows; there wasn't any glass.

He cleared the land to raise patches of corn and wheat to make bread for his family, and to feed his livestock in winter. He usually kept one or more horses or mules and from one to several cows for milk, butter, and cheese. He fattened from one to a dozen hogs for meat and lard. Pork and beef were supplemented by meat of the wild animals and fowls of all descriptions and kinds that abounded so plentifully in the woods around each mountain shack.

He raised cane to make sorghum molasses, which with maple syrup and wild honey provided his family's "long" and only sweetening. Salt wells were dug deep enough to provide this ingredient. From here it was often carried on horseback, or hauled long distances over rough roads on jolt-wagons.

Wood ashes were put in barrels and water poured over the ashes. After this water went down through the ashes and dripped from the barrel into a container, it was mixed with grease. From this, the wife and mother made all the toilet and laundry soap the family used. My mother made this, and I helped her. My wife makes it still; I used soap she made when I was in World War II, stationed at the Great Lakes Naval Training Station.

In the days of my parents and grandparents, each family kept a number of sheep to shear. The wool was woven on the old spinning wheel into yardage to make clothes for the family. Each mother had to be resourceful to keep her family fed and clothed. Each father had to be an expert axman to cut wood and hew logs for buildings, then rove boards to cover them; to make furniture and handles for tools, wagons, yokes for oxen, and about everything else he used. He had to be a blacksmith, a doctor with remedies, often a teacher and preacher, a skilled marksman and hunter. Betwixt himself and his wife, they had to do everything. Families lived far apart from each other, and without good roads. Later than anywhere else in America, our people were self-sufficient and got along without the pedlars and tradesmen.

In my growing up I can remember when my mother made our soap and clothes, canned, preserved, smoked or dried the wild and tame herbals, the wild and tame meats, the fruits, berries, and garden stuff. We raised, or found growing wild, practically everything we ate except pepper and salt; we ate most all we raised from our infertile soil. When a great flood in the Ohio River Valley cut everybody away from supplies except by boat, this didn't bother us. We had everything at my father's and mother's home to feed the flood refugees who filled our home to capacity. We didn't have coffee, so, unlike my uncle, Martin Hilton, we gladly accepted the coffee from the Red Cross. But Uncle parched corn and made his coffee from it rather than take their gift.

All of this independence we inherited honestly from our ancestors.

As the years passed we multiplied. Our large, hilly farms were divided among children, then subdivided among children's children; we gradually began to lose our independent way of life. Towns sprang up by the rivers, and began to industrialize. Coal was discovered to be a good fuel; our mountains had huge seams of this "black gold"; coal mining brought railroads, highways, and trucks. This brought in "outlanders," whose customs and ways of life were foreign to us.

A mountaineer dame

Our ancestors were without any schools in the pioneer days, except teaching by parents who had obtained some little schooling in the land they came from. The Methodist circuit riders were great teachers, as well as great preachers. Then there were roving teachers who taught "subscription schools" for a small tuition in addition to free lodging and board in the homes of their pupils. Even yet, many youths with excellent minds could not obtain a rudimentary education, so grew up without book knowledge and unable to read or write. My father was one of these. Mother had a second-grade education, and taught father to write his name.

This is one reason for so many different spellings of both given and surnames in our highlands today. Now, after such long and hard struggles to better ourselves in life, we are sharing almost equal educational opportunities with people of other segments of America. And our people are beginning to make as vast and far-reaching strides in all professional vocations as any other region. Belief that our mountain people prefer the barking hound, the music of the fiddle, the moonshine jug, and the dance floor to gainful kinds of employment is a misconception of the facts. Again due to our heritage, our people are good workers; with a little training they become skilled artisans.

Once I was pleased when Mrs. L. W. Singer, cofounder with her late husband of the L. W. Singer & Company, Educational Publishers, told me when I visited her firm in Syracuse, New York, that the reason so much of America's printing was done in east Tennessee was the decision reached after a survey was made to locate good reliable labor; it was found in our highlands among the descendants of an early Scots migration. These were the lineage of the mountain-men who marched to the midwest in coonskin caps with long rifles, under the leadership of General George Rogers Clarke, to capture from the British what is now Ohio, Indiana, Illinois, Michigan, Wisconsin, and part of Minnesota. These were our ancestors who fell, too, at King's Mountain fighting for our independence and requested that they be buried with their saddles.

America had need of us then. America still has need of us instead of such hostile remarks that a wall should be built around us "higher than the old wall of China," and we should be kept behind it and never let out again. We have been a hard-working, tough-fighting, God-fearing, independent but loyal segment of our Republic.

Although we are a portion of "Southern Earth," we are, generally speaking, different as oak from pine to all the other segments of lands and peoples that make the South, in its way of life and stubborn independence, almost a country in itself.

The mountain-men were not slaveholders. Only a few ever owned human beings; these, for the most part, freed them before 1860. The small minority who fought for the Southern Confederacy did so because of their loyalty to the South, not because they owned slaves and believed in slavery. My mother's father was one of these.

The great majority of the mountaineers were loyal to the Union. The mountaineers didn't understand the Negro as a race; why had they remained slaves as long as they had without fighting for their freedom? We had to; so did the Indians. Many in our region still do not understand the Negro as a race. My mother never saw a Negro until she was twenty-two. My father saw his first Negro when he was sixteen. Understanding them or not, they fought their own people for the Negro's freedom as they had fought their own ancestors for their own freedom and for the young Republic. My father's father was one of these.

Had our Southern Appalachian mountaineers been loyal to the South, it could be any historian's guess how much longer the Civil War would have been prolonged. There is yet, and always has been, a philosophy among us that we fight for what we believe is right, and will die before we'll be conquered.

The extent of our participation in this conflict has shown and still shows, though to a lesser degree now, in our voting. Mountain counties in Virginia, West Virginia, western North Carolina, east Tennessee, east Kentucky (mountaineers were so powerful here they kept Kentucky from seceding from the Union), plus a few mountain counties in north Georgia and one or two in north Alabama, still vote Republican.

Strong political pressures have often squeezed us into the overwhelmingly Democratic Southern states of which we are integral parts. These pressures have not been able to erase our political identity. But these, plus unionization of the miners into a body of collective votes, have changed a few of the industrialized coal-mining counties. Due to the feeling against taxation without proportionate benefits, as compared to other parts of the states, there is always a mountain area in revolt (there was one in eastern Kentucky in 1958) against the rest of the state. Strong feeling persists among mountaineers that mountain counties, populated by people of ancestral and hereditary ties and similar beliefs, should be joined together in a separate, single state.

The ink had hardly dried on an article I wrote, in which I said the young mountaineer generation rarely used our mountain dialect any more, when a former pupil of mine did an interesting paper on "Why high school pupils don't understand some of the stories in our textbooks." She stated our language barrier was the reason. Her pupils, whose ancestors had held to the old Chaucerian-Shakespearean-Elizabethan language so long, were such a part of this Anglo-Saxon tradition they couldn't fully understand dialect, idioms, and slang expressions from other parts of the nation. Monnie Roe, of Morehead State College, gathered only a few of the old words used daily in and around this college; the list approximated a vocabulary of more than 1200 words.

With this evidence, one can understand why primary- and secondary-school youth has difficulty with stories by writers from other parts of

A typical cabin home in Tennessee about 1910

America. Contrary to what I have earlier written about mass communications of radio, TV, magazines, papers, plus better highways and schools, and our extension of travel at home and abroad, we still use an Appalachian Mountain dialect that reflects its old Anglo-Saxon origin. In it may be found obsolete forms used by Chaucer and Shakespeare, and in the original King James Bible. It is most difficult for one who is a native of the mountains, and who writes from the inside looking out, not to have his work searched for folklore and obsolete forms of old English, even when he is under the impression he uses the modern words and definitions of his American tongue.

Whether we who live here and work, write, or teach, believe it or not, we perhaps cannot escape the early English, Welsh, Scottish, and Irish cultures. Even the distant lands of our ancestors have evolved beyond their early language, ways of life, and cultures more than we. We used their early ballads long after they lost them. Then forty years ago Cecil Sharp came, found them, and took many original ballads and their many, many variations back to his native England. I found epitaphs on gravestones at Chester, England, and in both old and new cemeteries at Stoke Poges and Luilithgow, Scotland, that are almost word for word the same as those carved on stones in our own mountain village, town, and city cemeteries. We held rural folk dances similar to England's—and as fast and furious as Scotland's Dashing White Sargeant—for a hundred and fifty years before the advent of TV. When video showed them to the rest of the United States they were gladly accepted, and since have become very popular. Our mountain ballads and songs, as native to our area as Negro spirituals are to the entire South, have echoed around the world.

Our humor is often grotesque, vigorous, with dry remarks, sky-high anecdotes, and roaring, whooping exaggerations. Often, as in English humor, a remark is planted among listeners, then explodes among them later. It is not hard for us in our area to realize why our cousins in the Ozarks surpass us in rich native humor. We inherited and held onto the mournful ballads; when we have not been engaged in one of the country's wars, we have been fighting private wars of our own. We have been and are still too much like the phlegmatic Spartans of ancient Greece, and not enough like our Celtic ancestors, to produce a great humor.

I was born after the beginning of the twentieth century. In my day and time the governor of this state has had to call out the National Guard many, many times to quell fights between families. World War II's coming when it did stopped a rough one; opposing clans were killing each other off despite the use of troops. Their scorched-earth policy left a wake of destruction and a no-man's land between them. Pearl Harbor stopped the feud; they went off together to fight a common foe.

The first half of the twentieth century brought us great changes, unparalleled in our way of life. Two worldwide conflicts took young mountaineers to about all parts of the world, and on the seas and through the skies. Systems of highways made almost every valley accessible by automobile throughout the year. Today public transportation can take us to any part of the world, in a hurry.

With plenty of electricity in our area, our homes can now have bathrooms, modern gadgets and appliances, the same as peoples of other parts of America have had for so long; they have become an accepted way of mountain life. The outside world of entertainment is brought to us by TV and radio; where areas are inaccessible to TV, it has been piped in. In some areas, we can get New York City newspapers the same day they are published. We can communicate with all other parts of America.

Our schools may not equal the best in America. But they are improved over what they used to be, with fair libraries (these are never good enough!) and the best available magazines, classics, and current books. School buses haul our pupils to and from school. Where the big buses can't go, feeder-buses carry pupils from mountaintops and valleys to the trunklines.

There is such a great renaissance in learning now that our colleges are filled to overflowing; youth must go outside to find institutions with room for them. One of our great exports is teachers. They leave us for all parts of the nation where salaries are better than at home. Teaching salaries in our area, generally speaking, are the lowest in the nation.

Instead of shooting it out with firearms as our clans did for more than a century, our young men now show spectators here and over the nation their skills at hitting the bull's-eye with basketballs. Basketball is a great game, and football too, in mountain areas.

Now with chainsaws to cut timber and wood to burn, with machines to dig and load coal, with farming confined to machinery that farmers ride and a machine to milk the cows, how long will it take our present generation to lose what their fathers had? Our forebears had to work harder than the "outlanders" for everything they got. Today America is a land of promises for all; there is no difference here and elsewhere. Many types are united to make the whole.

Maybe we will not lose all of the tenacious fight, the dream, the usefulness and skill of our hands, and the physical stamina of our rugged forebears. Maybe we will retain some of our heritage, and our Appalachian Mountain culture of music, ballad, song and dance, and our skills at crafts. Maybe with more enlightened youth we'll expand our rich inheritance into drama, book, music, and art! Maybe we shall! But we have definitely become, or we are fast becoming, America's last Original Type.

The cession of Louisiana and the Floridas by Spain to France works most sorely on the United States.

THOMAS JEFFERSON, 1802

RICHARD B. DUNLOP

Crescent Coast

STAND ON the tawny sand banks of Florida's Cape Sable, the southernmost point on the United States mainland. It is still easy to believe that at any moment Ponce de Leon's caravels will be sighted out on the blue waters. This unchanging sea brings yesterday close to family life on the Crescent Coast, sweeping in a vast arc from the Florida Keys to Padre Island, south of Brownsville, Texas. Yet the sea washing on the beaches and harbor jetties also brings the future to the Deep South. That is a curious trick that the Gulf of Mexico plays. It keeps the past alive and meaningful while ushering in the future.

Today it seems at first glance as if the Anglo-Americans are both the past and the future of the Crescent Coast. Four cannon in Lee Square in Pensacola testify that this is not so. One cannon bears the royal arms of George I of England, one is emblazoned with the crest of Charles II of France, and the other two bear the emblems of kings of Spain. The soldiers of these three powers all garrisoned Gulf ports at one time or another. The Spanish Trail running the entire length of the coast is concrete today and Detroit autos whir where Spanish friars once trudged. Gleaming new skyscrapers lord it over the heart of Creole civilization, the Vieux Carré in New Orleans. Read the Spanish and French names written on the coast; look at the architecture of the people and observe the élan of their way of life; it becomes evident that the Latin past has left its imprint for both present and future.

Nowadays religious conversions are accomplished from Florida to Texas with prayer, hymn singing, and sermons. The sword is finally out of fashion. But not when Panfilo de Narvaez landed on the Florida coast on April 14, 1528. De Narvaez was described by a contemporary as a "tall, one-eyed man with a voice deep and sonorous as though it came from a cavern." His thoughts came from deep caverns too. With four hundred armed men and eighty awe-inspiring horses behind him, he announced to the friendly Indians who came down to the beach, "You will be compelled to accept Christianity. If you delay agreeing to what I have proposed, I will make war on you from all sides; I will obtain possession of your wives and children. I will reduce you to slavery." De Narvaez made no converts. He found no gold. The Indians forced him to flee in a raft covered with horsehide. The lime of his bones has doubtlessly appeared from Key West to Galveston in the form of cockleshells and coquinas.

Hernando de Soto fared little better. One of his soldiers left a suit of armor in a meadow near modern Tallahassee. Not many years ago it was dug from the field by an English-speaking farmer planting his crops, mute reminder in the land of climbing scarlet honeysuckle and Cherokee roses. Can the incredible hardships of these men be comprehended? After astounding adventures, Cabeza de Vaca lived with the bloody Karankawa Indians on what is now Galveston Island. He feasted on ants and shellfish and sometimes human flesh before he escaped to Mexico. Somewhere he may have a descendant, who works perhaps in a Galveston office and wears a charcoal suit, yet has the sort of gene heritage which would make him "most likely to succeed" if aboard the first moon rocket.

The French who came to the Crescent Coast were hardly less redoubtable. What they lacked in fanaticism they made up for in tenacity, and have to this day never entirely relinquished their cultural influence over the coast.

Over the years the French and Spanish and later the British and Americans played a tumultuous, sometimes comic, sometimes savage game of empire. Pensacola traded hands half a dozen times. Eight flags—Spanish, French, British, Mexican, Texan, and West Floridan, Union and Confederate—have flown from the battlements at one place or another. Pirates such as Gasparilla and Billy Bowlegs in Florida and Jean Lafitte in Louisiana and Texas raised the skull and crossbones, then marauded up and down the coast.

The Gulf's tides brought freebooters and adventurers of every nation to mix their blood with that of French nobles and Spanish grandees, of Latin peasants and artisans. The heroic Acadians, displaced by the British Army from their Nova Scotia homeland, migrated by the thousands to the bayou country of Louisiana to give the coast its largest and most resilient French-speaking population. All in all there were close to three centuries of Latin predominance on the coast before Anglo-Americans began to push into the area in numbers. Although white native-born Southerners hoping to get a new start on the rich coast became the most numerous migrants in the nineteenth century, they were not the only ones. Negroes, more Latin people, Greeks, Slavs, Scotch, and Germans moved in, too. Among them were such fascinating individuals as Prince Murat, King of Naples, who fled his throne in 1816 and bought a farm at Tallahassee. The deposed king jumped into local politics and was appointed postmaster and elected alderman and mayor by what was by then a predominantly Anglo-American community.

Compared to Creole dandies in New Orleans or to Prince Murat, the Anglo-Americans were rough and blunt. In 1845 General Zachary Taylor stopped at a Texan frontier post established by Henry Kinney. One of Taylor's aides snorted that it was nothing but "a small village of smugglers and lawless men with but few women and no ladies."

Kinney snorted right back, "Ladies are all right, I reckon, but I've never seen one yet that was worth a damn as a cook."

In time, Kinney's post mellowed. When it grew enough to rate a post office, something a little fancier seemed in order for the postmark. So the name was changed to Corpus Christi. After that, the town fell to work living up to its new handle.

The historic old lighthouse at Biloxi, Mississippi

Perhaps their civilized descendants might lift an eyebrow at the antics of the Crackers, but the original Spanish and French explorers probably would have welcomed them into the fraternity of adventurous men. La Salle or De Leon would have approved of J. Brit Bailey, who founded Bailey's Prairie on the coast south of Houston. In 1832 the old "hell-raising alligator basher" died of cholera. At his own request he was buried in a standing position, facing west, his rifle on his shoulders. They say in Texas that on the darkest night of the year a weird light flickers about his grave, burning with the finest blue flame because of the jug of whisky entombed at his feet. Anglo-American adventurers made their contribution to the settling of the Crescent Coast just as had their French and Spanish predecessors.

As the nineteenth century waned, still other national groups came to the coast. For centuries divers have plunged for sponges off the isles of Greece. But sponges became scarce in the Mediterranean. Word reached Greece that the Crescent Coast was the home of magnificent sponges. Thus the first Greek divers arrived at Tarpon Springs, Florida. Today a whole colony of Greeks is grouped there around a stately Orthodox Church. Putting out to sea in brightly painted boats under the protection of Saint Nicholas, Greek divers risk sharks and the bends to explore rock and coral reefs. They bring to the surface jellylike creatures covered with a black skin. The skeletons of these animals are bleached and auctioned in the courtyard of the co-operative warehouse in Tarpon Springs and reach the market as sponges.

In Tampa there is a Latin settlement made up almost entirely of Cuban cigar makers. When these cigar makers first came to suburban Ybor City in the 1880's, alligators crawled casually along Seventh Avenue. Night-shift cigar workers had to carry lanterns to keep from stepping on them. This Latin community is a striking combination of traditional and up-to-date community life. As far back as 1887, the cigar workers founded a co-op medical service which for the sum of ten cents weekly provided medicine and doctor's care to its members. But although the Cubans of Ybor City pioneered with this simple Blue Cross arrangement, some still consult witch doctors for charms against everything from the alienation-of-affections to unemployment.

When the fishing fleet comes sailing into the Back Bay of Biloxi, the canneries shatter the silence with the scream of whistles calling the workers to pick the shrimp and shuck the oysters. The jokes and the jesting over the catch are incredibly multilingual; Cajuns, Slavonians, Austrians, and Jugoslavians as well as Anglo-Americans make up the polyglot town. They all came to the coast with the hope that the harvest of the sea would give them a good living.

One group of Germans had something else in mind. They built a sawmill at Panama City on the deep waters of St. Andrew Bay. Within the mill they secretly erected gun emplacements and made detailed plans against the day when the Kaiser's navy would take over the bay as a base which could dominate the Gulf of Mexico and the Panama Canal. Their plans came to disaster with the German defeat in World War I. Meanwhile, a band of Scots had formed a syndicate to exploit a new community at Sarasota, Florida. Characteristically, they laid out the New World's first golf course, while helping to build one of Crescent Coast's now-renowned resort towns.

On this subtropical coast vacationers from the interior of the South early found relief from the heat. Gulf winds not only cooled the spacious, high-ceilinged cottages and hotels, but in the nineteenth century it was assumed that they also blew away the miasma. The coast became known as the land of leisurely unconcern to which a family could go to escape yellow fever. Lavish hotels developed, particularly along the Mississippi and Alabama coasts. Down to the lovely Inn at Pascagoula in 1855, as though in reciprocation for the brisk trade Southern planters were giving the innkeepers of New England's coast resorts and New York's Saratoga Spa, Henry Wadsworth Longfellow came with portmanteaus, quill pens, and beard brush to research "an experiment in hexameter" about the Acadians. It would be called, of course, *Evangeline.* Today the inn is named for him, and Pascagoula's bustle as an important shipbuilding center reflects the spirit of two townsmen who haven't been talked about much since 1863: Admiral and ex-Justice of the Peace George and his son Admiral David ("Damn the Torpedoes") Farragut, commander of Union fleets at the Battles of New Orleans, Vicksburg, and Mobile Bay.

But the perennial tourist crop is far from being the only crop on the coast. Agriculture is as many-faceted as the lives of the people who live there. Cotton is still a major crop in the Coast's five booming states, but its production is largely confined to upcountry. Crosses on the stalwart, tick-resistant Brahman cattle and Texas-sired Santa Gertrudi now amble grassy pastures beside the bayous, or thoughtfully chew cuds as they stare over fences at decentralized chemical plants, eight-hundred-foot broilerhouses and supermodern pens for "integrated" pig production.

Yet despite the Crescent's vast agricultural complex of fruit, tobacco, rice, sugar, cotton, vegetables, and resurgent livestock, other magic wands have developed the area to gigantic industrial stature.

Razorback hogs, suffering from ticks, used to wallow in a sulphurous, oily mixture at the foot of a scraggly hill on the coastal prairie near Beaumont, Texas. Patillo Higgins was a man possessed by the inquisitive, restless spirit that the Gulf seems to imbue in Crescent Coasters. Observing the hogs, he began to sink a well into the hill, although every oil man from the East told him this was Texas foolishness. Why not be satisfied with the salt that coasters had been getting out of these "salt domes"? Higgins hit gas at sixty feet. When he was four hundred feet down, a gale knocked his derrick over. Quicksand slithered into the hole. It looked like the end. But Higgins joined forces with Anthony Lucas, who had been drilling without success at Jennings, Louisiana. The two redoubled their efforts. On January 11, 1901, Spindletop Hill blew in. A black spume of oil shot 190 feet into the sky and gushed for nine days before riggers could cap it. "It's too big," muttered Standard Oil's representative, refusing to buy. "There's more oil here than the whole world will need for the next century."

Beaumont overnight became the first of the Crescent Coast oil boom towns. Blankets and cots were unobtainable as roughs, thieves, lease gamblers, and blue-sky promoters swarmed in. Men slept on pool tables and sawdust heaps. Investors crammed their suitcases with greenbacks and padlocked them to their legs while they slept in barber chairs (for ten dollars a night). The police chief warned honest men to tote guns and to walk in the middle of the street after dark. "And tote 'em in your hand," he ordered, "not on your hips."

Louisianans hurried to Beaumont to help the Texans exploit the vast Spindletop field. Later on in Louisiana, on the land that Lucas had sold, the huge Evangeline Field came in. Texans then rushed to Louisiana. Folks have been rushing up and down the coast ever since. Derricks clanged up in out-of-the-way swamps, and even far out in the Gulf on the continental shelf. A tangle of silvery pipes and mushroom tanks unwound as if by magic in the very bayou fastnesses of the Cajuns. Descendants of the Acadians paddled about in ancient pirogues, first taking muskrat from traps and then checking the pumps and gauges for the oil companies. Louisiana's coast led the nation in fur pelts, and rivaled Texas in oil.

Refineries of incredible size and complexity grew up. Arthur Stillwell, Port Arthur's founder, was a great believer in pixies. He maintained that it was the brownies who picked the site of the city he named for himself. His brownies knew what they were doing; today at Port Arthur one refinery alone sprawls over 4800 acres. It contains twenty-two miles of rail and 1400 steel tanks and can handle 23,000,000 barrels of petroleum daily. Across town is a plant almost as large.

World War II gave further impetus to the industrial boom that Spindletop started. Sulphur was taken from beneath the swamps below New Orleans where the pirates of Jean Lafitte had once skulked. The yellow mineral was mined from beneath the coastal plains of Texas as well. At Freeport, Texas, magnesium, so valuable in the construction of lightweight aircraft, is

A mobile oil-drilling unit, designed to drill in up to 100 feet of water, operating out of Corpus Christi, Texas (*Ewing Galloway*)

produced from sea water. Texas City became the site of the nation's first tin smelter. Men bubbled air through butanes to make an acid which was mixed with cotton linters or wood pulp to create wrinkle-resistant cloths. Inks, paints, and artificial rubber were produced from petroleum by-products. In the decade after World War II the chemical industry alone invested eight hundred million dollars in plants on the Mississippi between Baton Rouge and New Orleans. Cadmium and zinc added to the mineral wealth of the coast. Steel mills and shipyards flourished.

To old folks, sitting on the farmhouse gallery with a chinaberry tree planted close by to ward off the fevers, all these changes seem too strange and incredible for belief. But to the millions of Crescent Coasters taking home comfortable pay checks, "living it up" with long weekends at the beach or in flower-hedged yards, the black plume of Spindletop was J-Day . . . the arrival of Justice-long-delayed.

The vast array of industry, from Houston clear around the great Crescent's curve to Fort Myers and Naples, has come providentially at a time when science permits decentralization for both factory and workers. No longer need the plant be hemmed by tenement slums because of horsecar-and-buggy shortcomings. And only the Pacific Coast can rival the Crescent Coast in the United States for year-round environmental pleasures allowed by the forty-hour work week. So the old dream of Spanish and French explorer, of Creole and Scotch-Irish pioneer, of the Longfellows, Farraguts, and Davises, as well as the Prezewskis, Anastasias, and all the other polyglot peoples of four centuries, is come to pass. The day will come, Crescent Coasters fervently believe, when all the South will be remade in their socio-economic image.

Part 5
The Heritage

Preceding page:
Bull Street, Savannah, Georgia

Whom shall we consecrate and set apart as one of our sacred men? Sacred, that all men may see him, be reminded of him, and, by new example added to the old perpetual precept, be taught what is real worth in man. Whom do you wish to resemble? Whom you set on a high column, that all men looking at it, may be continually apprised of the duty you expect from them.

CHARLES FRANCIS ADAMS, 1907

HODDING CARTER

Statues in the Squares

GIVEN ENOUGH MONEY and sculptors and the consent of the states and the communities concerned, I could spend a pleasurable and useful lifetime placing new statues in a multitude of Southern town and courthouse squares.

They would not replace but only supplement the marble figures, "like as like" with their broad-brimmed campaign hats and blanket rolls and grounded muskets, brooding beneath the catalpas and live oaks, the elms and magnolias and sycamores that shadow the public lawns. These weather-stained guardians, doing sentry duty above the inscriptions to the beloved dead, have earned the right to unending vigil. Each is an idealization of the vanished, tatterdemalion legions of the Lost Cause, the typical and the untypical men of a homogeneous region who, most of them, made a poor man's fight of what the rank and file jibed at as "a rich man's war"; who, poor and affluent, gentleman and yeoman and redneck alike, etched with their life-blood a record of courage and perseverance and fealty to homeland so unique as to have earned for it in defeat a brighter page in the annals of combative man than has been allotted to the victors of a myriad of wars.

But the statues in the squares are more than symbols of gallantry in defeat, or the defeat of gallantry. They are also the reminders of, and, in an unstated way, a kind of recompense for the inexcusable aftermath of military subjugation; for they supplanted the plunderers of Reconstruction, whose memory still brought in my boyhood ready curses from the aging veterans of whom we were so proud and not a little afraid. And it was these old men and their ancient womenfolk, unreconstructed and unforgiving, who passed on to sons and grandsons the truth and legends of wrongs which, in the commission and the remembering, make up the saddest of our nation's multiple legacies.

And statues are reminders, lastly, of the true nature of the Southern past and of the South's folk heritage; for beneath the romantic overlay so greatly inspired by a Scots novelist's tales of knightly derring-do was a frontier land, the stamping ground of Davy Crockett and Mike Fink, of Andy Jackson and Sam Houston, of Nolichucky Jack Sevier and Oglethorpe's paupers and the unsubdued sons of the clansmen who fought at Culloden. The warriors in marble bespeak that frontier whose hallmarks are the ready rifle and the white-hot temper, the violent workings of a code of honor, a mistrust of the intruder, and the feudal unity of a people whose fields were bounded all around by wilderness.

Because this is so, because the chiseled sentinels of the Confederacy evoke the frontier as surely as they recall a war and a defeat and a needless, consequential humiliation, I would choose first as their companion figures the likenesses of men whose abilities the frontiersmen respect above all others, or whom they could identify with themselves. They should come, or so I think, from the rosters of warring man and political man, man the singer of songs and teller of tales and preacher of sermons, man the underdog, and the unregimented, maverick man.

Not that the men of other talents—the scientists and the artists and the scholars and the builders of cities—are not as useful or do not require more exacting apprenticeships. They too belong in the courthouse squares. But the others have prior place.

The fighting man . . .

It is understandable, since the vanquished always remember the longest, that the South should have so lavishly memorialized her Confederate dead. They died in a war that their survivors lost. Above their graves a nation-in-being was pounded to nothingness. Understandable, and sad. For before and after them were other Southerners who fought in other wars. While some among these have been remembered, few of them have been honored enough.

What of Nathaniel Bacon of the Colony of Virginia who tested with his life the tyranny which was once the divine right of kings? What of the New Orleans Creoles who died resisting the empire of Spain? What of South

Carolina's Sergeant Jasper, the pirates and the backwoodsmen who destroyed the British at the Battle of New Orleans, and the Southern adventurers who made the War for Texas Independence their jubilant cause? Where are the statues to Jeff Davis' Mississippians and those other soldiers of the Deep South who principally fought the Mexican War?

There should be places for them in many a square which has neglected to honor them; places for the men of San Juan Hill and the fever swamps of Cuba, and of Château-Thierry and Tarawa and Bastogne and the Chosen Reservoir. These Southerners battled as bravely for their country as did their ancestors for the nation that did not live. They belong in the company of Bedford Forrest, the Confederate Jehu, and rollicking Beauty Stuart and young Pelham and dour Stonewall Jackson. It would be better for us all if they stood together in the squares.

And the spellbinders . . .

The argument can be made successfully, I believe, that the English and Scots and Scots-Irish have a peculiar genius for political philosophy and political action, and that a notable characteristic of Protestantism is its evangelical concern with the social order. The frontier South was settled mostly by Protestant migrants from England and Scotland and the north of Ireland and their sons. No wonder, then, that the South has produced and that its people—sometimes to their own detriment—have listened so attentively to the spellbinders of the hustings and the pulpit.

We have honored fully the Southern giants who were our nation's political architects—Jefferson and Madison and Monroe who helped put the colonial jigsaw pieces together, and Henry Clay who strove to keep the pieces joined, and gaunt John Calhoun who made his compatriots willing to take them apart again. But we have not recognized sufficiently the less successful and the later statesmen. It should not be forgotten that for every five men who spoke for secession in the Congress of the United States and in the legislatures of the South, at least one other spoke for moderation and the preservation of the Union. We could do worse than recall them now, and with them the obscure pleaders for the little man in the day of domination by the great landowner and the railroaders. They were in the Southern tradition, the frontier tradition.

So, too, the preachers. The churchmen were among the South's builders; they were the founders of such colleges as Randolph-Macon and Hampton-Sidney, Wofford and Mercer and many another, largely guiding them and staffing their faculties. The preachers of the Second Awakening, inspired by tough James McGready, the South Carolina Presbyterian; Louisiana's Benjamin Morgan Palmer, another Presbyterian, who fought the infamous Louisiana Lottery to a standstill; the circuit riders of Methodism, who brought the gospel to outcasts and renegades and doubters; the ministers who died by the hundreds nursing believers and scoffers alike in the terrible century of Yellow Jack—surely they are as worthy of the South's recognition as of God's. They too should be enshrined in the communities where they were born or where they worked and lived and died.

And the writers . . .

The orator and the preacher have ever thrived best among frontier and rural folk whose pleasures are simple and few and whose hearts and minds are easily captured by the political debaters' thrust and parry, and by the ministers' warnings of sins of the flesh. Greatly welcome too are the ballad makers and the tellers of folk tales. But this has not been as true of the dealer in words that are written instead of spoken or sung; for book learning was not as easily come by in the frontier South nor was as much store set by it as in the cities of the settled eastern seaboard. A suspicion of scribblers or an indifference to what they write, coupled with the extraordinary contribution of the South to American literature, has given rise to the wry jest that more Southerners write books than read them, an exaggeration that may make the point better than does unadorned fact.

Because of this oversight, I would erect many a statue to remind region and nation of the South's writers, so diverse in their output, so numerous, and so studded with the brilliance of genius as to dwarf even New England in the time of her flowering. Save for a handful, among whom Edgar Allan Poe and Sidney Lanier alone surmounted regionalism, they arrived late on the scene, rising from the ashes of the Confederacy to plead its cause in verse and story, and to discover for themselves and thereby to reveal to the nation the many-faceted South of mountaineer and lowlander, seafarer and former slave and an aristocracy in travail. Their patriarchs were William Gilmore Simms and Robert Y. Hayne, and the frontier satirist Joseph C. Baldwin. But they escaped in part from the mold. The South could and did inspire and accommodate a host of local-color writers: Joel Chandler Harris, James Lane Allen, Irwin Russell, and Lafcadio Hearn; and such historical novelists as Mary Johnson and Thomas Nelson Page, romanticists who had little save talent in common with those Southerners who came later and who today all but dominate the American literary scene. Though most of them wrote, then and now, of the frontier South, the South has looked upon them with a wonder that is not always friendly. Prophets more honored beyond their region than in it are Ellen Glasgow, the precise Virginia realist, and Thomas S. Stribling, Thomas Wolfe, Erskine Caldwell, and William Faulkner. Yet some day, they and others will be spoken of with understanding and pride in the land they wrote of and loved. The South may yet recognize its creative critics, whose barbs are needful if only because they prick.

And the mavericks . . .

It is a Southern contradiction that a region which prides itself, and rightfully, upon the individualism and independence of its people has nevertheless demanded of them a nearly blind conformity in matters having to do with regional loyalty, political preferences, and racial attitudes. As even the most casual reader of history knows, this disciplinary demand was the result of the presence of the Negro as a slave, the war which freed him, his utilization as a political pawn after that war, and the determination of the white South, once the end of Reconstruction had been brought about, never again to permit any threat to its political and economic dominance. So it is that the nonconformist, especially if his apostasy is a challenge to this determination, is a rare and a brave person and one against whom the pressures of the entire community are usually exerted. But a democracy requires mavericks; so, in our region which looks upon the challenger with

Monument to the Confederate Dead, at Marietta, Georgia

suspicion, I would pay homage to the sincere and visionary minority who have stood up throughout the tormented generations and said, "But on the other hand—."

There were more of them than might be supposed. They were among the hardiest of Southerners; they not only walked almost alone but were easy targets as they walked. No Southern memorial has been raised to the little New Orleanian, George Washington Cable, who in the '70's and '80's ranked as author and lecturer with Mark Twain and whose characterizations of the Louisiana French remain unsurpassed in our regional literature. The reason for this neglect is that Cable's conscience impelled him to speak against injustice to the Negro, and to criticize certain Southern shibboleths that to his fellows were sacrosanct. George Washington Cable deserved better treatment. So did Walter Hines Page, the North Carolina newspaper editor who likewise protested inequities and dared to lampoon the professional Southern veteran. Two courageous professors of ante-bellum Virginia, George Wythe and St. George Tucker, must have been even more vulnerable than these, for a generation before the War they dared, as members of the William and Mary faculty, to denounce the institution of slavery.

There were dissenters in matters other than race. I would single out men like Charles W. Macune, the Texan who accomplished seventy years ago the consolidation of the small, badly organized farmer groups and with his Farmer's Alliance brought at least passing benefit to desperate men, and unease to the interests that despoiled them.

Above all Southern mavericks I would recognize stubborn Andrew Johnson of Tennessee who loved the South but not its aristocratic secessionists; who, as a Union Democrat, won the Vice-Presidency under Lincoln in 1864; and who, coming to the Presidency when the Great Emancipator was assassinated, suffered and weathered the efforts of his vengeful political foemen to impeach him because they thought him too lenient toward his native South.

And the underdogs . . .

The frontier has ever been lodestar and refuge for the outcast, the dispossessed, and the underdog, for its forests offer sanctuary and its fertility another chance; its indifference to antecedents gives a man the right to prove himself on his own. There were more underdogs than gentry among the pioneers and the landseekers who thrust southward and westward from the Atlantic periphery. Some of them found on the Southern frontier what they were looking for; many did not.

But of all the underdogs of the unfolding South, none had the cards so stacked against them as those who came as slaves. Surely there should be statues here and there to some of the Negroes of the South who in the time of slavery, and in the after-years which were often little better, won honor for themselves and their race and region and nation. The free Negroes of the ante-bellum South—there were 250,000 of them on the eve of the War Between the States—numbered such men as Henry Evans whose North Carolina Methodist congregation was biracial; Austin Dabney, veteran of the Revolution whose farm was a gift of the Georgia legislature and who had been the guest of the governor of his state; rich John Jones, whose Charleston Hotel was among the South's most popular; and Thomy Lafon, New Orleans merchant, money-lender, and philanthropist whose charities knew no color line.

In the near century since Emancipation the list of meritorious Negroes has become so long, and the achievements represented thereon so varied, as to win the prideful admiration of most of their fellow Southerners and fellow Americans. Who would deny an accolade to Booker T. Washington, foremost of his people's spokesman in the early years of freedom; or George Washington Carver, who wrought scientific miracles with the products of the South's farms; or William C. Handy, the music master to whom the city of Memphis *is* rearing a monument; or the poets, James Weldon Johnson, Countee Cullen, Langston Hughes? It is good today for all of us to know that in every field of human endeavor—the arts, science, government, and the rest—can be counted Southern Negroes who for three hundred years have given dignity to the name Underdog.

And the fighters not in uniform . . .

Lastly, I would erect somewhere in the South, preferably deep in the lower Mississippi Valley, another statue, as anonymous and as representative as the graven Confederates of the courthouse squares, but, unlike these, neither armed nor uniformed. This figure would be clad in the work clothes of a farmer or the rough garb of a riverman or the unstylish everyday suit of a small-town citizen. His face would reflect the toil, the frustrations, and the sufferings of a people who have passed through a succession of ordeals such as no other American region has known: the ordeals of flood and of decimation by malaria and of yellow fever; the ordeals of military defeat and of political grinding-down and agricultural ruin and long poverty. The eyes of this unknown and unsoldierly warrior would be fixed upon the far horizon of the frontiersman; and in the set of the shoulders a sensitive observer would perceive the glory of an indestructible people whose struggle for their rightful place in the sun is all but ended.

The dramatic is not the unusual. It is happening daily in our lives.

Attributed to DR. FREDERICK H. KOCH
by Thomas Wolfe

PAUL GREEN

Symphonic Outdoor Drama

A STRANGE THING is happening in the southeastern part of the United States. Along with good roads, new industries, schools, motels, tobacco, vegetables, electronics, and farm fish ponds, the people are going in for a new sort of enterprise in a big way—symphonic outdoor drama.

King Cotton is dying and dramatic art is flourishing!

Well-equipped amphitheaters, some of them costing hundreds of thousands of dollars and subsidized into being by interested citizens, municipalities, historical commissions, and in some cases by actual financial aid from the state governments themselves, as in North Carolina and Virginia, are springing up all over the place.

Local and professional playwrights are writing historical dramas for these amphitheaters. And each summer hundreds of young people—one could say thousands—actors, singers, dancers, technicians, and production staff personnel are assembled from neighboring communities and colleges to put these plays on. And professional talent from the larger Middle-Western cities and from Broadway is most often recruited to help out.

And everybody gets paid for his services.

These are plays, not old-timey pageants. Some of them do incline to the pageant notion in looseness of structure and temporal sequencing of scenes. But the concept behind them and working in them all is one of organic dramatic form. Each has a story to tell, each has suspense as to outcome, characters are arrayed against characters, and issues and results develop from the inner motives, ambitions, feelings, and opposing moral forces.

The South is busy dramatizing its history.

So popular is this form of entertainment becoming that it can be spoken of as something of a people's theater movement—at least the beginning of it. And it is spreading into other parts of the country. Whether it will develop to any sort of fine maturity comparable to the outdoor drama of the ancient Greeks, of course no one can say. But at the moment it looks as if it might. For the productions are getting better as they are getting more numerous all the time.

However, as they thrive they are already threatened. The two most obvious enemies are television and air-conditioning. As time goes on, more and more people may want to stay at home of nights snug in their cool sitting-rooms watching the spew of commercialism and grim gun shooting, or sit in their cool hotel lobbies doing the same.

But for the present the movement is growing. And since millions of automobiles are being sold in America each year and people like to get in them and go somewhere, it may be that these plays will still continue to draw their homefolk crowds and tourists as well, and so things will equal out.

The first of these symphonic outdoor dramas was staged on Roanoke Island, North Carolina, in 1937. The local citizens there got the idea of commemorating the three-hundred and fiftieth anniversary of Virginia Dare's birth on that island and the tragic settlement which Sir Walter Raleigh had attempted there. It was in 1584 that Raleigh first sent out a band of explorers to find a place for a colony in the New World. They hit on Roanoke Island, which they described on their return to England as "the goodliest land under the cope of heaven." In 1585 a hundred men arrived and built a fort there which they called the Citie of Raleigh. But after a year of discouragement they returned home with Sir Francis Drake, leaving fifteen of their fellows to hold the place.

Within a few months Sir Walter sent out what he hoped would be a permanent colony, consisting of a hundred and twenty-one men, women, and children. They found that the fifteen men had been killed by the Indians or drowned trying to escape. The newcomers took possession of the fort and began to clear the land, build houses, and plant fields. Here on August 18, 1587, Virginia Dare was born, the first child of English parents in the New World and the granddaughter of the governor of the colony, John White. And here two days later the Indian chief, Manteo, was baptized in the Christian faith. A few weeks later White returned to England for supplies and was caught up in the war with Spain. He did not return to Roanoke Island till some three years had passed. When he arrived, he found the fort ruined, the houses fallen in, and the people gone. And no one knows to this day what happened to the colony. It has been one of history's greatest mysteries.

The citizens of this island and nearby communities decided to memorialize these historic events. They got together and raised money among themselves and with the additional help of the WPA in labor and materials built an amphitheater for the celebration near the water's edge right where the ancient Citie of Raleigh had stood.

The play written for this commemoration was called *The Lost Colony*, and it told of the sufferings and trials of this tragic band of pioneers. Most of the action had to be imagined, for the historical records as to individuals were of the scantiest. The play ended with the colonists marching off into the wilderness to escape a threatened attack from the Spaniards, disappearing "into the vast unknown, out of our sight forever," as the old historian in the drama said.

Now this story had to deal with the entire group of people and not with just a few, for all had suffered, all had struggled, and all had perished. Naturally as the action proceeded, some characters rose to more prominence than others as always happens in life. But essentially it was a drama of them all that had to be told.

It turned out that in bringing these people to dramatic life before a big outdoor theater audience, I found use for nearly all the elements of theater art—spectacle, music, song, dance, pantomime, chorus (we had the services of the fine Westminster Choir from Princeton, New Jersey), sound effects, and a microphone with amplification for narration when needed.

But all these elements had to do service to the story line of the piece, and they were made to adhere and cohere into a thickened unity of effect, helping to keep the narrative moving and infused with feeling as it moved right on up to the dynamic and explosive climax. Otherwise we would have had something of the dull pageant chronicling mentioned before.

The characters in the play and the theatrical elements accompanying and surrounding and sometimes spilling in on them were used much like the instruments, say, in an orchestra—each coming forward to fulfillment, sometimes singly and sometimes in company, and then retiring and giving place to others, and they in turn yielding to others likewise, and all strongly controlled by the definite story line. And always there was music, music!

A true dramatic democracy.

In looking around for a term to describe this sort of play, I hit on the word "symphonic," using it in the original Greek sense of "sounding together," that is, a working and the co-operating of all matters each with the other. It seemed to fit.

The Roanoke piece was meant to run only the nine weeks of the one season celebration. But it proved so popular that it was repeated the next season and has been repeated every summer since, except for a blackout period during the war years, running six nights a week from late June to Labor Day. (This is the usual schedule for all of these plays.) So it has gone on playing summer after summer, some seasons good, some bad, but still managing to survive these twenty-three years.

Other localities around the South got interested in having their history dramatized. In 1939 the people of Fayetteville, North Carolina, celebrated the founding of their town by staging *The Highland Call*, a play of the same type written about the Scotch settlers in the Cape Fear River valley and their famous heroine Flora McDonald who lived among them there and who suffered a tragic upheaval of her life because of her Tory sentiments in the Revolutionary War.

Then, in 1947, the people of Virginia, under the leadership of the former governor, Colgate W. Darden, Jr., later president of the University of Virginia, built a beautiful brick amphitheater on the shore of Lake Matoaka (Pocahontas) at the edge of the College of William and Mary woods in the outskirts of Williamsburg, and *The Common Glory*, another symphonic outdoor drama dealing with Thomas Jefferson's fight for democracy was staged there. Working with Darden were a number of young theater people from the University of Virginia and William and Mary—Althea Hunt, Roger Boyle, Howard Scammon, Roger and Sue Sherman, Al Haak, Carl Fehr, Myra Kinch, Anthony Manzi, and especially the dedicated Allen Matthews. The play caught on from the first and was a success. It has played every summer since then, this being the thirteenth season.

In 1950 a group of citizens in western North Carolina built a stunning mountainside amphitheater at the village of Cherokee in the Great Smokies, and Kermit Hunter, a talented young playwright at Chapel Hill, was commissioned to write the story of the tragic Cherokee Indian people and their "trail of tears." Hunter turned out an imaginative and touching script, and the production became a resounding success.

Following this, Hunter turned his attention to the Revolutionary history of the North Carolina piedmont. An amphitheater was built by the citizens of Boone, and here was staged in 1952 his *Horn in the West*, which told the story of the patriots' rebellion against the royal governor, William Tryon. It was a success too and has been playing to appreciative audiences every season since.

Of course tourism often has something to do with the local citizens' interest in these plays. That is only normal and healthy. But commercialism is not the first interest. Southern history is.

A statistician friend of mine recently worked up a few figures on the dramas that have been staged in North Carolina and Virginia since the movement got started. He found that some four million people have attended the plays in the two states, paying between eight and nine million dollars in at the box office. And with the addition of tourist items of gas, hotel, food, and purchased doodads added, he concluded that some of the localities had made more money out of symphonic drama than any other preceding business. He estimated, for instance, that the eight plays in North Carolina and Virginia have already brought to these two states forty to fifty million dollars in new income.

And so it has gone—with other projects starting up in Tennessee, Kentucky, Florida, and here and there a sporadic one in the middle Atlantic states, in the midwest, in the northwest, the west and the southwest—with their own local writers, actors, directors and staffs.

If the Roanoke Island drama was the first of these plays and somewhat set the type, the beginning of the matter goes back further than 1937 for its inspiration. It goes back to one man—to Professor Frederick H. Koch, or "Proff" as we students at the University of North Carolina affectionately called him.

Koch came to Chapel Hill from North Dakota in 1918 as a professor of dramatic literature. He started a class in playwriting—an unheard-of thing in the whole sand-and-clay reaches of the South. He founded the Carolina Playmakers, with folk plays as his hobby.

He had the wild theory that everybody was an artist—more or less. And most everybody was a playwright too if he only knew it, he said, and his business as a teacher was to show that this was so.

He was an enthusiast, and he filled his students with something of his own joy and enthusiasm. He taught us all—Thomas Wolfe, Jonathan Daniels, Betty Smith, Hubert Heffner, George Denny, Legette Blythe, Kay Kyser, Whitner Bissell, Robert Armstrong, John Harden, Lamar Stringfield, Shepperd Strudwick, Douglass Watson, Robert Dale Martin, Frances Gray Patton—to call some names at random—and dozens and dozens of others. He taught us all to look around us with fresh eyes, to write about our own localities, about what we knew, about our own folklore, legends, customs, and traditions, and especially about our own local folk history.

During his more than twenty-five years at Chapel Hill, Koch and his associates kept a ferment of playwriting and producing of original folk-plays going on. And through touring groups, published volumes, and university extension services, the cause of playmaking was spread throughout the state.

When the time came for the writing of *The Lost Colony* Koch gave me a lot of encouragement and was the advisory director of that play for its first two seasons. "Proff" died in 1945—as he would have wished to die—suddenly and in the midst of a fine creative activity.

And the work went on.

Samuel Selden, a quiet gracious man, but also an enthusiast, succeeded Koch as head of the dramatic arts department at the University and director of the Carolina Playmakers. And he has been a key figure in pushing forward the symphonic drama movement beyond the borders of the state. He has directed a number of these plays, among them *The Lost Colony*, *Forever This Land*, *Wilderness Road*, *The Confederacy*, and *The Stephen Foster Story*.

Closely associated with Selden have been Harry E. Davis, John W. Parker, Kermit Hunter, Foster Fitz-Simons, Irene Smart, Kai Jurgenson, and Thomas Patterson—to mention a few—all disciples and hard-working evangelists in the Koch tradition.

I believe Koch's instinct was right in coming to the South to put his dramatic theories to work. I don't think he and his followers would have had the same success in any other part of the country. The South was the one place to do it.

And there are a number of reasons why.

We are a people and a land rich with dramatic material—stuffed with folklore, superstition, folksongs, folk hymns, ballads, Negro spirituals, legends, wild tales, night-riders, feuds and murders, and even a stew of prejudice. And above all we are a land chock-full of history and historic characters, of battles, of heroes, of statesmen, and of colorful stentorian demagogues.

We are a people who have suffered mightily. And suffering is the very heart of dramatic literature, of any literature no doubt. We have known the long grind of poverty, have groaned with the tortures of our conscience over the evils of slavery and race prejudice, have endured defeat in war, been overrun and occupied by an invader (even our brother!), had our homes and cities burned, our fields devastated and stained with the blood of thousands of our young men. And we ourselves helped do the burning and the staining. The rest of the country has never felt these evils to any like extent.

Our very existence as a people here in the South has been something of an epic tragic drama—a sort of huge and terrifying Job story, if the truth were acknowledged. And no doubt it was but logical that as time went on and the bent of the age got right that we should—for sympathy's sake if for no other reason—begin to set forth to the world something of our story not only in fiction and poetry but in drama.

Our different experience and conditioning have helped, I believe, make possible our present literary renaissance as well as the symphonic drama movement. And the South is different. We have an almost idolatrous love of the past, of our heritage, of our tradition, for instance. We also have a strong sense of place. We love our neighborhood, our home, our friends and kinsfolk with a passionate love. And we are agrarian people, an outdoor people. We belong to the outdoors. There is something about gathering under stars to witness one of these dramas which naturally works its magic in us. And our Southern summer nights, never too cold and rarely too hot, are conducive to such gatherings.

We Southerners especially love spectacle. We like flag-waving, marching men, bugles sounding, and drums beating. We delight in battle scenes, cannon flashing, and the smoke and turmoil of clashing arms and Indians on the warpath. We like dancing and singing, music and good speech-making too. We usually get a good dose of all these in the outdoor dramas. And the people listen with joyous intentness as, say, one of our pioneer leaders turns from his bloody warring and mounts a stump to declaim the principles he believes in and for which he and his followers are fighting: "Let the wilderness drive us forth as wanderers across the earth—scatter our broken bones upon these sands. It shall not kill the purpose that brought us here. Yea, hear what once Sir Walter said, the victory lieth in the struggle, not the city won!"

And we heartily applaud General Robert E. Lee when in the play, *The Confederacy*, he declares to an emissary from Lincoln who offers peace for surrender, "I will carry on to the last ounce of my strength, fight on till here in my heart I know I have done all that can be done. My men, they will not quit, and I will not quit. Let it be said of us in future generations if anything be said—they gave all they had, they would not weaken, they stood and failed not to the last!"

The heroes in these plays then are usually he-men and the heroines she-women, and most always they are depicted as being up against terrific odds and enemies—all healthy outside enemies and not inside self-sick and teeny pathological ones. These characters need a lot of room to strut their stuff in, to wage their struggles in, and sitting outdoors we like to see them have plenty of space to do that strutting, that struggling. A small intense psychological drama would die in its tracks in one of these amphitheaters.

And finally these symphonic dramas often gain a strange and gripping sense of living actuality and dramatic realism from being staged on the spot or near where some of the heroic characters lived and died and the historic events themselves took place. And throughout the land there are hundreds of such places—waiting.

However successful the movement has been to date, it is still in its infancy. But as our people learn more and more about the theater, as our public becomes more and more conditioned to seeing these plays, I think the writing and the production will vastly improve. And the subject matter will broaden too. History will no longer be the main source to draw on. The imagination of the poets will be turned loose to new creations of their own. And the greatest need at the present is for talented playwrights. A mighty storehouse of native dramatic subject matter already awaits their using.

Long before Aeschylus, Sophocles, and Euripides made their glowing contributions to the world's dramatic literature, a multitude of now nameless writers helped prepare the way with their beginning dramatic spectacles on the scattered hillsides of Greece. Perhaps it is not too much to hope that we, too, here in the South in this symphonic outdoor drama movement, are helping prepare the way for something wonderful to come in this land of ours.

I'd like to believe so.

I do.

The family has transcended all other interest and affections in the South. It acts as a bridge linking the Southerner to his past.

ELLINGTON WHITE—"The View from the Window"

RUPERT B. VANCE

The Southern Family Today

HARDLY ANYTHING seems more remote from the changing South of today than the frontier and the plantation. Yet if one wishes to understand what is different and distinctive about the Southern family, one must begin with the frontier farm and the plantation family. This is where tradition and social class were fixed; this indicates whence the family came and what it lost when it became urban, middle-class, and modern.

On the frontier and on the farms of the yeomanry, the family was a self-contained unit, the one major social institution. Young people married early, had many children; and those children were trained in the physical tasks necessary for subsistence and survival. Nobody had much, but what they had they owed to themselves and to the land. Every boy learned work —hunting, fishing and frontier farming; every girl learned to do rough household tasks, to listen to the menfolks and not talk back too much. The family was homespun, rough, self-reliant, patriarchal, and stable. There were few other institutions either to help or to adjust to.

If the frontier family did not teach urbanity and poise, it did much to fix character. Personality was direct, frank, and sometimes aggressive. Children got what education they got at home; they minded their parents; and when they could stand discipline no longer, the boys left home and set up homes of their own. When they were asked, girls married and likewise departed.

This was the first nursery of the life of the common man and woman of the South; this is what they had, and this is what they could expect. Nearest this mode of life today are the farm tenants, the small mountain farmers; in fact, the life of the small Southern farmers. As Ellen Glasgow made the distinction, they and their descendants are "good people but not good family." The particular values of the South—what most people wanted but never had—came out of the traditions of the agrarian ruling class, the planter and the limited plantation aristocracy. Here were economic competence, gracious living, influence, and even power. Family stability ranked high, and Southerners were credited with being "traditional, romantic, chivalrous, and incurably idealistic."

"At their best," Francis B. Simpkins writes, "the governing families possessed modesty and good breeding": in other words, much informal geniality without formality, marked social distinction. "Southern charm reached its culmination in the Southern lady, a creature who could be decorative without sacrificing any privilege except the masculine prerogative of holding office."

On farms and plantations, however, the rural family was the producing unit. The father was the foreman who organized the work. There was no place for mature females outside marriage and the family. If a sister was so unfortunate as not to marry, she came to live with a married brother or sister as the Maiden Aunt—"that household drudge with social status." Here were horrible examples of what divorce would mean for a woman who had to go back to her parents.

This picture serves to indicate how far the Southern family has gone in social change. In some parts of the region and in some classes of Southern society, a wife's relation to her husband may have resembled that of a child to a parent or of a servant to a master. But, if such patriarchal families once existed, those days are gone.

Central to the structure and interaction of the family is the position of woman. There are two sides to this position, respect and equality. In the Older South, woman was placed on a pedestal of respect—the respect due woman in her role of wife and mother. For a brief coming-out period, the girl drew admiration in the role of glamour girl—the Southern Belle, a type that F. Scott Fitzgerald was able to depict in several revealing portraits, for he married one. The emancipation of women moved South when, to girls as to men, a period of independence came to intervene between childhood and marriage. Formerly, a farm girl at the age of sixteen to eighteen passed out of the control of her father and mother and into that of a husband with no taste of intervening freedom. Now that college or employment intervenes between parental control and the beginning of married life, the Southern girl, like her sisters elsewhere, awakens to ideas of her own independence and equality.

Divorces are more frequent when women are able to support themselves, when wives are in demand, and when they can use the law for their own protection. A marriage based on equality will sooner end in divorce than in the subjection of the wife, and the divorce will more often be of the wife's seeking. In spite of these changes, the Southern family still remains more stable than its national counterpart and proportionately fewer divorces are granted in the South on the wife's petition.

In the two main currents of migration—one from the rural districts to the cities, the other from settled areas to newly opened territory—family breakdown is more often found where the current stops, not where it begins. Divorce is higher in the West than in the South; it is higher in the South's growing cities than in the countryside. Disorganization of the Negro family is greater in Northern cities, least on Southern farms.

Emancipation means that the roles of the Southern Belle and the Southern Lady have given way to the problem of the career woman. There are women in the South who give themselves unreservedly to their families, and ask no other boon. Sometimes these families are grateful; sometimes they find "Mom" too possessive. As elsewhere, the intelligent housewife finds a need to divide herself among husband, children, and home, and still build something for herself. In the South today, there are women working not because they have to, but because they want to. The significant thing is that with its traditions and its aspirations, Southern opinion is not especially dismayed by the present picture of the middle-class working wife and mother.

The new generation has settled the problem of a career and a home with the decision characteristic of youth. Faced, in a prospective loss of her man to the services, with the independent life of the Career Girl once advocated by feminists, "nice" middle-class girls learn pothooks and typewriting, marry their men, put them through college, bear their babies, and live in veterans' villages all the while.

"What has become of chivalry?" writes an unreconstructed Southerner. "I waited for my wife until I could support her. My daughter married her fiancé in order to work *his* way through college. And as far as I can tell, he thought it was a good thing, too." So has passed the legend of the Southern Belle along with that of the flapper.

The temptation is to take the rural family and the ruling class as the mode and to neglect the family life of the working class and the new middle classes rising in the South. For the common man, the working-class family made its first transition from agrarian to industrial regime by moving into the company-owned cotton mill village: "home of buried Anglo-Saxons," Frank Tannenbaum called it in the early 1920's. Here the working class family in the South went through its Industrial Revolution. For the farm family this meant the assimilation of the work of wage-earning women to the workaday world of men. Yet marriage continued to have its basis in the difference between the sexes. Insofar as women's work and training have been masculine, ability and motivation for homemaking may be lowered. In the wage-earning classes where standards are lower and harder to maintain, "a great deal of the misery to which the working classes are subjected in their homes," according to an older report of the proceedings of the London divorce court, "arises from the inability of women when they get married to render their homes comfortable and attractive."

Astute observers drew convincing pictures of the three periods of poverty associated with the family cycle of the unskilled working class. As a child in a large family he lives at a poverty level. For a while before he marries, the grown young man lives at the level of competence of his wages. Then, as his children begin to arrive, the family again goes below the poverty level. The growing youngsters go into child labor. With the aid of their wages, the family once more rises above the poverty line. The children leave home to set up homes of their own. The old couple, now unable to work, sink back into poverty for the last time.

This was the conventional picture of the Southern cotton-mill village before Social Security and higher wages—a company-owned town of working wives and mothers, of child labor and low incomes. The Southern working-class family has since outlived this portrait. Working-class families are no longer called "lintheads" simply because they live in cotton-mill villages; they have escaped the drab limitations of the "one-crop industry" and its child labor. Employment for the wage-earning family is diversified along a whole industrial range. Village housing has been sold to workers. The better-paid workers constitute a new middle class, and the South no longer buries wage-earning Anglo-Saxons.

The size of the family continues to be larger in the South than elsewhere, but birth rates among rural people are declining, partly through a differentiation into what can be called "reflective" and "unreflective" family types. Certain studies indicate the difficulties the common folk have in finding in the institution of the family satisfaction for a multitude of desires—for affection, security, sex, and improved living standards—while carrying the burden of "involuntary" reproduction. This area of involuntary reproduction is, however, continuously being narrowed by the spread of education and knowledge of health measures. Urbanization has lowered the birth rate; the distinction between the "reflective" and "unreflective" family now appears to depend on whether the wife has had a high school education—a change which also has meaning in the transition from the "patriarchal" to the "companionship" family.

In spite of education and urbanization, the age of marriage grows younger. Thus, with the great decline in infant deaths, family planning is the one force making for the small-size family. The Negro family remains large. The rural white family still shows decline in the average number of its children. The middle-class family in the South is now as likely to have four children as three or two. This is generally accepted as representative of the new prosperity which is reaching professional and white-collar groups, rather than indicating a return to involuntary reproduction. Along with the revival of interest in children has grown a less harsh family discipline and a longer period of schooling.

The Negro family, as Franklin Frazier has presented it, is an essential part of this picture. Under slavery the Negro family emerged as a matriarchy—"a natural organization based upon the physical and emotional ties between the mother and her off-spring." The attitude of "husband and wife," whose "marriage" had no legal basis, was influenced in the early family by the degree to which the Negro had assimilated the sex and family morality of the whites. Among the house servants and those of mixed bloods, and in areas where the plantation became a social as well as an industrial institution, the father and husband played a more important role; gradually the Negro family acquired institutional characteristics, with traditions of sex and family morality.

In its struggle against poverty, limited education, and instability, the Negro family has also achieved new institutional sanctions among those acquiring middle-class status. The break in domestic manners, in household care, and in family mores between upper and lower classes are as complete among Negroes as in any group in our Western culture. Girls brought up in middle-class homes are shielded from contact with boys whose behavior may be uncouth because of class origins. Hylan Lewis in *Blackways of Kent* has distinguished between "respectable" and "unrespectable" lower classes among Negroes, largely on the basis of whether they have developed habits of sobriety and assimilated middle-class family morality. While the urban Negro family may show stability less than the traditional rural family of the South, it is nevertheless on its way to assimilation of the democratic standards of middle-class family life.

In this account of family life, what is essence and what is accident? The family has its inner life of conflict and affection in a unity of interacting personalities—man and woman, parent and child, brothers and sisters.

It may be that the inner, subjective elements are universal; only the environment and status aspects are regional and thus Southern. Certain notable Southern novelists fuse the two. While Ellen Glasgow is able to portray the Virginian's concern with questions of family background and social status, Erskine Caldwell caricatures family life among the "poor whites"—rough frontier humor applied to sensuality and sex, subjects that frontier writers never treated as humorous. William Faulkner has what is rare in the novels of our time, writes Malcolm Cowley: "a warmth of family affection, brother for brother and sister, the father for his children—a love so warm and proud that it tries to shut out the rest of the world." In comparison Cowley feels that married love in Faulkner seems coldly calculating and illicit love an irresistible flame. Thomas Wolfe depicts the compelling force of family life and in *Look Homeward, Angel* tells in the round of the growth of a "strange, wild boy in a strange, wild family" without recourse to Freudian myths. And, no one since Charles Dickens—not even Dickens—has dealt so powerfully with death and bereavement in the family.

The Southern family has moved to town; it has become working class and middle class; its women are emancipated; they work "for gain" before and after marriage. Its children are less numerous; they are fashioned by the school, the public playground, the scout troop, and the church; their discipline is less authoritative and more permissive.

The Southern family, in short, is going through all the changes that have happened to the family elsewhere as society shifted from agriculture to industry, from the simple life to a more complex environment.

In their unfavorable opinion of the nature of the soil of our country, our forefathers were utterly mistaken. The native weeds were scarcely destroyed before white clover and different kinds of grass made their appearance.

JOSEPH DODDRIDGE, 1824

EUGENE BUTLER

Tall Grass

WE HAD RIDDEN forty miles through a rich green countryside, lush with tall grass interspersed here and there with forests of stately pine. Cattle, fat and indolent, stared at us as we rode by. Finally, my friend, a Southerner by birth but long gone from his native land, exclaimed: "You know, we haven't seen but three or four cotton fields in the last hour. What's happened to cotton down here? Looks like this country has 'gone to grass.' "

Between 1940 and 1958, the South cut cotton production by ten million acres; with these lost acres went five million people. Cotton is still important in parts of the South and adds hundreds of millions of dollars to its annual income. But in an area whose political and economic life was once dominated by King Cotton, farm operations now revolve around grass and cattle and trees. It is said that:

"Negroes are moving north
Yankees are coming south
Cotton has gone west
Cattle are shifting east."

Certainly, the cattle are shifting from the West into the Southeast, and the South is fast becoming the "tall grass" region of the nation.

In 1940, the South harvested 103 million acres in crops. In 1958, the acreage fell to 86½ million acres. Meanwhile, since 1930, pastures of all kinds have climbed from 152 million acres to 222 million acres—about 75 per cent; the number of cattle is up 130 per cent.

Nearly half the beef cows in the United States old enough to drop a calf are in the South, if we include all of Texas and Oklahoma as South. And this increase in the number of Southern cattle is not so startling as the tremendous improvement in quality. Only a few years ago, a cattle buyer would seldom see a Prime calf (i.e., top grade) in Southern feeder calf sales. By 1958, most of them were at least Choice or Good (second and third grade) calves, and many of them were Prime. It is safe to say that Southern cattle jumped two market grades in fifteen years.

Stockmen are finding in the South a grassland utopia. With land values and the outlay for feed and storage comparatively low, the South can offer a lower capital investment per cow than any other section of the nation. So it is that stockmen seeking greener pastures have come South from all parts of the nation.

Favored by forty-five inches annual rainfall and two hundred days of growing weather over most of its area, the South has a marked advantage in the production of meat and milk. Contemporary grazing records are almost unbelievable, particularly since only a few years ago Southern pasture was being defined as "a grassless area enclosed with two strands of barbed wire."

Sam Neville of Bulloch County, Georgia, who won his state's 1957 Grazing System and Feed Production Contest, carried his livestock through the summer on three-fifths of an acre per mature beef animal; in winter months, his pastures did even better.

From Florida comes a report of a half-ton of beef per acre per year from a heavily fertilized pasture with fourteen to sixteen inches of irrigation water. Each day the cattle were on this pasture, they put on 1.8 pounds per head. Days of grazing figured out 696 cattle days per acre. There is another report of a ton of beef per acre from the Everglades Experiment Station, Belle Glade.

The carrying capacity of our best Southern pastures is equal, or superior, to top pastures in other parts of the nation. Stock may not gain quite as much per day on these Southern pastures due to hot weather part of the year. But add up the grazing from a much longer period, and the total for the year is unsurpassed in any other section.

Grassland agriculture was a long time returning to the South. In the earliest days, there was unlimited range. Little attempt was made to improve pastures or quality of stock. And for many years the South had more livestock and less meat and milk than any other part of the nation. Periodically, particularly after a few years of low cotton prices, there were interest flurries in crop rotations, improved pastures, and livestock. Merino sheep were "in style" in the early 1800's; so were Berkshire hogs in the 1840's. But always the pasture enthusiasts rammed hard against a general disrespect for grass. Even crab grass, the "poor man's hay," was looked down upon. And swift-spreading, deep-rooting Bermuda was considered a pest, the mortal enemy of cotton choppers and corn hoers.

Tall grass finally gained ascendancy in the South through a combination of fortuitous circumstances. Long years of excessive production of row crops had challenged nature to do its worst to Southern soils. Ravaged fields bearing the unsightly scars of erosion became the trademark of Southern agriculture. Now, finally, farmers turned to grass. At first, soil and crop authorities promoted winter legumes. Legumes are the Samaritans of the crop world. With the help of bacteria, they take nitrogen from the air and store it in the soil, where it is used by less fortunate crops. Later, when grasses were used with legumes, the South began to make substantial progress in restoring soil vigor and productiveness. It is the permanent grasses that send roots deep into the ground and, by adding organic matter to the soil, restore lost youth and vigor. On a steep slope, grasses do a ten-times better job than cotton in holding soil and water. Usually, land in grass and legumes half the time will produce more bales of cotton, bushels of corn, or pounds of peanuts or tobacco during a ten-year period than similar land in these row crops all the time.

Erosion and soil exhaustion would not have been enough to bring grassland farming had they not coincided with the great exodus from row crops due to heavy surpluses and low prices of cotton and other cash crops during the early thirties. It was only when the South reached the point of no possible return to a system that produced ravaged soils and a cash crop crisis that grassland agriculture finally came to stay. Here, at long last, was a practical way to rebuild exhausted soils, while producing a living income.

Bermuda grass, Dallis grass, Johnson grass, and carpet grass have been with us for many years. And there have also been well-adapted legumes, such as white and crimson clovers and Lespedeza. Then, with the time ripe for a tremendous surge of interest in grassland farming, scientists found and developed several super-duper grasses specifically adapted to our regions. In the Upper South, tall fescue gave many sections their first real opportunity to "go into livestock." In the Lower South, Bahia and Pangola revolutionized pastures. But of all its forage plants, Coastal Bermuda is the South's most amazing. Developed at, and named for, the Coastal Plains Experiment Station at Tifton, Georgia, "Coastal" is a hybrid with an unprecedented capacity to produce an immense tonnage of high-class forage. Moreover, it is a greedy deep-rooted grass that laps up fertilizer the way a hound-dog swills pot licker. It is a standard performance for "Coastal" to send out

Jersey cattle grazing on sweet Sudan grass, Alabama

runners ten feet long, covering an area twenty feet in diameter.

Today, livestock farmers are finding that commercial fertilizers can be made to pay as well on pastures as on row crops. Two hundred pounds of nitrogen, properly balanced with phosphoric acid and potash, have produced nearly seven hundred pounds of beef to the acre on Coastal Bermuda. Every pound of this two hundred of nitrogen produced an additional two pounds of beef. This means that if cattle market at twenty-five cents a pound, a twelve-cent investment in nitrogen for Southern grasslands will return fifty cents' worth of beef. Virginians claim that proper fertilization makes it possible for stock to graze two weeks later in the fall and two weeks earlier in the spring. Yes, indeed, commercial plant food is a splendid investment for the man who has pasture and wants more meat and milk to the acre. A dollar so invested can bring a three- to five-dollar return in grazing.

What of the future? Amazing new developments in pasture improvement and in the livestock world promise to revolutionize the production of meat and milk before the young grow old. If we are to have 225 million people by 1975, and 300 million by the year 2000, they will each want as much meat and milk as we do. Food needs are expected to double by 2000 A.D. And 70 per cent of the undeveloped land resources of the United States suitable for cultivated crops and pastures are in the South. We are the last great frontier of productive land in the nation; we have all the advantages required to make Dixieland the Meatland of America.

It was only about twenty-five years ago that Southerners began to think it important to learn pasture "know-how." Already, there is talk of a ton of beef per acre of pasture; a thousand-pound yearling is the goal of the commercial beef herd of the future. Probably when we do produce a thousand-pound beef animal at twelve months of age, it will be a Brahman-cross calf grazing Coastal Bermuda pasture. Such a calf will make our present day six- or seven-hundred-pound yearling look mighty puny.

We have already come a long way. A piney-woods cow needed ten to fifteen acres of native grass to keep alive. She lost in weight from September to March just about what she gained from March to September. And the calf she brought every other year weighed about three hundred pounds at weaning. Dr. Glenn Burton, leader of the science team that discovered Coastal Bermuda, estimates that annual gains on such pastures at best would not have exceeded fifteen pounds of beef per acre. With two-hundred pounds of nitrogen per acre, the Coastal Plains Experiment Station has produced 696 pounds of beef to the acre of Coastal Bermuda in one season. Over a period of several years, an average of three and one-half animals per acre have grazed this pasture 220 days per year, with average daily gains of 1.2 pounds per head. Speculating on what might be done with more know-how in the years ahead, Dr. Burton forecasts that an annual gain of 2680 pounds of beef per acre per year is not beyond the realm of probability.

A pasture potential of 2680 pounds of beef is well over a hundred times that of the South's native grasses. Yet a hundred years ago, a prediction that Southern pastures would one day produce fifty pounds of beef a year would have been equally rash.

Aside from the vast potential of Southern pastures, new developments in the livestock field, such as beat-the-heat research, systemic insecticides, and chemical tenderization of meat, all seem to be designed to give the South decided advantages in the production of meat and milk.

A warm moist climate has always been a ready invitation to insect pests to take heavy toll of Southern livestock, particularly internal parasites. Already great progress has been made in the control of internal parasites. Now that we have systemic insecticides, the pests that prey on Southern livestock are in for a rude surprise. Taken internally and circulated through the animal's system, these wonder-working insecticides enable "the cow to bite the bug." They promise to take the insect curse off of Southern livestock. Poultry and hog parasites, now presenting growers with a 350-million-dollar bill annually, may be completely eliminated by 1965.

Using the heat tolerance of the humpbacked Brahman and other breeds from hot countries, Southern cattle are being bred to produce well under our high summer temperatures. Insulation and air conditioning of barns and other shelters, plus new ideas about night grazing and shade in pastures, are making Southern livestock more comfortable. Research workers are finding that there is such a thing as a "cool" ration for livestock. As the housewife offers her family a cooling meal on a hot summer day, so we can expect that Southern livestock farmers will soon be providing their stock a ration to maintain a lower body temperature, resulting in greater efficiency in meat and milk production.

Until recently it has been believed that fat makes beef tender and that cattle must be fattened on expensive grain for an extended period in the feed lot to produce the highest-quality beef. But researchers are now finding that the old idea that fat invariably makes meat tender is all wrong. A vast amount of research is under way to put tender beef within the range of the average guy's pocketbook. Efforts are being made to tenderize and otherwise influence the quality of meat, both before and after the death of the animal. Such things as feeding sugar to cattle and hogs, subjecting animals to stress and exercise, injection of enzymes, and the use of tranquilizers are being tried.

Chemical or enzymatic tenderizers injected into the carcass are under experimental test at state colleges and elsewhere. Beef carcasses, with a minimum of fat, will be processed with chemicals to produce tender steaks. Tough beef muscles will no longer present a challenge to artificial teeth. In fact, scientists contend that best results are obtained by tenderizing steaks from tough lean types of beef. Regardless of just what method is found most acceptable in tenderizing meat, it is a development of large significance. Anything that is done to improve the tenderization of beef is certain to have a tremendous economic impact on the cattle industry. And it seems a safe prediction that once tenderization really gets in high gear, it will be a great boon to the Tall Grass stockmen of the South.

Let's admit the South still has a way to go before it can hope to reach its tremendous potential as the dominant livestock-producing area of the nation. We had too long a tradition as a one-crop area, and too recently departed from it, to develop all our natural advantages for yet a while. We still face the difficulty of making "cowhands" out of "hoe hands." Nonetheless, the signs show that Tall Grass, the pest of King Cotton's reign, *is* rebuilding the South.

There is a new spirit abroad in the South which is building modern factories in ancient cotton fields.

WILLIAM T. POLK—"Southern Accent"

J. W. FANNING

The Job

FROM ONE END of the South to the other, factories are rising and new businesses are being created. This is the industrial South in the making, long the dream of its leaders. From thirty thousand industries in 1939 to fifty-four thousand industries in 1954 is a story of tremendous progress. And the number continues to grow.

Equally fantastic is the approximate 800 per cent rise in the "value added by manufacturing" during this same period. This expansion of industry across the South has provided employment for thousands of persons from its farms, and has reduced the rate of migration of young people. The gain in the number of business firms in the South has been at a rate much faster than that for the United States as a whole. Agriculture is finally being "balanced with industry."

What has the South to offer to industrial establishments? It's a good question. For many years the majority of industries in the South concentrated on textiles, lumber, and food processing. They were generally associated with low capital investment per worker, and developed to utilize the abundant stocks of cotton and timber. In the early 1950's these industries still employed around 60 per cent of all the area's manufacturing workers.

World War II and postwar years brought exciting new developments. An amazing growth is taking place in those industries which require a relatively large capital investment per worker. Among these are chemical plants, pulp and paper mills, and primary and fabricated metal plants. The development of Kingsport and Nashville, Tennessee, as printing centers and the appearance of "Tanner of North Carolina" and the "Tog Shop" in fashion advertisements in *The New Yorker* and other ultrasophisticated publications are among examples in evidence. The world's familiarity with Oak Ridge, Cape Canaveral, and TVA is, in itself, indicative of the tremendous surge in electronic and atomic industry developing below the Potomac.

Many reasons have been given for industrial development in the South. The promotional activities of trade groups have been prominently mentioned. So have community and regional developmental corporations. The provision of facilities by local communities is another method to which progress is attributed. All of these have been effective. But the basic reasons for industrial development in the South are its social and economic advantages in people, in climate, and in natural resources. These are assets of considerable proportions. By no means a minor factor has been the rural environment of the South. Industry finds more pleasant homes in the Southland's villages and countryside.

Despite the trek into the cities, the majority of people remain in rural settings. Much of the rural environment is and will be retained. Community planning and the development of "greenbelts" around urban centers is under way. The evidence exists in better rural roads, the extensions of urban facilities, and the encouragement given to "hold your residence in the country." How successful these efforts will be in maintaining a large rural population is yet to be determined; progress is significant.

In common with the rest of the nation, the South has experienced a sharp decline in its farm population. Within a span of less than twenty years, five million people left southern farms. This rate will probably not be maintained, but the trend toward fewer farm people in the South will continue. As the farming population drops, the region logically develops its urban centers, and extends city facilities to those suburbs and RFD's where so many Southerners choose to live even though working "in town."

The South remains proud of its rural heritage. It has looked with favor upon a large farm population and strong rural communities. Its ante-bellum philosophy has largely revolved around small farms, large families, rugged independence, and the dignity of work. Thus today the South finds itself in the midst of both industrial and agricultural crises, trying as best it can to guide the dynamic developments into a better balanced and stronger economy. The single goal is, obviously, to achieve living standards for Southerners equal to those of other American regions.

In 1950, for the first time, the number of full-time workers employed in manufacturing exceeded the number engaged in agriculture.

Between 1940 and 1950, too, more than 60 per cent of the off-farm migrants between the ages of twenty and twenty-four years were leaving the

An aerial view of the International Paper Company mill at Georgetown, South Carolina

rural South. The South has a heavy financial investment in these young people. Expanded employment opportunities will hold more of these youngsters within the South to help develop our resources and economy.

Yet this progress toward a balanced economy has not caused a decline in agriculture at acreage or output. There are fewer and larger farms. The average Southern farm now contains 170 acres; commercial farms average 236 acres in size. Those farms selling above $2500 in products annually contain better than 330 acres. Farms are largely mechanized, with almost 1,500,000 tractors furnishing most of the power, a 600 per cent increase since 1940. Modern power machinery and equipment represents almost one-third of the total capital investment of Southern farms. Behind each full-time farm worker of the South is now almost $15,000 in capital assets—a 500 per cent increase over 1940.

Larger income per person continues to be a pressing need in Southern agriculture. As capital assets per worker rise to even higher levels, so will per capita production and income. The record of progress in increased production per worker is magnificent and is indicative of better years ahead.

The Southern sharecropper is on the way out. More prominently identified in the total operations of the farms of the South are owners—both full- and part-time. The tenant continues to be an important farm operator. But he is fast becoming an owner of considerable capital with long-term lease arrangements. Greater stability in farming is resulting.

The South has held firmly to its position as the top producer of peanuts and tobacco. However, the more rapid enterprise expansions have come in food products. Tremendous and spectacular growth has come in cattle, hogs, dairying, and poultry. From a minor position in the production of broilers, the South now furnishes more than two-thirds of all broilers bought by consumers in the United States. We continue, too, to expand our fruit and vegetable industry. Our laying flocks come nearer supplying our egg needs than ever before.

Indications point strongly, as Dr. Butler shows in "Tall Grass," to the development of intensive systems of livestock production in the South. Improved hybrid grasses and forage crops with high fertilization are producing fantastic amounts of beef per acre. Recent research has found pelleted Coastal Bermuda grass equal to alfalfa in beef gains. Experimentation at the University of Georgia's College of Agriculture revealed that feed-conversion rates in pork production can be reduced to less than three pounds per pound of gain from weaning to 200-pound weight. Such findings as these, together with the experiences of hundreds of farmers, serve as the basis upon which small- and moderate-size farms can add profit through livestock enterprises.

Southern farmers look to the growing local consumer markets as opportunities for continued expansion in a truly diversified agriculture. The ratio of food and fiber consumers to producers is becoming larger. Thus, with rising per capita incomes and greater demand for quality production, some of the finest consumer markets in America are being created.

The economic progress of any area is closely associated with the growth and development of transportation and communication facilities. The improvement and addition of highways and the construction of modern airports have been added to the South's excellent rail facilities to provide a splendid network for freight and express movements. Barges, operating on precise schedules, serve the Mississippi and Tennessee valleys. The leveling-out of transportation rates facilitates the interchange of products with other sections. The New South is no longer isolated from important markets and our great centers of industry and finance.

A modern oil-tank farm at Carthage, Texas (*Ewing Galloway*)

Prophetically, the South has increased its personal incomes much faster than the rest of the United States. From 1930 to 1954, the gain in the South was 420 per cent as compared with 272 per cent for the United States. Florida made the fantastic gain of almost 700 per cent. From a per capita income of $307 in 1930, the South moved to $1233 in 1954. Since then, per capita incomes have continued upward at a faster rate than for the United States as a whole. Yet, even though the gap is narrowing, the South still lags behind the nation in average per capita income. In 1954, the South's per capita income was 70 per cent of that of the United States. Here lies a vital challenge. It is being met.

Equally basic in the changes under way throughout the South are adequate financial resources. Long-term savings have shown a remarkable increase, also rising much faster in the South than the national average. This story is repeated in the growth of bank deposits. Mr. L. B. Ralsty, vice president of the Federal Reserve Bank of Atlanta, in a paper on "Economic Resources: Development in the South and Southeast," states: "The United States had a gain in bank deposits of 290 per cent from 1935 to 1954, whereas the eleven Southeastern states had a gain of 549 per cent. Florida, in particular, experienced a spectacular gain in bank deposits, rising from $244 million in 1935 to $2700 million in 1954, a gain of more than 1000 per cent." In 1935 the South had 6 per cent of the total bank deposits of this country against 10 per cent in 1954.

These gains in financial resources should enable the South to overcome a serious problem in economic development. A wide gap continues to exist between the financial resources per capita of the South and those of the United States, but it has been narrowed. Further progress seems assured.

Another dramatic expansion has taken place in the production of electric power. Eleven Southeastern states moved from producing 12.0 per cent of the United States' electric power in 1935 to the production of 21.5 per cent in 1954. The gain reflects both the extension of TVA generating capacity and the expansion of private power companies. Power lines have crisscrossed the entire South, to the most remote mountain coves. Hence, people have more time to devote to activities other than supplying their own food needs; industry is added; a new culture comes into being.

In doing over its way of life, the South has come up against a multitude of tough problems. But, such is progress. The self-contained rural community, with its pleasant living patterns, has been replaced by the hustle and

A branch bank of the Trust Company of Georgia in the Atlanta area

bustle of a commercial economy with all of the risks of an industrial society. Instead of "ten ears of corn and a bundle of fodder," it's "twenty gallons of gasoline and a quart of oil." Rather than all farmers living at home, almost 40 per cent earn more of their income in city employment than from farm production.

Cities and towns, as they sprawl out across the surrounding countryside, wonder how all of their needs can be met from the new economic base. Disruptions come to agricultural communities. Confusion often prevails among town and country people. Yet, here, too, a light is shining; the city and country—rural and urban—are coming to understand they live in the same community.

An encouraging trend in this direction is the expanding co-operation between city and county governments in planning for this total community. Rapid industrial growth and urban sprawl have created "no-man's land" around cities and in metropolitan areas. A recent survey of Southern states showed more than seven hundred fifty city planning commissions. Most of these are including in their planning the immediate area beyond the city limits. Both city and county governments are coming to realize that they must join co-operatively in programs for good land use, wise subdivision development, desirable housing, recreation, roads, and other aspects of sound community growth. With this end in mind, more than one hundred joint city-county planning commissions are at work. This movement is well under way and promises to spread rapidly. Spearheading this imperative program are State Planning Commissions and other responsible boards of central government. Every state, aware of its needs, moves toward a full and effective program of planning for sound growth.

Thus, the pattern of the future seems well outlined, with tomorrow's challenges clearly in focus, for the forty-five million people who now reside in this great section of the United States. In the New South, industry, business, and agriculture are joining hands to develop a new economy. The goal is a balanced economy with full and productive use of all resources, employment of all its people with opportunities galore for its youth, and strong communities heavily flavored with rural influences and values. Truly, the South expresses its feelings in the little poem which says:

"Change and change, and never rest;
Not what we are, but what we
hope for is best."

Part 6

For Kissin' Cousins

Preceding page:
On the road to Asheville

ROY H. PARK

Eatin' Out

"EATIN' OUT?" Not many years ago, such a suggestion to a guest anywhere in the South would have been as rank an insult as whistling *Yankee Doodle* at the foot of Stone Mountain or admitting a dislike for fried chicken. The only fit place to dine was "t'home."

Some of the best Southern cookery is still confined to the home-place. But for the past twenty years the diner-out has been able to grin at the excellent cuisine developing in public restaurants across Dixie. The best of these restaurants have charmingly blended a careful preparation of famous old recipes with the casual graciousness and environmental décor of that tradition we still label "Southern hospitality."

Even though some restaurateurs have been tempted to "drag heel" a bit on this, they have been forced to go along. The home had always been the center for hospitality in the South. Whenever friends were invited over, the best meals we could provide and the most comfortable beds we had were underlined components in the invitation . . . even when it meant that the youngsters had to sleep on the floor. Consequently, there wasn't much trade floating around for public restaurants—particularly restaurants that weren't up to the folks' standards.

That's why—glory be—today's bushy-tailed and booming Southland has hundreds of good restaurants where the décor of candlelit tables, sparkling silver, and fireplaces twinkling with old brass and copper "tools" chorus *Home Sweet Home* as naturally as the hot buttermilk biscuits cuddling in the wicker baskets and the waitresses who chirrup, "Tha's real good. Ah ate it m'self." Now, most families below the Potomac concede that suffrage for Mother should include a dinner a week, at least, away from the kitchen.

Since mealtime was, is, and will be a major Southern ritual of conviviality, one indication of a "good" restaurant anywhere in the South is to count the number of *local* license plates on the autos parked beside a public dining room at mealtime. If Hometown eats there, you'll probably like it, too. But if there are only one or two *local* license plates in the parking lot, proceed cautiously; our Southland, as elsewhere, still has its quota of hash-joints and "greasy spoons."

Beyond this standard rule—and it applies in Iowa and Montana as vigorously as in Georgia or along the Gulf Coast—the best eatin'-out counsel to any visitor must be conditioned by individual taste. Here, then, I offer those restaurants that have created pleasures on the Park palate. This particular palate was weaned in North Carolina and has spent much of the last decade in savory chores for the Duncan Hines Institute.

Let's start with that delightful Southern tradition—morning coffee. The demitasse of jet-black, savory coffee the waiter wordlessly serves as you settle in for breakfast in a railway diner anywhere across the South is a hand-me-down from ancient habit. The blissful perk-up of three ounces of strong, hot coffee before the citrus course was a day-starter that won as much approval from French and Spanish governors of New Orleans as it did from leaders of the Confederacy. At the Dinkler-Andrew Jackson Hotel in Nashville, I always leave a call for "morning coffee." At the Hotel Sir Walter in Raleigh, North Carolina, you will be awakened, unless you leave specific instructions to the contrary, by a knock on your door and a waiter bearing your morning coffee.

Virginia preserves this custom, too, whether you cross the lovely countryside by train or rise at cock's crow to tour the amazing restoration of Colonial Williamsburg. If you choose to take the Williamsburg "breakfast" at Christian Campbell's Tavern, don't miss the spoon bread as a grand companion of the country-cured bacon or ham. Luncheon or dinner will be equally good at the eighteenth-century reproduction of Chowning's Tavern (excellent Brunswick Stew here!), King's Arms Tavern (Sally Lunn

Greengage-Plum Ice Cream, and Virginia Ham are specialties), and Williamsburg Inn (I favor their Spiced Layer Cake and Orange Cake).

Downstate, at Roanoke, the Hotel Roanoke sits in a ten-acre park in the heart of town. I order their Virginia Peanut Soup and the old-style sausage cakes and usually succumb to Peanut Brittle Delight for dessert.

Smithfield, Virginia, is, of course, the home town of the delectable Smithfield Ham. Sykes Inn there serves it plentifully in those paper-thin slices that bring out the full savor of this unique meat. Top it off with their Damson Plum Pie. Another place serving excellent spoon bread is the Tides Inn at Irvington. On an island in the Rappahannock River, it is noted for its colonial foods and serves an excellent oyster stew.

Neighboring North Carolina, my home state, has its share of outstanding restaurants. I like two, because of their artistry in vegetable cookery. Sunset Farm Restaurant of Cherokee raises its own meats, dairy products and vegetables. Settle in with sweet potato puffs, fried yellow squash, scalloped okra, broiled tomatoes, country-cured ham, and chicken. If you like rhubarb pie, this is the place.

At Burnsville, don't rush by the Nu-Wray Inn. At this country hotel, you will just pull up your chair with the rest of the boarders and help yourself to a half-dozen kinds of jelly for the hot biscuits and Wray-cured Ham. The smothered lettuce and the corn pudding are delicious here, too.

Way atop North Carolina are two lovely resorts with excellent inns. General (and U.S. Senator) Wade Hampton lived near Cashiers, mountain-ringed at an altitude of 3500 feet. The old inn he developed on his 2200-acre estate has been rebuilt and operates, in season, as High Hampton Inn. It is quiet and informal, with superb scenery—provided you can take your eyes away from the Apple Casserole or Sunny Silver Pie.

Just twelve miles west nestles the historic resort town, Highlands, the highest incorporated town in the state. The Highlands Inn there has a homey loveliness that enhances its family-style meals. Editor Bob Howard learned this in June, 1958, when he stayed there a day and a half to finish a speech scheduled for Atlanta delivery before a critical audience of ministers and theologians at the Church & Community Workshop. The first morning, the Howards were awakened by a light tap at the dor. A smiling waitress swirled in, carrying a bridge table in one hand and a tray with coffee and hot rolls in the other. "Miss Kennerly," she announced, "said to tell you breakfast ends heah at 9:30. But youh got that ol' speech t'do so we fix to bring it up wheneveh youh ready. Th' sooneh you finish," she said, "the moah you can git of this *free* sunshine." Miss Georgia Kennerly, the Highlands Inn manager, hadn't known the Howards "from beans" when they registered.

Similar gracious hosting waits after a breath-taking fifty-mile drive southeast to South Carolina and modern Clemson House on the Campus of Clemson State College of Agriculture. Try the roast beef, peach preserves, and school-grown fruits and vegetables here, by all means. South Carolina has two fine inns at Summerville too. The Squirrel Inn, famed for its continental cuisine and good wines, is in a beautiful setting of azaleas and Spanish moss. On the road to Charleston, the attractive Carolina Inn excels in fried chicken and homemade ice cream. There are few appropriate similes for the cookery of Charleston. The word "devastatin'" best expresses it. Exotic marrow hors d'ouevres are still served here. You can buy marrow-spoons in the silver shops. She-Crab Soup, Resin-baked Potatoes, Shrimp Creole, gorgeous roasts of beef are among my favorites at the Francis Marion or Fort Sumter hotels and, of course, Brewton Inn. Then, *do* bust the diet wide open to indulge in some benne-seed and "peach leather" candies.

In Georgia, many restaurants have built a reputation on regional specialties. The Pirate's House in Savannah is justifiably proud of its crab soup. Likewise, the aptly named Deck at Brunswick, down by the Sea Isles, is famous for barbecued crab and its superb specialty, Shrimp Mull.

At the north end of Ashburn, Georgia, set on a beautiful estate, is the House by the Road, with such memorable specialties as Guinea Squash (eggplant) Pie, Sweet Potato Soufflé, and Banana Bread. Aunt Fanny's Cabin in Smyrna is famous for baked "sweet taters." Georgia Peach Ham is grand at the Lankford Manor in Tifton and the Terrace Hotel in Thomson, Georgia. Peach cobbler is a "must" at the Hotel Richmond in Augusta. And in the Bon Air Hotel, Augusta, try the Southern-fried Chicken with Banana Fritters or the Charleston Roast Beef Pie and Savannah Rum Layer Cake. In Atlanta, I go to the Frances Virginia Dining Room for their deviled eggplant and corn sticks.

Up northwest, atop Lookout Mountain at Chattanooga, Tennessee, is the charming Chanticleer Lodge. Its antique furnishings and breath-taking view are rivaled by the Soufflé of Summer Squash and Maid-of-the-Mist Pie.

Florida cuisine is varied, perhaps because the state is more cosmopolitan than any other Southern states. There's excellent Southern cooking at the Lee Manor, Boynton Beach, a lovely old colonial home set amid nine acres of tropical beauty. Creighton's in Fort Lauderdale also has fine Southern dishes and pastries. And, sweet glory, they make *good* apple pie.

No tour of Florida is complete without a visit to Tarpon Springs, where most of the sponges come from. Louis Pappas' Riverside Café, located on the water front, is noted for seafood and Greek specialties, especially the Greek Combination Salad. Proceeding on down this gorgeous stretch of Gulf Coast, I can dine happily on Shrimp-Steamed-in-Beer at

Fisherman's Wharf in Venice, at the Viking Room of Sarasota's Azure Tides Motel, or at Sarasota's famed Spanish restaurant, The Plaza.

My central-Florida favorite is the Chalet Suzanne near Lake Wales. Actually it isn't a restaurant but an unforgettable hostelry, with thè dining room only a part of its charm. The name suggests a Swiss atmosphere, but Chalet Suzanne has no real nationality. It is a potpourri of architecture and decorations from all over the world. The tables in the dining room are of tile from Mexico, Spain, Egypt, and Italy. The furniture is English, the crystal Egyptian. The Chalet is set in orange groves beside Lake Suzanne. The dining rooms and lobby are built directly over the water. The menu has such delicacies as baked grapefruit, and steaks with mint ice.

The luxury hotels of Miami Beach, are of course, too numerous to mention. They offer every type of cuisine imaginable, beautifully prepared and served—and expensive. If you tire of them, traipse west across the Everglades to the splendid home-cooking of Clewiston Inn at Clewiston, or whisk south across the Keys for Conch Chowder, Key Lime Pie, and a host of soulful seafood dishes.

So much for the seaboard route. Now come the times when I head toward New Orleans, the "eating capital" of the South, and saunter lovingly across Kentucky to the land of Ol' Man River.

The Beaumont Inn at Harrodsburg, Kentucky, serves appetizers and mint juleps on the lawn all summer. It features Kentucky Ham, corn pudding, corn cakes and ham loaf, and little pig sausages with fried apples. Then Chess Pie for dessert.

Not too far away is another distinguished inn, the Boone Tavern of Berea College. Berea students hand-wove the attractive fabrics in its upholstery and curtains. Many of the foods served are fresh from the college farms, gardens, dairy, creamery, and bakery.

In west Tennessee, I race my appetite toward the Britling Cafeterias in downtown Memphis or one of the Dobbs House restaurants. The Poplar Street one specializes in roast beef carved at your table; the Airport one will swoon you with pompano, trout, and Fresh Lime or Black-Bottom Pie.

Across the river in Arkansas, I favor the trout or catfish at the Spring Lake Restaurant near Harrison. They have their own trout pond just outside the glass-front dining room. Baked stuffed eggplant and baked scallops are fine at the Sam Peck Hotel in Little Rock. For unforgettable Grated Sweet Potato Pudding, go to the Mayfair Hotel at Searcy.

In Mississippi, the old Southern Tea Room in Vicksburg serves a great Plantation Breakfast and surpasses in Southern Stuffed Ham and Corn Pudding.

Wandering over into Alabama, perhaps after a boisterous meal on Blue

Channel catfish or fine homegrown steaks at Greenville, Mississippi, I'm tempted toward the Vilulla Tea Garden at Seale. (Can't help it. I adore their watermelon pickle.) Then, on the way to Tuscaloosa, my hunger's up again for roast pig and Spiced Nut Pie at the McLester Hotel. The Alabama and Mississippi Gulf Coasts are great shrimp and seafood country.

New Orleans' supremacy in cuisine traces, obviously, to those lovely ladies who learned the secret of "jus' so much" powdered sassafras leaf (called "file" and pronounced "fee-lay") as a seasoning.

These powdered leaves give much of the flavor to Gumbo-File, a thick soup and probably the best known of the Creole dishes. Another basic type of gumbo, called Gumbo-Fevi, uses okra to give the distinctive flavoring. There are many gumbos—chicken, oyster, shrimp, fish, pork, ham, and other meats—all served on boiled rice. Some of the finest are served at Corinne Dunbar's, a dignified old house on St. Charles Avenue.

Oysters Rockefeller, as everyone knows, originated at Antoine's in the French Quarter. Founded by Antoine Alciatore in 1840, the old-fashioned, four-story frame building with wrought-iron trim, so typical of New Orleans, has never been altered. Jules, Antoine's son, created Oysters Rockefeller and offered the dish to some of his friends. One of them commented that it was "very rich." Jules thereupon named it after the richest man he could think of at the time. If oysters aren't your dish, but you like seafood, order Pompano en Papillotte.

Another of New Orleans' historic places is Commander's Palace, known for Oysters à la Poulette, Soft-Shell Turtle Stew, Crabmeat Impériale, and Stuffed Flounder. Arnaud's Restaurant was founded by Arnaud Cazenove, originally a wine salesman. His daughter, Germaine Cazenove Wells, carries on her father's gourmet tradition. I favor the celebrated Shrimp Arnaud, Filet de Fruite Amandine, Lake Shrimps Maure Pas, and Oysters Bienville. Galatoire's, too, specializes in Creole and French cooking.

Smart and modern in décor is the Caribbean Room of the Pontchartrain Hotel, where such New Orleans delicacies as Trout Marinière or Veronique and Louisiana Gumbo Creole are menu standards. Lysle Aschaffenburg, the owner-manager, has issued a standing challenge to all of his guests that, providing they will let him select their meal, there will be no check if they don't agree that it's one of the finest meals they have eaten in New Orleans.

And, finally, another breakfast. To me, the "French breakfast" at Brennan's French Restaurant in the Vieux Carré is the high note of a New Orleans' visit. Creole ladies and gentlemen "of fashion" used to breakfast after midmorning Mass, a charming custom that somehow or other disappeared. Owen Brennan revived it in 1948. Today you'll have to wait in line. In 1955 Owen, at an early age, passed on to his culinary reward. His sister

Ella, and the rest of the Brennan clan, carry on. Here is that Brennan breakfast: First, an Absinthe Suissesse to get the eyes open, and a fresh Creole Cream Cheese. Next, an Egg Bénédict, followed by a sirloin steak with fresh mushrooms, French bread and marmalade, and a chilled rose wine. For the finale, Crêpes Suzette, cafe au lait, and cognac. How wise the suggestion on the menu: "Important . . . DON'T HURRY"!

I find it wise, after Brennan's, to let the appetite whet up for a day or two, especially when heading toward the Old South–Old West border in Texas. There are gastronomic paradises beyond the Trinity, too. In northeast Texas, I've enjoyed meals at Town House Restaurant in Tyler, at Byrce's Cafeteria in Texarkana, and at Seller's Cafeteria in Sulphur Springs. But south along the lovely sweep of Crescent Coast is the true eatin'-way. The Caribbean Seafood Restaurant in Port Arthur is justifiably famous for stuffed shrimp, red snapper, and flounder. Only fourteen miles south, at Sabine Pass, there are devastating barbecued crabs and fried shrimp at Grangers'. Houston beckons with a dozen excellent spots.

Still Old South, even though King Ranch is a brief jog down the road, Corpus Christi is a logical stop for Texas steak and seafoods. Take your choice here of Lochabay's Grill, Robert Driscoll Hotel, or The Vagabond; I like them all.

Frontier of the South is, of course, Dallas. Amon Carter was right: the West does begin in Forth Worth. Even Texas' most sophisticated rancher, Stanley Walker, concedes that. I have ten favorites in Dallas. Their names, alone, are indicative of this cosmopolitan city: Arthur's, Dobbs House, Dunton's Cafeterias, The Golden Pheasant, La Vielle Varsovie, the S & S Catering Shop, the Southern Kitchen, The Torch, Town & Country, and Vick's.

Most appropriately, a last meal in the Old South should be taken at Dobb's House out at Love Field. There I'd order shrimp cocktail, prime ribs, and Black-Bottom Pie, dream a bit of the glorious past, and then, as a jetliner screamed down the runway, drink a toast to the future.

Places to See

THE FUN and education involved in a trip South should begin long before one leaves home. Advance planning over and beyond the routines of road map, AAA Directory, et al., will yield a far richer harvest of memories.

Illustrated brochures about any state can be obtained, without charge, by writing to the Director of Public Relations, State Department of Conservation and Development in any capital city. A postcard request to Superintendent of Documents, Washington 25, D.C., will bring a listing of the *Historical Handbook Series* of National Parks and Monuments in the South.

Finally, a browse through the *State Guides* of your trip route can produce fascinating side-trip explorations and environmental detail. These *Guide* books were produced by the Federal Writers Project of WPA before World War II. Most state governments in the South found them worthy of perpetuation, so have prepared new editions since 1946. They may be ordered through any bookstore, allowing a week or two for delivery, at an average cost of six dollars per volume. Each volume is titled in the state's name, such as *South Carolina—A Guide to Palmetto State.*

The following Places-to-See recommendations were developed from "favorite places" lists of the authors of *This Is the South.* Each community or area in this "authors' favorites" list merits from two days to two weeks of leisurely prowling. It is arranged under five categories:

THE HISTORY PLACES. Jamestown and Williamsburg, Va.; Richmond, Va.; Charleston, Georgetown and Pawleys Island, S.C.; St. Augustine, Fla.; Biloxi and Natchez, Miss.; New Orleans, La.

THE SEA PLACES. Cape Hatteras area, N.C.; the Sea Isles, east of Brunswick, Ga.; the lower Gulf Coast of Florida, the Everglades, and Key West; the Bayou country of Louisiana.

THE HIGH PLACES. The Great Smokies (U.S. 19 from Asheville to Cherokee and U.S. 441 through Newfound Gap to Gatlinsburg, Tenn., is the classic route; Route 28 from Franklin, N.C. through Highlands to Clemson, S.C., is equally breathtaking); the Ozark country, best approached in our estimation via historic St. Genevieve and Cape Girardeau, Mo.; Virginia's lovely Blue Ridge, easily accessible out of Washington, D.C., to Winchester, then southeast, through Front Royal, via the Skyline Drive. This route was, in 1959, being extended to a "Top of the Appalachians" Thruway.

THE NEW-SOUTH SPECTACULARS. The northwest sections of Atlanta, Ga., in the vicinity of Paces Ferry Road, which are among the loveliest urban-residential areas in the United States; the air-view of Dallas–Fort Worth, Texas, long regarded as the dividing line between Old South and the West but now a dazzle of suburbia and decentralized industry; the industrial "complex" of Baton Rouge, viewed from the trans-Mississippi bridge; TVA's dams, hydro-power stations, and land-development projects in the Tennessee River valley; Miami and Florida East Coast hotels and homes north through Daytona Beach; Oak Ridge, Tenn., and other "restricted area" centers for atomic-age development; the industrial centers of Nashville and Kingsport, Tenn.; International House at New Orleans.

THE BATTLEFIELDS. Chattanooga, Tenn., and vicinity; the Cyclorama painting of the Battle for Atlanta in Grant Park, Atlanta; Virginia battlefields, largely available in a drive from Washington to Harpers Ferry, Warrenton, Richmond, Petersburg, and Yorktown; Shiloh battlefield, nine miles south of Savannah, Tenn., near the Tennessee-Mississippi-Alabama border; Vicksburg, Miss.; the forts south of New Orleans; and, because it marked the high-tide of the Confederate States of America, Gettysburg, Pa.

Expanding this on a state-by-state basis, the authors feel the following are essential "taste-samplers" for each state in the South:

ALABAMA. Bellingrath Gardens, Mobile. Wilson Dam. Tuskegee Institute, Tuskegee. Point Clear, on Mobile Bay. Horseshoe Bend battlefield, scene of Andrew Jackson's defeat of the Creek Confederacy. The caverns near Guntersville. Montgomery, first capital of the C.S.A. The Vulcan statue on Red Mountain and its view of Birmingham steel mills. Dothan, scene of the National Peanut Festival each October. Nearby Enterprise, with its famous statue to the boll weevil. The Dismals, prehistoric gardens near Russellville. Indian mounds near Moundville.

ARKANSAS. Hot Springs National Park with forty-seven government-owned and operated thermal springs. Oil fields near El Dorado. The U.S.A.'s only diamond mines, near Murfreesboro. Bull Shoals in the Ozarks. Ouachita and Ozark National Forests. Fayetteville and environs, particularly the University of Arkansas campus where mountain crafts are featured exhibits.

FLORIDA. (You might as well see all of it, while you're about it. Every section of the state has biased devotees. A few of our brash observers suggest: East Coast for fashion-and-dazzle; West Coast for quieter delights and natural beauty; the inland lakes areas for uninhibited life-in-the-sun.) Kissimmee, the most authentic cow-town east of the Mississippi. Suwanee River valley, where the Stephen Foster Memorial at White Springs is a favorite center for choral and folk singing. Pensacola, closely related to New Orleans and Mobile in both history and architecture. St. Augustine, still impressive despite its "tourist traps" as "the oldest city in the U.S.A." Nearby Marineland, with 11 A.M. and 4 P.M. performances by trained porpoises and an amazing collection of sea life. Bok's Singing Tower and sanctuary near Mountain Lake. Cypress Gardens—and, despite the spectacular water-ski show, don't fail to stroll through the beautiful gardens. Tarpon Springs, for the glamour of its Greek colony and sponge divers. Tampa and St. Petersburg, a maze of old and new, with interest-range from some of the nation's best Latin-American restaurants to the Gulf-edge motels and apartment houses.

Sunshine Skyway, an amazing complex of parkway and bridges, spans the twelve-mile mouth of Tampa Bay from St. Petersburg to Bradenton. The Charlotte Harbor area, vowed by some to be the loveliest in all Florida, includes Boca Grande, Captiva, and Sanibel Islands (all world-famous to shell-collectors) as well as Fort Myers, Thomas A. Edison's winter home. Fort Myers and West Palm Beach are starting points for the circle tour across the state via Lake Okeechobee, the Clewiston sugar-cane fields, the vast truck gardens of the Belle Glade area, Naples, and the U.S. 41 route along the boundaries of Everglades National Park. West Palm Beach through Miami to Homestead is so luxurious that it becomes monotonous, yet is an essential experience. Key West, for gourmet delights as well as atmosphere, is well worth the bumpy processional down U.S. 1. Everglades National Park, a 1,258,000-acre preserve of the great Everglades Swamp, is accessible via State 27 out of Homestead or via U.S. 41 from the West Coast. (Guided tours of the Park can be arranged at travel agencies, hotels or Audubon Society offices.)

GEORGIA. Atlanta, because it is "the New South at its best." Rome and the sixty buildings of the Berry Schools, developed under the leadership of Miss Martha Berry (1866–1942). Brasstown Bald (4784 ft.) and the beautiful Georgia Highlands country along U.S. 19–129 between Atlanta and the N.C. line. Dahlonega, scene of the United States' first Gold Rush in 1828. Stone Mountain, on Atlanta's outskirts. Callaway Gardens, near La Grange. Ocmulgee National Monument, near Macon. The Uncle Remus memorials at Eatonton. Athens, with University of Georgia campus and ante-bellum homes. The Coastal Plains Experimental Station at Tifton, birthplace of Coastal Bermuda, Suwanee and many of the South's new miracle grasses. Okefenokee Swamp Park, 660 square miles of jungle preserve, with many wildlife exhibits and boat trips, east of Waycross. The Sea Islands, northeast of Brunswick, with the ruins of Fort Frederica and the Bloody Marsh battleground on St. Simon, plus the new state park with a nine-mile public beach and camp sites on Jekyll Isle. Savannah, for its picturesque self.

KENTUCKY. Berea College, its handicraft shops and summer theater. The Jesse Stuart country around Riverton and Greenup. Abraham Lincoln's birthplace at Hodgenville. Paducah, gracious in memories of Irvin Cobb, and approach to the lowlands sweep of the Tennessee. The Louisville-Lexington area as heartland of the Bluegrass country. Middleboro as the west-portal of Cumberland Gap. Highway 15 from Winchester to Whitesburg, along the Trail of the Lonesome Pine. The Mammoth Caves National Monument. Pioneer Memorial Park at Harrodsburg.

LOUISIANA. New Orleans vies with Charleston, S.C., as the South's most picturesque city. (Indeed, in the estimation of some of our authors, it is *the* most picturesque). Give ample time to explorations here, from the matchless Vieux Carré and Jackson Square out through the new city to the Lower Delta, the Bayou country, the industrial maze of Lake Pontchartrain.

Also visit: Avery Island for its jungle aviary, tabasco factory, sugar cane, oil wells, and salt mines. The bayou plantation homes north and south of New Orleans. St. Martinsville and the Evangeline country. Boothville, because it is "end of the line" for the drive down the Delta past Port Sulphur through the Jean Lafitte country. Natchitoches, the oldest town in Louisiana Purchase. Baton Rouge for the impressive State Capitol and new industries.

MISSISSIPPI. Natchez for stately architecture, lovely gardens and gorges of loess soil. Vicksburg and its historic battlefield, Greenville, and nearby Stoneville, for full flavor of Delta-country plantations and the New South shift from cotton to livestock and diversified crops. Piney Woods School, southwest of Jackson on U.S. 49, the amazing achievement of Laurence C. Jones. Sections of the Natchez Trace, now serviceable for automobiles, off U.S. 51 north of Jackson. Beauvoir, the home of Jefferson Davis, and other ante-bellum houses at Biloxi. Jackson for its Old Capitol. The Choctaw Indian Reservation near Philadelphia. Oxford for its associations with William Faulkner. The adjacent University of Mississippi. Tupelo for its monumental industrial rehabilitation program of the 1940's. Pascagoula, reborn from moss-oak isolation to booming shipyard city.

NORTH CAROLINA. The Cape Hatteras area. Roanoke Island, with Paul Green's drama, *Lost Colony*, a summer-long feature. Kittyhawk, nearby, with monument to the Wright Brothers' first airplane flight, as well as the parent-plant of the South's famous grape, the Muscadine. Asheville, its handicraft and folk singers. The adjacent Biltmore Estate. The pioneer mountain country west from Highland. Cherokee Reservation, its summer-long classic, *Unto These Hills*, and Indian crafts shops. Chapel Hill, home of the University of North Carolina. The Asbury Trail, Lake Junaluska, and adjacent summertime religious centers. Winston–Salem and the gracious Moravian "planned community" at Old Salem. The architectural perfection of mansions at New Bern and Tarboro. The Historical Museum at Greensboro, with its replica of the drugstore where William Sydney Porter (O. Henry) worked as a boy. Raleigh and the brashly modern State Fair arena, a 9500-seat parabolic with glass walls and its roof supported on cables. Wilmington, birthplace of the world-famous subject of Whistler's painting, *My Mother*, as well as logical base for a tour of historic Cape Fear.

SOUTH CAROLINA. Charleston and all its historic and beautiful environs, including Fort Sumter; Fort Moultrie; the Magnolia, Middleton, and other gardens; Battery Walk; the Citadel; Catfish Alley; St. Michael's and St. Phillip's churches; the grave of Calhoun, and the splendid Charleston

Museum. (Charleston is one of the most hauntingly beautiful cities in North America. You can't "do justice to its charms" in less than a week of intensive exploration.) Georgetown and the area of "great plantations" extending north past Pawleys Island and south to Charleston. Beaufort, the early Spaniards' Santa Elena and early Frenchmen's Port Royal, with adjacent plantations and the U.S. Marine Corps' Parris Island Base. Columbia for its State House, University of South Carolina, Shaw House, and picturesque Curb Market. Abbeville, in the Calhoun country, with nearby Sumter National Forest. Clemson, the State Agricultural College, named for John C. Calhoun's son-in-law and centered by Calhoun's mansion, Fort Hill.

TENNESSEE. Great Smoky Mountains National Park soars along the Tennessee-North Carolina line. It contains 29 peaks more than a mile high, 152 varieties of trees, and more than 4,000 types of plant life. Gatlinburg, Tennessee's west gate to the Park, is nationally famous for handicraft shops. Also worth visiting are: Chattanooga for Lookout Mountain and Chickamauga Battlefield. Hermitage, the home of Andrew Jackson, near Nashville. The home of James K. Polk at Columbia. Andrew Johnson's tailor shop and museum in Greeneville. The Davy Crockett country around Lawrenceburg. The pottery kilns at Pigeon Forge. The TVA country and Oak Ridge. The livestock and Walking Horse countryside around Pulaski. Memphis, the world's largest cotton market and, as possessor of Beale Street, a "blues" shrine. Reelfoot Lake, the 14,000-acre wildlife preserve formed by an earthquake in 1811. The Casey Jones Museum in Jackson. Elizabethton, site of the Wautega Republic created by the Long Rifles in 1772. Roan Mountain, in Cherokee National Forest, for summer displays of rhododendron.

TEXAS (EAST). Downtown Dallas, the city that oil built. The Beaumont-Port Arthur area for examples of Gulf Coast industry. Houston because, in some respects, it is the most remarkable city in North America. The nearby San Jacinto battlefield. The lower Trinity River valley, a contrast in primitive and ultramodern. The Dwight Eisenhower birthplace at Denison. The Alamo at San Antonio because, while technically across the western boundary of the South, it is a memorial to pioneers from the South who, in heroic death, fired the Texas War for Independence and the U.S. War with Mexico.

VIRGINIA. The unique restorations at Colonial Williamsburg. Nearby Jamestown (south) and Yorktown (east) National Parks. A tour of the James River valley to Westover, Shirley, and other old plantations. The Newport News–Portsmouth–Norfolk area for its shipyards, U.S. Navy Yard, Cape Henry, and Virginia Beach. The trip down U.S. 17, south from

Norfolk, along the east border of Great Dismal Swamp. Smithfield, on the south shore of the James River estuary, made world-famous by its "Smithfield Ham." Petersburg for Civil War memories. Richmond, capital of the C.S.A. and one of the loveliest cities of the South. Charlottesville for the nearby homes of Thomas Jefferson and James Monroe, the birthplace of George Rogers Clark and Meriwether Lewis, and the beautiful campus of University of Virginia. Appomattox Court House National Park. Staunton for the birthplace of Woodrow Wilson. Danville, last capital of the C.S.A. Mount Rogers in Jefferson National Forest (5720 ft. elevation), the highest peak in Virginia. Skyline Drive and the beautiful Shenandoah National Park area along the Blue Ridge summits. Winchester—not only for history but for the spring beauty of gardens and flowering apple orchards and the year-round delights of its apple products. Alexandria, logical starting place for a tour of Civil War battlefields because of Arlington National Cemetery, the Custis-Lee Mansion, and its many memorials. Mount Vernon, home of George Washington and a jewel of architecture and landscaping. The Lower Potomac shore, east from Fredericksburg, past the birthplaces of George Washington (Wakefield) and Robert E. Lee (Westmore). The loveliness of Delmarva Peninsula.

West Virginia. This is a land of amazing contrasts. Allow yourself time to absorb it. The memorials to John Brown's Raid at Harpers Ferry in 1859 will prove a "must" for tourists through the years of the Civil War Centennial. Brown's trial and execution took place in nearby Charles Town (don't confuse this with Charleston, the state's capital). Visit Martinsburg, too, only fifteen miles away, for the gracious Martin House, Parks House, Boydville, Norbourne Hall, and other splendid examples of Georgian and Federal architecture. (West Virginians believe that the transition from the camp-meeting tune *Say, Brothers, Will You Meet Me* to *John Brown's Body* occurred in Martinsburg during the winter of 1859–60.) Near Halltown, four miles from Harpers Ferry, is Beall Air; John Brown kidnaped Colonel Lewis Washington here and also appropriated, for symbolic reasons, the sword given George Washington by Frederick the Great. Now as famous for stained glass as for clothespins, for chemicals and steel as for mountain parks, lumberjacks, and John Henry legends, West Virginia offers spring and fall Music Festivals at Morgantown; an October Mountain State Forest Festival at Elkins; a September Song Festival at Wheeling; the Rhododendron Festival at Webster Springs in July; the Strawberry Festival at Buckhannon each June. The State Museum in the capitol at Charleston is excellent. Hawks Nest State Park, forty-three miles east of Charleston, has notable views and a museum. Don't miss the Kanawha or Greenbrier State Forests.

Appendix

The Authors

ROBERT GREENHALGH ALBION, Gardiner professor of oceanic history and affairs, Harvard University, is world-famous as an authority and author.

OREN ARNOLD, native Texan who judiciously adapted to Pacific seashore summers and Phoenix winters, is a student of America's regional humor, has twenty books in print, contributes to national magazines, and writes the popular quips-page of *Kiwanis Magazine*.

GEORGE H. AULL, student of the South's economic history since his teaching career began in Georgia in 1919, is head of the Department of Agricultural Economics and Rural Sociology, Clemson Agricultural College, Clemson, S.C.

EUGENE BUTLER, native of Mississippi, joined the staff of *Progressive Farmer* as an assistant editor in 1917, is now president of Progressive Farmer Company as well as sage and active editor of the magazine's Texas Edition in Dallas.

HODDING CARTER, Louisiana-born, has published his own daily newspaper, *The Delta Democrat-Times*, in Greenville, Miss., for twenty-three years. Recipient of the Southern Literary Award (1945) and the Pulitzer Prize (1946), he has written nine distinguished books about the South, coauthored four others. His latest work, *The Angry Scar*, the story of Reconstruction, was published in January, 1959, as one of Doubleday's "Mainstream of America" series.

JOHN CHASE is the editorial cartoonist of *The New Orleans States-Item,* author of the prize-winning narrative history of New Orleans, *Frenchmen, Desire, Good Children*, a special lecturer in New Orleans history at Tulane University, and, best of all when you're with him, a gourmet who knows most—perhaps all—of the kitchen secrets of the Vieux Carré.

THOMAS D. CLARK has been head of the Department of History, University of Kentucky, since 1942, and Visiting Professor on campuses ranging from Chicago to Vienna. His regard for the country editor and the general store led to his authorship of *Pills, Petticoats and Plows* (1944), *The Southern Country Editor* (1948), and *Frontier America* (1959).

MARGARET COIT received the Pulitzer Prize in biography for her *John C. Calhoun: American Portrait* (1950), won numerous book awards and citations with *Mr. Baruch* (1957), and, since 1950, has been beloved author-in-residence at Fairleigh Dickinson University, Rutherford, N.J.

JAMES MCBRIDE DABBS, whose book *The Southern Heritage* (1958) was nationally acclaimed, farms and writes at the old McBride plantation, Rip Raps, near Mayesville, S.C., after a career as a professor of English. He is president of The Southern Regional Council.

PHILIP G. DAVIDSON, JR., historian and teacher, became the president of University of Louisville in 1951, was the author of *Propaganda and the American Revolution* in 1941, but has obviously pursued a scholarly love for plantation life since his Mississippi childhood.

IVY W. DUGGAN lists himself as an "agricultural economist" despite nation-wide respect as a humanist and student of American history. Governor of the Farm Credit Administration in Washington, D.C., 1944–53, he returned to his native Georgia to become vice president of The Trust Company of Georgia.

RICHARD DUNLOP, former editor of *Home & Highway* and a cofounder of *Best Articles and Stories* magazine, is a contributor to *Readers Digest* and other national magazines as well as the author of forthcoming books on St. Louis, Burma, and the Boy David. This achievement from a home in Arlington Heights, Ill., is, friends aver, "uniquely Dunlopian."

J. W. FANNING, admired throughout the South for scholarly magazine articles and lectures is director of agricultural economics, University of Georgia.

G. ROSS FREEMAN teaches as realistically as he writes. He is assistant to the dean and director of field work, Candler School of Theology, Emory University, Atlanta, and director of the Church & Community Workshop for rural preachers held on the Emory campus each July.

WAYNE GARD, editorial writer for the Dallas *Morning News* since 1923, is an authority on pioneer life in both South and West. His latest books, *Frontier Justice*, *The Chisholm Trail*, and *Fabulous Quarter Horse: Steel Dust*, have enhanced this reputation. His sixth book, *The Great Buffalo Hunt*, has been scheduled for 1959 publication.

AUBREY GATES is an Arkansan who likes to tell stories about his grandfather, a C.S.A. veteran wounded in the right arm at Shiloh, in the right hip at Chickamauga, in the left arm at The Wilderness. But story-times are a rarity when you are director of field services for the American Medical Association.

PAUL ELIOT GREEN first won fame when his play, *In Abraham's Bosom*, received the 1927 Pulitzer Prize in drama. His name has since become an international synonym for "history relived" as *The Lost Colony*, *Common Glory*, *Faith of Our Fathers*, *Wilderness Road*, *The Confederacy* surged from his workshop at Chapel Hill, N.C.

SALLIE HILL gets away, now and then, to her stock farm in Parker County, Texas, and collects old family recipes en route. But, workaday-wise, she is a vice president of *Progressive Farmer*, editor of its Home Department, author of *Our Southern Food Ways*, and recipient of such honors as Theta Sigma Phi's National Headliner Award and the University of Alabama's Distinguished Service Award.

ROBERT WEST HOWARD, son of an upstate New York preacher, traveled extensively in the South as magazine editor and correspondent. He edited *This Is the West* (1957), is author of *Rodeo—Last Frontier of the Old West*, *Two Billion Acre Farm*, *The Real Book About Farms*, *Educational Planning for Communities*, etc., plus several hundred magazine articles. His home, currently, is in Chicago, Ill.

LAURENCE CLIFTON JONES, native of St. Joseph, Mo., and graduate of Iowa State University, came to Smith County, Miss., in 1909 to establish a school for the impoverished Piney Woods' families of his race. The sagalike story of Piney Woods School and its founder was dramatized by Ralph Edwards' *This Is Your Life* TV-show in 1954, and in 1956 was the subject of Leslie Harper Purcell's book, *Miracle in Mississippi*.

WEYMOUTH T. JORDAN, native of North Carolina and professor of history at Florida State University, is the author of *George Washington Campbell of Tennessee*, *Hugh Davis and His Alabama Plantation*, *Rebels in the Making*, and *Ante-Bellum Alabama*. He is currently working on a book about town-life in the Old South.

HARNETT T. KANE has published twenty books since *Louisiana Hayride* first placed his name on the "best seller" list. The N.Y. *Times* in 1958 called him "today's most literate spokesman of the traditional South." His *Southern Christmas Book* was published in the late fall of 1958, followed three months later by *The Golden Coast*. Between lecture trips in the spring of 1959, he was typically working twelve hours a day in his New Orleans office on "a book that I hope will give a human portrait of the Old South."

APPENDIX

HUGH McGARITY, choral director and arranger, is professor of music, Clemson Agricultural College, Clemson, S.C. His choral arrangements of *Jennie Jenkins, Come All Ye Fair and Tender Ladies, Golden Harp, Saw Ye My Saviour* are favorites with high-school and college choruses.

ALEXANDER NUNN, veteran spokesman for the New South and one of its best-known editorialists, is executive editor of *The Progressive Farmer*, Birmingham.

ROY H. PARK, native Tar Heel, began to unveil his abilities as an editorial and advertising consultant for farmer co-operatives in Ithaca, N.Y., hit his stride as the "Park" in Hines-Park Foods, and currently saunters through his orange groves as vice president of Duncan Hines Institute.

WILLIAM S. POWELL, another native Tar Heel, is librarian of the North Carolina Collection at Chapel Hill. He is the author of two volumes on the Colony of Carolina in the seventeenth century and, as a Guggenheim Fellow, lived in England during 1956 while researching records on the Roanoke colonists and explorers of 1584–90. And he's a grand guy to work with.

JAMES W. SELLS, as "The Preacher" testifies, is a native of Mississippi and one of the glory-road host of Methodist circuit riders. Forthright, keen, big-hearted "Rev. Jim" is a beloved figure to both ministry and laymen throughout the South. He pioneered the Church & Community Workshops at Emory and the Protestant Radio and Communications Center nearby, and in 1959 was tirelessly raising funds for creation of the Stanley E. Jones Communications Center where ministers of every creed could perfect skills in public speaking, writing, and human relationships. Officially, he is Executive Secretary, the Southeastern Jurisdictional Council of the Methodist Church, with headquarters in Atlanta.

CELESTINE SIBLEY, columnist and reporter for the Atlanta *Constitution*, received a Christopher Award (1953) and two Associated Press prizes for reporting. She is the author of a Crime Club mystery, *The Malignant Heart*, and has written for *Saturday Evening Post* and other magazines. She is currently working on a book on Atlanta.

ALFRED STEFFERUD would, if he had his "druthers," label himself "Former Schoolteacher, Adoptive Virginian and Former Newspaperman." But, while Steff whispers, his achievements shout. A veteran of A.P. and O.W.I., he has edited the U.S. Department of Agriculture's *Yearbook* since 1945, with a total staff of one secretary-assistant; The *Yearbook* consistently wins awards for editorial and typographical excellence. In 1952, he edited *Wonderful World of Books*, a collection of original writings by sixty-three authorities on literature and reading-appreciation. The book, a "labor of love" sponsored by the American Book Publishers Council, has been reprinted in twenty languages; more than 3,000,000 copies have been distributed. Mr. Stefferud is also author of *The Wonders of Seeds, The Book of Wildflowers,* and *The Story of Photosynthesis.*

JESSE HILTON STUART has made "Greenup, Ky." a postal address revered throughout the United States and Europe. His poems and stories of the Kentucky mountains, from *Man with a Bull-Tongue Plow* through *Taps for Private Tussie* and *The Thread That Runs so True*, are classics of regional mood and folkway realism. He apologized for being a few days late with the manuscript of "Up the Branch": been out chopping firewood, and time just got away from him.

RUPERT BAYLESS VANCE, born in Plumerville, Ark., studied and taught in Tennessee, Oklahoma, Georgia, Louisiana, and Texas. It proved a logical route not only to the Kenan chair in sociology at University of North Carolina but to Dr. Vance's position as one of the United States' most distinguished, and literate, authorities on social science. In addition to his many works on population studies, rural sociology, et al., he is coauthor of *New Farm Homes for Old* (1946), *Exploring the South* (1949) and *Urban South* (1954).

WILLIAM D. WORKMAN, JR., uses his keen historian's instinct every day of the year as statehouse reporter for the Charleston (S.C.) *News & Courier*, the Greenville *News*, and WIS-WIS-TV. There are book manuscripts under way in his Columbia study, too.

All-time Books About the South

IN A MAIL BALLOT, the authors submitted most of the following list of "Books About the South Every American Should Read." The need for "editor's prerogative" loomed when it became apparent that the thirty-one had not included their own definitive books in their recommendations. Some of these have been added, but not all; the authors of *This Is the South* have written, and published, more than 200 books. Nor does this list constitute a Bibliography; the indications are that approximately 1,100 books and resource-files were consulted during the research for these chapters.

Abbott, John S. C. *South and North*. New York: Abbey & Abbott, 1860.

Agar, Herbert, *The Price of Union*. Boston: Houghton Mifflin Company, 1950.

Alden, John R. *John Stuart and the Southern Colonial Frontier*. Ann Arbor: University of Michigan Press, 1944.

Allen, William Francis, Ware and Garrison. *Slave Songs of the United States*. New York: Peter Smith, 1867.

Angle, Paul. *The American Reader*. Chicago: Rand McNally & Co., 1958.

Benedict, Agnes Elizabeth. *Progress to Freedom, the Story of American Education*. New York: G. P. Putnam's Sons, 1942.

Benton, Thomas H. *Thirty Years' View*. *2 vols*. New York: D. Appleton & Co., 1854–1856.

Billington, Ray Allen. *Westward Expansion*. New York: The Macmillan Company, 1949.

Binns, John G. *Recollections*. Philadelphia: Parry & McMillan, 1843.

Bowers, Claude G. *The Tragic Era*. Boston and New York: Houghton Mifflin Company, 1929.

Boyd, Minnie C. *Alabama in the Fifties*. New York: Columbia University Press, 1931.

Bridenbaugh, Carl. *Cities in the Wilderness*. New York: The Ronald Press Company, 1938.

———. *Myths and Realities*. Baton Rouge: Louisiana State University Press, 1952.

Bruce, William C. *John Randolph of Roanoke*. *2 vols*. New York and London: G. P. Putnam's Sons, 1922.

Caldwell, Erskine. *You Have Seen Their Faces*. New York: Viking Press, 1937.

Calhoun, John C. *Correspondence of John C. Calhoun, J. Franklin Jameson, ed., Annual Report of the American Historical Association (1899), Vol. II*. Washington: 1900.

APPENDIX

Cash, W. J. *The Mind of the South.* New York: Alfred A. Knopf, 1946.
Carter, Hodding. *Lower Mississippi* (Rivers of America Series). New York: Rinehart, 1942.
———. *Where Main Street Meets the River.* New York: Rinehart, 1953.
———. *The Angry Scar* (Mainstream of America Series). New York: Doubleday & Company, 1959.
Chase, John C. *Frenchmen, Desire, Good Children.* New Orleans: Robert L. Crager & Co., 1949.
Chestnut, Mary Boykin. *A Diary from Dixie.* Boston: Houghton Mifflin, 1949.
Chitwood, Oliver Perry. *John Tyler: Champion of the Old South,* New York: D. Appleton-Century Co., 1939.
Clark, Thomas D. *The Rampaging Frontier.* Indianapolis: Bobbs-Merrill Company, 1939.
———. *Frontier America.* New York: Charles Scribner's Sons, 1959.
———. *Pills, Petticoats, and Plows.* Indianapolis: Bobbs-Merrill Co., Inc., 1944.
———. *The Southern Country Editor.* Indianapolis: Bobbs-Merrill Co., 1948.
Clay, Henry. *The Works of Henry Clay. 10 vols.* Calvin Colton, ed. New York: A. S. Barnes & Co., 1904.
Coit, Margaret L. *John C. Calhoun: American Portrait.* Boston: Houghton Mifflin Company, 1950.
———. *Mr. Baruch.* Boston: Houghton Mifflin Company, 1957.
Cotterill, Robert S. *The Southern Indians.* Norman: University of Oklahoma Press, 1954.
Crane, Verner W. *The Southern Frontier 1670–1732.* Ann Arbor: University of Michigan Press, 1929.
Dabbs, James McBride. *The Southern Heritage.* New York: A. A. Knopf, 1958.
Dabney, Charles William. *Universal Education in the South. 2 vols.* Chapel Hill: University of North Carolina Press, 1936.
Dacy, George H. *Four Centuries of Florida Ranching.* St. Louis: Britt Printing Co., 1955.
Daniels, Jonathan. *A Southerner Discovers the South.* New York: The Macmillan Company, 1938.
Dau, Frederick W. *Florida Old and New.* New York: G. P. Putnam's Sons, 1934.
Davenport, H. Garvin. *Ante-Bellum Kentucky: A Social History.* Oxford, Ohio: The Mississippi Valley Press, 1943.
Dick, Everett. *The Dixie Frontier.* New York: Alfred A. Knopf, 1948
Dodd, William E. *The Cotton Kingdom,* (The Chronicles of America, Volume 27). New Haven: Yale University Press, 1919.
———. *Statesman of the Old South.* New York: The Macmillan Company, 1921.
Dyer, Oliver. *Great Senators of the United States Forty Years Ago.* New York: R. Bonner's Sons, 1889.
Eaton, Clement. *Freedom of Thought in the Old South.* Durham: Duke University Press, 1940.
Farish, Hunter D. *Journal and Letters of Philip Vickers Fithian, 1773–1774.* Williamsburg, Virginia: Colonial Williamsburg, Inc., 1943.
Federal Writers Guide Series (Compiled by the Writers' Program of the Works' Progress Administration in the various States, after 1936).
Alabama, A Guide to the Cotton State. New York: Hastings House, 1949.
Arkansas, A Guide to the Wonder State. New York: Hastings House, 1949.
Florida, A Guide to the Southernmost State. New York: Oxford University Press, 1955.
Georgia, A Guide to Its Towns and Countryside. Atlanta: Tupper & Love, 1954.
Kentucky, A Guide to the Bluegrass State. New York: Hastings House, 1949.
Louisiana, A Guide to the Pelican State. New York: Hastings House, 1949.
Mississippi, A Guide to the Magnolia State. New York: Hastings House, 1946.

North Carolina Guide, Edited By Blackwell P. Robinson. Chapel Hill: University of North Carolina Press, 1955.
South Carolina, A Guide to the Palmetto State. New York: Oxford, 1949.
Tennessee, A Guide to the Volunteer State. New York: Hastings House, 1949.
Texas, A Guide to the Lone Star State. New York: Hastings House, 1949.
Virginia, A Guide to the Old Dominion. New York: Oxford, 1949.
West Virginia, A Guide to the Mountain State. New York: Oxford, 1943.

Furnas, J. C. *Goodbye to Uncle Tom*. New York: Sloane, 1956.

Gaines, Francis P. *The Southern Plantation*. New York: Columbia University Press, 1925.

Gard, Wayne, *Fabulous Quarter Horse: Steel Dust*. New York: Duell, Sloane & Pearce, Inc. 1958.

———. *Frontier Justice*. Norman: University of Oklahoma Press, 1959.

Garrett, Franklin M. *Atlanta and Environs*. New York: Lewis Historical Publishing Company, 1954.

Graves, John Temple. *The Fighting South*. New York: G. P. Putnam's Sons, 1943.

Gray, Lewis C. *History of Agriculture in the Southern United States to 1860*. Washington: Carnegie Institution of Washington, 1938.

Green, Paul. *The Common Glory Song Book*. Chapel Hill, N.C.; University of North Carolina Press, 1948.

———. *Dramatic Heritage*. New York: French, 1953.

———. *Out of the South*. New York. Harper and Bros., 1939.

Hamilton, Peter J. *Colonial Mobile*. Boston: Houghton Mifflin Company, 1897.

Handlin, Oscar, and Others. *Harvard Guide to American History*. Cambridge: Harvard University Press, 1954.

Holley, W. C., Winston, Ellen, and Woofter, T. J., Jr. *The Plantation South 1934–1937*. Washington: U.S. Government Printing Office, 1940.

Hollis, Christopher. *The American Heresy*. New York: 1930.

Howard, O. O. *Zachary Taylor*. New York: 1892.

Hubbell, Jay B. *The South in American Literature*. Durham: Duke University Press, 1954.

Jackson, George Pullen. *White Spirituals in the Southern Uplands*. Chapel Hill, N.C.: University of North Carolina Press, 1933.

James, Marquis. *Andrew Jackson: Portrait of a President*. New York: Grosset & Dunlap, 1937.

———. *The Raven, Sam Houston*. Indianapolis: Bobbs-Merrill Co., 1929.

Jefferson, Thomas. *The Writings of Thomas Jefferson*, Paul Leicester Ford, ed. New York: 1899.

Johnson, Gerald. *America's Silver Age*. New York: Harper & Bros., 1939.

Johnson, Guion G. *Ante-Bellum North Carolina: A Social History*. Chapel Hill: University of North Carolina Press, 1937.

Jones, Katherine M. *The Plantation South*. Indianapolis: Bobbs-Merrill, 1957.

Jordan, Weymouth T. *Hugh Davis and His Alabama Plantation*. Tuscaloosa: University of Alabama Press, 1948.

———. *Rebels in the Making*. Tuscaloosa: Confederate Pub. Co., 1958.

Kane, Harnett T. *Louisiana Hayride*. New York: William Morrow, 1941.

———. *Deep Delta Country* (American Folkways Series). New York: Duell, Sloan, & Pearce, 1944.

———. *The Southern Christmas Book*. New York: David McKay, 1958.

———. *The Golden Coast*. New York: Doubleday & Company, Inc., 1959.

Kendrick, Benjamin B. and Arnett, Alex M. *The South Looks at Its Past*. Chapel Hill: University of North Carolina Press, 1935.

Kennedy, John F. *Profiles in Courage*. New York: Harper & Bros., 1956.

Kennedy, John Pendleton. *Swallow Barn*. New York: G. P. Putnam's Sons, 1929.

King, Edward. *The Great South*. Hartford: American Publishing Company, 1875.
Knight, Edgar Wallace. (ed.). *Documentary History of Education in the South before 1860. 5 vols.* Chapel Hill: University of North Carolina Press, 1942–1952.
Knight, Edgar Wallace. *Education in the United States*. Boston: Ginn and Company, 2d rev. ed., 1941.
Lomax, John and Alan. *Best Loved American Folk Songs*. New York: Grosset & Dunlap, 1947.
Madison, James. *Letters and Other Writings of James Madison. 4 vols.* Philadelphia: J. B. Lippincott & Co., 1865.
Malloy, Robert. *Charleston*. New York: D. Appleton-Century Co., 1947.
Malone, Henry R. *Cherokees of the Old South, A People in Transition*. Athens: University of Georgia Press, 1956.
Mayo, Bernard. *Henry Clay: Spokesman of the New West*. Boston: Houghton Mifflin Company, 1937.
McAdoo, William G. *Crowded Years*. Boston and New York: Houghton Mifflin Company, 1931.
Mecklin, John Moffatt. *The Ku Klux Klan*. New York: Harcourt, Brace and Company, 1924.
Mitchell, Broadus. *The Rise of Cotton Mills in the South*. Baltimore: John Hopkins Press, 1921.
Monroe, James. *Writings of James Monroe. 7 vols.* New York: G. P. Putnam's Sons, 1902.
Moore, Glover. *The Missouri Compromise*. Lexington: University of Kentucky Press, 1953.
Nevins, Allan and Commager, Henry S. *America: The Story of a Free People*. Boston: Little, Brown & Co., 1942.
Olmsted, Frederick Law. *The Cotton Kingdom*. New York: Alfred A. Knopf, 1953 (re-printing).
Owsley, Frank L. *Plain Folk of the Old South*. Baton Rouge: Louisiana State University, 1949.
Parrish, Lydia. *Slave Songs of the Georgia Sea Islands,* Vols. I and II. New York: Creative Press, Inc., 1942.
Phillips, Ulrich B. *Life and Labor in the Old South*. New York: Grosset and Dunlap, 1929.
Pike, James. *The Prostrate State*. New York: D. Appleton & Co., 1874.
Polk, James K. *Diary of James Knox Polk. 4 vols.* Chicago: A. C. McClurg & Co., 1910.
Pollard, Edward. *The Lost Cause*. New York: E. B. Treat & Co., 1868.
Rights, Douglas L. *The American Indian in North Carolina*. Durham: Duke University Press, 1947.
Roark, Eldon. *Beale Street Bragabouts*. New York: McGraw-Hill, 1945.
Robertson, Ben. *Red Hills and Cotton: An Upcountry Memory*. New York: Alfred A. Knopf, 1942.
Roosevelt, Eleanor. *This I Remember*. New York: Harper & Bros., 1949.
Rubin, Morton. *Plantation County*. Chapel Hill, North Carolina: University of North Carolina Press, 1951.
Sandburg, Carl. *Abraham Lincoln: The Prairie Years*. (Blue Ribbon Edition). New York: Harcourt, Brace & Co., 1926.
Savage, Henry, Jr. *River of The Carolinas: The Santee* (Rivers of America Series). New York: Rinehart and Company, 1956.
Scherer, James A. B. *Cotton As a World Power*. New York: Frederick L. Stokes, 1916.
Schlesinger, Arthur M., Jr. *The Age of Jackson*. Boston and New York: Houghton Mifflin Company, 1945.
———. *The Crisis of the Old Order*. Boston: Houghton Mifflin Company, 1957.
Seymour, Charles. *Woodrow Wilson and the World War*. New Haven: Yale University Press, 1921.

Shay, Frank, *Judge Lynch*. New York: Ives Washburn, 1938.
Simkins, Francis Butler. *A History of the South*. New York: Alfred A. Knopf, 1956.
———. *Pitchfork Ben Tillman*. Baton Rouge: Louisiana State University Press, 1944.
———. *The South Old and New: A History 1820–1947*. New York: Alfred A. Knopf, 1947.
Smith, Justin H. *The Annexation of Texas*. New York: Baker & Taylor Co., 1911.
Smith, Rixey, and Beasley, Norman. *Carter Glass*. New York: Longmans Green & Co., 1939.
Stefferud, Alfred. *The Wonderful World of Books*. Boston: Houghton Mifflin, 1953.
Stokes, Thos. L. *The Savannah* (Rivers of America Series). New York: Rinehart, 1951.
Street, James H. *South*. New York: Doubleday, 1955.
Stroude, Hudson. *Jefferson Davis*. New York: Harcourt Brace, 1955.
Stuart, Jesse Hilton. *Man with a Bull-Tongue Plow*. New York: E. P. Dutton, 1934.
———. *Taps for Private Tussie*. New York: E. P. Dutton, 1943.
———. *The Thread That Runs So True*. New York: Charles Scribner's Sons, 1949.
Swanton, John R. *The Indians of the Southeastern United States*. (Bureau of American Ethnology, Bulletin 137) Washington: Government Printing Office, 1946.
Sydnor, Charles S. *Gentlemen Freeholders*. Chapel Hill: University of North Carolina Press, 1952.
Tannenbaum, Frank. *Darker Phases of the South*. New York and London: G. P. Putnam's Sons, 1924.
Tate, Allen. *Jefferson Davis, His Rise and Fall*. New York: Minton Balch & Co., 1929.
Taylor, Rosser H. *Ante-Bellum South Carolina*. Chapel Hill, North Carolina: University of North Carolina Press, 1942.
Thompson, James Westfall. *A History of Livestock Raising in the United States, 1607–1860*. Washington: Agricultural History Series, No. 5, U.S.D.A., 1942.
Thorp, Willard. *A Southern Reader*. New York: A. A. Knopf, 1955.
Tryon, Warren S. *A Mirror for Americans. 3 vols.* Chicago: University of Chicago Press, 1952.
Twelve Southerners. *I'll Take My Stand*. New York: Harper & Bros., 1930.
Underhill, Ruth M. *Red Man's America*. Chicago: University of Chicago Press, 1953.
Vance, Rupert Bayless. *All These People*. Chapel Hill: University of North Carolina Press, 1945.
———. *Human Geography of the South*. Chapel Hill: University of North Carolina Press, 1932.
Van Deusen, John G. *Economic Basis for Disunion*. New York: Columbia University Press, 1928.
Warren, Robert Penn. *All the King's Men*. New York: Modern Library, 1953.
Wecter, Dixon. *The Age of the Great Depression*. New York: Macmillan Co., 1948.
Wentworth, Edward N. and Towne, Charles W. *Cattle and Men*. Norman: University of Oklahoma Press, 1955.
Wertenbaker, Thomas Jefferson. *The Golden Age of Colonial Culture*. New York: New York University Press, 1942.
———. *The Old South*. New York: Charles Scribner's Sons, 1952.
Wissler, Clark. *The American Indian*. New York: Oxford University Press, 1938.
Woodmason, Charles. *The Carolina Backcountry on the Eve of the Revolution*. Chapel Hill: University of North Carolina Press, 1953.
Woodward, C. Vann. *Reunion and Reaction*. Boston: Little, Brown & Co., 1951.

Index

Index

Index

Index

PRINTED IN U.S.A.